Palgrave Studies in New Religions and Alternative Spiritualities

Series editors
James R. Lewis
University of Tromso – The Arctic University
Tromso, Norway

Henrik Bogdan
University of Gothenburg
Gothenburg, Sweden

Palgrave Studies in New Religions and Alternative Spiritualities is an interdisciplinary monograph and edited collection series sponsored by the International Society for the Study of New Religions. The series is devoted to research on New Religious Movements. In addition to the usual groups studied under the New Religions label, the series publishes books on such phenomena as the New Age, communal & utopian groups, Spiritualism, New Thought, Holistic Medicine, Western esotericism, Contemporary Paganism, astrology, UFO groups, and new movements within traditional religions. The Society considers submissions from researchers in any discipline.

More information about this series at
http://www.palgrave.com/series/14608

Jessica Moberg • Jane Skjoldli
Editors

Charismatic Christianity in Finland, Norway, and Sweden

Case Studies in Historical and Contemporary Developments

Editors
Jessica Moberg
University of Gothenburg
Gothenburg, Sweden

Jane Skjoldli
University of Bergen, Norway
Bergen, Norway

Palgrave Studies in New Religions and Alternative Spiritualities
ISBN 978-3-319-69613-3   ISBN 978-3-319-69614-0   (eBook)
https://doi.org/10.1007/978-3-319-69614-0

Library of Congress Control Number: 2017960949

© The Editor(s) (if applicable) and The Author(s) 2018. This book is published open access.

Open Access This book is distributed under the terms of the Creative Commons Attribution 4.0 International License (http://creativecommons.org/licenses/by/4.0/), which permits use, duplication, adaptation, distribution and reproduction in any medium or format, as long as you give appropriate credit to the original author(s) and the source, provide a link to the Creative Commons license and indicate if changes were made.

The images or other third party material in this book are included in the work's Creative Commons license, unless indicated otherwise in the credit line; if such material is not included in the work's Creative Commons license and the respective action is not permitted by statutory regulation, users will need to obtain permission from the license holder to duplicate, adapt or reproduce the material.

The use of general descriptive names, registered names, trademarks, service marks, etc. in this publication does not imply, even in the absence of a specific statement, that such names are exempt from the relevant protective laws and regulations and therefore free for general use.

The publisher, the authors and the editors are safe to assume that the advice and information in this book are believed to be true and accurate at the date of publication. Neither the publisher nor the authors or the editors give a warranty, express or implied, with respect to the material contained herein or for any errors or omissions that may have been made. The publisher remains neutral with regard to jurisdictional claims in published maps and institutional affiliations.

Cover illustration: Karen Ilagan / Getty Images

Printed on acid-free paper

This Palgrave Macmillan imprint is published by Springer Nature
The registered company is Springer International Publishing AG
The registered company address is: Gewerbestrasse 11, 6330 Cham, Switzerland

Foreword

I commend this volume to you wholeheartedly. This volume on Pentecostalism in the Nordic region is full of intriguing multidisciplinary studies that have relevance not only for this region, but for the study of Pentecostalism elsewhere. Despite the difficulties of definition mentioned by several authors in this collection, I have always been fascinated by how what we may term "Pentecostal and Charismatic" movements often present surprises. That Scandinavia and Finland, with their relatively low populations, became the founding region for European Pentecostalism as a whole, is one of those surprises. Relative to its position in the rest of western Europe, Pentecostalism became a significant movement within Nordic Christianity within a short period of time and was probably as well established there as anywhere else in the world. Undoubtedly, the towering figures in this remarkable story were those of Thomas Ball Barratt of Oslo and Lewi Pethrus of Stockholm. Both these early leaders were to have enormous international significance in the development and expansion of Pentecostalism. They were not the first or the only significant figures, as papers in this book show. But it was from Norway and Sweden that Pentecostalism spread to the other Nordic countries, and also to Britain, Germany, Switzerland, and Russia.

Pentecostalism was from its beginnings fundamentally a missionary movement. The Spirit had told them to "go." From the earliest years before the First World War, Nordic missionaries went out not only to other European countries, but also much further to Brazil, Argentina, Mexico, and to Southern and Eastern Africa, Ceylon (Sri Lanka), India, and China. The largest "classical" Pentecostal denomination in the world, the Assembleias de Deus in Brazil, was started by two Swedish migrants to the United States, Gunnar Vingren and Daniel Berg. The enormous Pentecostal denominations in present-day Ethiopia owe their origins to Finnish and Swedish missionaries (Haustein 2010). We must also not overlook the significant role also played by Danish missionaries, whose impact was far greater abroad than it was at home (Christensen 2017). To say that Scandinavia was one of the epicenters of global Pentecostalism is no exaggeration. If we understand Pentecostalism as being essentially a missionary and evangelistic movement (Anderson 2007), we will also understand the outward thrust by Nordic missionaries, and particularly women, amply illustrated in the chapter in this volume by Mikaelsson. Pentecostalism was relatively weak compared to the dominant Lutheran state churches in Nordic countries, but the Nordic impact on the rapid internationalization of Pentecostalism far outweighed its small numbers at home. This was especially the case in Denmark, where the growth of Pentecostalism was relatively small, aggravated by internal schisms early on in its history, as the recent history by Nikolaj Christensen (2017) shows. Because there is no article on Denmark in this volume, I will give some attention to the related events there. Although contemporary Danish Pentecostalism is extremely small, this does not mean that nothing significant has happened there. Christensen reveals that an important factor for the lack of Pentecostal growth in Denmark (unlike other Nordic countries) was the absence of active religious minority groups. The state church monopoly in Denmark was still virtually intact, and though the earliest Pentecostals were largely members of the state church, even this was perceived as a threat by traditionalists and especially by Evangelical and Holiness factions. Denominational organization also made the Swedish, Norwegian, and Finnish Pentecostals more robust, whereas early Danish Pentecostals tended to pursue obscure doctrines like universalism and the ineffective restorationism of the Welsh-led Apostolic Church.

I have long advocated a "multiple origins" theory of Pentecostalism in contrast to the many attempts at making this a movement whose primary genesis comes from the United States. At the same time I have avoided suggesting that the American forms springing from Los Angeles and other centers were not influential, as indeed they were in many places. There are at least three considerations that the present volume illustrates. Firstly, there was much *continuity* with Evangelical, Holiness and healing revivalist movements that preceded early Pentecostalism in the nineteenth century. Stenvold's chapter on Norway makes this clear. The links with

American Methodism also had great significance in the beginnings of Pentecostalism in India, Chile, and West Africa, among others. Pentecostalism did not suddenly appear from heaven, as some would have us believe. Even speaking in tongues, one of the most divisive aspects of the early movement, did not suddenly appear at the beginning of the century. Tongues speaking has been recorded throughout the history of Christianity among various groups and revival movements. In Finland, the Laestadian movement (briefly mentioned in the chapter by Mantsinen) is an example of this. Furthermore, in Europe at least, many of the early Pentecostals remained in their church denominations until forced to leave. In some cases, they never did leave the old churches.

Secondly, there was *no one place of origin*, despite the fairly widespread claims that it all began at Azusa Street in downtown Los Angeles in 1906. It is true, as these chapters show, that Nordic Pentecostalism was at first influenced by events in the United States, but that was a transitory period. Contemporary Charismatic Christianity in Nordic countries (as throughout the world) is the product of a long process of development with precedents going back to a much earlier time. Its history was in continuity with the revivalist movements out of which it emerged. Azusa Street was indeed an important centre for the early internationalizing of the movement, but there were other significant networks and centres of influence worldwide. Perhaps the most significant in Europe was that initiated by Methodist pastor T.B. Barratt in Oslo. In Barratt's mission, the founding father of Pentecostalism in Britain, Anglican vicar Alexander Boddy, had his first experience of Pentecostalism. Boddy never left the Church of England. Of course, there are many new examples of centres that have appeared over the past century in many places worldwide. One of the more recent was that of Ulf Ekman in Uppsala. Pentecostalism as we know it today has had many beginnings, which are sometimes connected, but sometimes isolated. It was in a process of formation for at least its first two decades and arguably, it has never stopped being in a process of formation and reinvention.

Thirdly, there have been many iterations or *waves* of Pentecostalism throughout the past century. Even the threefold classification of Hollenweger and others into "Pentecostal", "Charismatic," and "Neocharismatic" can no longer be applied without countless exceptions and additions. It is as incorrect to speak of three "Waves" of Pentecostalism in North America as it is anywhere else in the world. Besides the threefold typology of classical Pentecostalism, the Charismatic movement, and the so-called "Third Wave," there were other significant movements in North America that do not easily fit into this schema like the "Latter Rain" movement beginning in the late 1940s and the "Jesus People," from the late 1960s. All of these movements impacted on events in Europe, and vice versa. One could also speak of the "Word of Faith" movement that dominates several global megachurches today, based on the doctrine of the late Kenneth Hagin, Jr. in Tulsa, Oklahoma. The most prominent Nordic center was of course the Livets Ord in Uppsala under the enigmatic Ulf Ekman, with significant influence in Eastern Europe and Russia. Much more could be written about this but perhaps that has already been done (Coleman 2000). As a side issue, it would be interesting to look at Ekman's more recent conversion to Roman Catholicism and what the nature of his journey from Lutheran priest to "Word of Faith" leader to Roman Catholic adherent was. Perhaps it was not as great a leap as some have thought.

We cannot discuss Pentecostalism in Europe without mentioning the enormous impact of the so-called "migrant" or transnational churches, many of which have now become national churches in their own right in the countries where they have been planted. Migration has brought new life to Pentecostalism in the Western world, although it might be argued that this is a different kind of Pentecostalism. After the 1980s, the "Pentecostalization" of older churches outside the Western world, especially in Africa and Asia, accelerated as these churches adjusted to the rapid growth of new churches in their midst. They began to adopt the latters' methods, particularly appealing to the young and urbanized. Simultaneously, the new form of Pentecostalism exhibited a fierce independence that eschewed denominations and preferred associations in loose "fellowships." The Pentecostal megachurches operate in cities like Lagos, Rio de Janeiro, Seoul, and Singapore, but also in unexpected European places like Kyiv (a Ukrainian church with a Nigerian leader), Budapest, and of course, Uppsala. Each of these European cases is (or was at one stage) the largest congregation in its respective country; and in London the largest congregation is predominantly Nigerian. The megachurches form networks of similar churches across the world, and these transnational associations are not only North–South, but also South–South and East–South. In most cases, the transnational churches in the North have been unable to break free from their ethnic minority character. However, the migrant churches have not inflated the numbers of Pentecostals in Nordic countries as much as they have in other Western countries like Britain, France, or Germany or, indeed, in the United States itself.

Within a century of their commencement, Pentecostal and Charismatic forms of Christianity now exist in most countries and have affected all forms of Christianity in our contemporary world—however we regard or manipulate the statistics on affiliation. Pentecostalism has certainly changed world Christianity in the twenty-first century, and perhaps religion as a whole. Whatever our opinion or personal experience of Pentecostalism might be, these are movements of such vitality that Christianity has been irrevocably changed. The mushrooming growth of Pentecostal and Charismatic churches and the "Pentecostalization" of older, both Protestant and Catholic churches—especially in the majority world—is a fact of our time. With all its failings and schisms, these complex movements continue to expand and increase across the globe. The growth may well have halted or even decreased in northern Europe, but the enormous growth of Charismatic Christianity in Asia, Africa, and Latin America also means that it may continue to expand and influence all types of Christianity there. In creative ways Pentecostalism has promoted a globalized Christianity that has not lost touch with its local context. It is able to preserve both global and local characteristics, making it possible to speak at the same time of "Pentecostalism" and "Pentecostalisms." So at least for the foreseeable future, the continued vitality of Charismatic Christianity is probably assured. Where it will go in Nordic countries is anyone's guess. This volume gives us a glimpse into that possible future, but also reminds us that Pentecostalism in Europe itself is really insignificant in comparison with other forms of Christianity that have been here much longer.

University of Birmingham   Allan H. Anderson

References

Anderson, Allan H. *Spreading Fires: The Missionary Nature of Early Pentecostalism*. London/Marynoll/New York: SCM & Orbis, 2007.

Christensen, Nikolaj. 2017. *Flickering Flames: The Early Pentecostal Movement in Denmark, 1907–1924*. Ph.D. thesis. University of Birmingham.

Coleman, Simon. *The Globalisation of Charismatic Christianity*. Cambridge: Cambridge University Press, 2000.

Haustein, Jörg. *Writing Religious History: The Historiography of Ethiopian Pentecostalism*. Wiesbaden: Harrassowitz, 2011.

Acknowledgments

No book is created in a vacuum, and the present volume is the product of cooperation with and support from colleagues, friends, and institutions. Most essential among these have been our contributing authors, whom we would like to thank for their contributions and their patience during the editing process. We are especially grateful to James R. Lewis for introducing us to one another and setting us upon this path in the first place, and for his everlasting encouragement and continuous support. We would also like to extend special thanks to Allan H. Anderson for generously agreeing to write the Foreword. Finally, we would like to thank the University of Bergen for funding Open Access for this volume, making it available to a wider audience than otherwise would have been possible. On a more personal note, we thank our supportive friends, partners, and family members.

Contents

1 Introduction 1
Jessica Moberg and Jane Skjoldli

Part 1 Historical Perspectives on the Early Pentecostal Movement 23

2 Paving the Way for Pentecostalism: A Historical Exploration of Post-Reformation Revivals in Norway 25
Anne Stensvold

3 The Norwegian Pentecostal Foreign Mission: A Survey of Mission History with an Emphasis on Organization, Expansion, and Gender 49
Lisbeth Mikaelsson

Part 2 Internal Dynamics 79

4 In the Wake of God's Fire: Transforming Charisma and Charismata in the Reconstruction of a Local Church 81
Jane Skjoldli

5 The Finnish Pentecostal Movement: An Analysis of Internal Struggle as a Process of Habitual Division 109
Teemu T. Mantsinen

6 Knutby Filadelfia: A Schismatic New Religious Movement Within the Pentecostal Context 137
Liselotte Frisk

Part 3 Novelties and Contemporary Innovation 159

7 Faith Healing Revisited: A Charismatic Christian Intervention to the Therapy Culture in Finland 161
Tuija Hovi

8 Sharing and Holy Hugs: The Birth and Development of Intimization in Charismatic Stockholm 187
Jessica Moberg

9 Televangelism in Sweden—Now? Is Channel 10 in Älmhult in Fact a Telechurch? 213
Jan-Åke Alvarsson

10 Postscript: Embers from a Global Fire 239
Jessica Moberg and Jane Skjoldli

Index 243

Notes on Contributors

Jan-Åke Alvarsson is a professor of cultural anthropology at Uppsala University, and the Director of the Institute for Pentecostal Studies in Uppsala. Among his publications are several works on Pentecostalism among indigenous peoples in Bolivia, Pentecostal missionaries in Latin America, as well as the American origin, history, and developments of the Swedish Pentecostal Movement.

Liselotte Frisk is a professor of religious studies at Dalarna University and Vice-chairman of the Association for Research and Information on Alternative Spirituality (FINYAR), Sweden. Frisk has published extensively on New Age and new religious movements in Sweden. Recently (2008–2011), Frisk has, together with Peter Åkerbäck, mapped new spiritualities in Dalarna. She presently studies children in minority religions. Between 2010 and 2013, Frisk was coeditor of the *International Journal for the Study of New Religions* and the Director of the International Society for the Study of New Religions. She is currently coeditor of *Aura*.

Tuija Hovi is a senior lecturer and an adjunct professor in comparative religion at the University of Turku, Finland. She teaches ethnography and methodology in the study of religions, as well as psychology of religion. Hovi's research interests include the diversity of Charismatic and Pentecostal Christianity, social psychology of religious experience, identity construction, vernacular religion, and narrative inquiry. She is a member of the steering group of the recently founded Centre for the Study of Christian Cultures.

Teemu T. Mantsinen is a researcher and anthropologist of religion at the University of Turku, Finland. His main research interests include Pentecostalism and apostasy. His PhD dissertation (2014) explored the relationship between Pentecostal religiosity and social class in Finland, based upon ethnographic fieldwork.

Lisbeth Mikaelsson is professor emerita of the study of religion at the University of Bergen, Norway. Having published in both English and Norwegian, her research focuses on Norwegian Christian mission, with special emphasis on mission literature and gender, New Religious Movements, Lutheran church religion, and contemporary pilgrimage in Norway.

Jessica Moberg is a senior lecturer in religious studies at the University of Gothenburg, Sweden. Her main research interests include contemporary Neo-Pentecostalism and various forms of new spiritualties. Moberg has taken interest in issues of religious change, and in the lived religiosity, emphasizing ritual, narrative, and material dimensions. Moberg is on the editorial board of the *Alternative Spirituality and Religion Review*.

Jane Skjoldli is a PhD candidate in the study of religion at the University of Bergen, Norway. Her research interests focus on contemporary Christianity, primarily Catholicism and Charismatic Christianity. Particular aspects of interest are World Youth Day, public events, digital game studies, ritual studies, pilgrimage studies, Weberian charisma, and evolutionary approaches to religion.

Anne Stensvold is a professor of history of religion at the University of Oslo. Her academic interests mainly center on modern and contemporary Christianity. She has published on a wide range of topics including Catholic piety, religion and television, and contemporary religious developments in Norway. Lately, she has worked on interrelations between religion and politics.

CHAPTER 1

Introduction

Jessica Moberg and Jane Skjoldli

Somewhere in Finland shoppers at a local mall saturated by sale offers and lounge music are approached by a group of amiable strangers. The strangers offer them healing and therapeutic methods with which to confront their everyday problems. Solutions are offered through intercessory prayer. Many of the intercessors are women involved in Charismatic churches. Their aim is to carry out missionary work but, as they engage with potential converts, they are careful to avoid open proselytization and speaking in tongues during the prayer sessions. Both are strictly forbidden. Elsewhere, in Sweden, an elderly Pentecostal sits down in front of her television and tunes in to Channel 10 in order to enjoy "old-fashioned" Pentecostal songs and sermons, many of which are but a memory in contemporary Pentecostal congregations. Watching the church service on TV, a quite recent phenomenon in the country, she feels at ease, reminded of her childhood as a young Pentecostal. Turning to Bergen in Norway, members of the country's formerly largest independent church, previously part of the Faith Movement, are taking on the herculean task of recreating

J. Moberg (✉)
University of Gothenburg, Gothenburg, Sweden

J. Skjoldli
University of Bergen, Bergen, Norway

their organization after a collapse a few years back, when over half of the members dropped out following the ousting of their founder and leader.

These three snapshots provide a small glimpse into the diversity of contemporary Charismatic Christianity in Nordic countries. The region is home to "classic" Pentecostal organizations and Faith Movement churches, as well as Charismatic immigrant groups, Charismatic Lutherans, newer networks like Hillsong Church, and various offshoots. A hundred years ago, all three scenarios would have been unthinkable, and not just because of the technological advances that had not yet been made then. At that time, early pioneers had recently introduced Norway, Sweden, and Denmark to the Pentecostal Movement, bringing influences from the Azusa Street revival. The first preachers traveled widely, spoke in tongues, and called people to "turn to Christ" before the end (see Anderson 2014, 93–94).

If we permit ourselves to indulge in a thought experiment whereby the first Nordic Pentecostals travel to the present day, we can imagine they would probably be surprised—perhaps even shocked. Vast changes have occurred in culture, politics, technology, and administration. Additionally, increased religious and ethnic pluralization has occurred within and without the Pentecostal Movement. How might they have perceived developments within the Charismatic traditions? Would they marvel at the many new orientations, ethnic minority churches, and new forms of organizational networks? Would they condemn alterations to traditions for which they helped lay the foundation? So much has transpired in the span of a mere century. Can we even claim to be speaking of the same tradition? Such questions beg reflection, not only when we consider our hypothetical time travelers; they also bear implications on the academic level.

Definitions and Terminology

Like all terms and categories, those native to Pentecostal studies come with their own sets of problems. As this field of study has developed, it has attracted the attention of sociologists, psychologists, anthropologists, theologians, historians, and scholars of religion. Today's researchers struggle to consolidate disparities that arise from the terms' usage spanning the last 100 years, and to encapsulate transformations that create distance to Pentecostalism's early heritage. Another problem is how interchangeability between the terms "Pentecostal" and "Charismatic" is frequently taken for granted. On the one hand, this problem reflects the emergence of interdisciplinarity in Pentecostal studies. On the other, it conceals a lack of consensus regarding problems of definition and delineation of the objects of study.

In its nascency, Pentecostal studies focused on early movements, leading to challenges in reconciling the categories and concepts that were created early on with the descriptions and analyses of later developments. In response to these complications, old ways of categorizing and naming different phenomena have been revisited. Although contemporary scholars are careful in emphasizing local variation, there is still some consensus regarding Pentecostal-Charismatic Christianity as a distinct category, set apart by the centrality of the gifts of the Spirit (see Droogers 2010). Some scholars have defended this position by focusing on similarities in theology, common roots, or practice. Norwegian theologian Nils Bloch-Hoell, who studied the Pentecostal Movement of the early twentieth century, focused on the doctrine of baptism in the Holy Spirit as distinct from conversion, manifested in the speaking of tongues (1964, 2). Another way of justifying Pentecostal-Charismatic Christianity as a specific category has been by stressing the common historical roots. Theologian Walter J. Hollenweger's work has been particularly significant to the field's development in this respect (see Hollenweger 2005). Hollenweger's account traced the movement's origins to the Azusa Street revival, and then followed its spread to various corners of the world, its influence on existing churches, and transformation into a much wider Charismatic movement. This view is still prevalent (Anderson 2014; Cox 2001; Westerlund 2009).

Attempts have been made to complicate and deconstruct "Pentecostalism" and "Charismatic Christianity" as categories. Previously, the view that speaking in tongues amounts to "evidence" of baptism in the Spirit was seen as being a universal trait among Pentecostal-Charismatic Christians. Important criticism has been leveled against this notion, revealing that the view was shared only by a small number of early American Pentecostals (van der Laan 2010). More recently, critique has gravitated towards two topics: The first regards phenomenological approaches that focus on common features in order to justify the construction of Pentecostal-Charismatic Christianity as a unique category. The second concerns the analytical value of the categories thus constructed (cf. Bergunder 2010). Other critiques reflect the globalization of Pentecostal-Charismatic Christianity, growing scholarly interest in such groups, particularly in the developing world and the postcolonial turn (Anderson 2005, 2014; Jenkins 2006, 2007; Lindhardt 2014; Martin 1990; Meyer 2010). Furthermore, global studies scholars have called into question the "common origins" hypothesis, highlighting its Americentrism. Allan H. Anderson has pointed out that this form of Christianity did not originate at Azusa Street, but emerged in various places in the world at about the same time, emphasizing the importance of early movements in India, Korea, and Chile. These findings were formulated in the now famous "multiple beginnings thesis" (Anderson 2005, 2014).

Others have gone even further. Michael Bergunder and André Droogers, among others, consider "Pentecostal" and "Charismatic" to be constructs of scholarly discourse (Bergunder 2010; Droogers 2010). Taking such perspectives into consideration, it has become a vital task to inquire into what alternative perspectives the category Pentecostal-Charismatic Christianity obscures; it conceal diachronic developments and synchronic connections to other Christian and non-Christian religions. As pointed out by Bergunder, it also clouds Pentecostalism-Charismatic Christianity's roots in previous Protestant revivals, as well as its immediate heritage in the twentieth century's broader revivalist milieu (2010, 60–64). In a similar vein, Donald E. Miller suggests that what are often described as "Neo-Charismatic movements" may be seen as a kind of second Reformation, with roots stretching back to the sixteenth century (1997, 11). As illustrated by George Chryssides (2000, 66), Mary Jo Neitz (2012), and Linda Woodhead and Paul Heelas (2000), there are also striking similarities between Pentecostal-Charismatic movements and non-Christian new spiritualities.

Attempts have also been made to defend the umbrella category "Pentecostal-Charismatic Christianity," and to outline suggestions for how this form of Christianity may be studied. Anderson, drawing on Ludwig Wittgenstein, notes that Pentecostal-Charismatic movements share traits of "family resemblance" in terms of "character, theology and ethos" (Anderson 2010, 15). Another option, hinted at by Droogers, is to think of it as a Weberian ideal type (2010). Other more recent suggestions involve network analysis (Bergunder 2010, 52–56).

We generally agree with the critique presented above, and concur with Droogers regarding classifications in that they are scholarly constructs that inevitably entail simplification and universalization of local perspectives. However, we also share his opinion that they are necessary and useful (2008; cf. Bergunder 2010). As such, we treat Pentecostal-Charismatic Christianity as an umbrella category for the purpose of this anthology. There are two main reasons for this: Firstly, as an established category, it grounds the anthology in a global field of research, thus enabling us to communicate with other scholars of Pentecostal studies. Secondly, it offers us a way of pinpointing certain historical and contemporary processes that have been important influences on the religious Nordic scene in the last 100 years. Furthermore, it invites comparison with similar movements on the global level.

Our approach is inspired by Anderson's "family resemblance." The features that we would consider key to our understanding of this category are: emphasis on connecting with the Holy Spirit; the centrality of healing and *charismata*; the prominence of individual experiences; and bodily involvement in ritual participation (cf. Lindhardt 2011). That said, we aim to avoid the pitfalls of essentialization by presenting case studies from different historical periods and settings, all of which situate and exemplify "Pentecostal-Charismatic Christianity" in broader religious landscapes. We also hope to inspire, but also demonstrate, continuing elaboration of the nuances denoted by Pentecostal-Charismatic religiosity as a distinct category.

One of the pleasures of academia involves the recognition that new problems arise whenever a solution to an existing problem is reached. Applying this category includes the classification and labeling of different strands and movements, and their terminological disentanglement. Hollenweger distinguished between the early "classic" Pentecostals, the "Charismatic Movement" within mainline churches, and indigenous Pentecostalism in the developing world (2005). His approach has been rethought and new categories developed. A presently strong threefold model involves distinguishing between "classic" Pentecostalism, the Charismatic Movement, and Neo-Pentecostalism, which emerged in the postwar period. The latter is characterized by emphasis on well-being here and now, worship, global church networks, and so on (see Anderson 2010, 19–20; cf. Hunt 2010, 184). Of course, this "triad" has also been scrutinized; the label Neo-Charismatic in particular has been criticized for being a "leftover category," lumping together highly diverse movements with different roots and orientations (van der Laan 2010, 204). Moreover, this approach may be a blunt tool when researching contemporary groups, since their origins as Pentecostal or Neo-Pentecostal may say little about their current orientation. As illustrated in Teemu T. Mantsinen's chapter, Pentecostal organizations may transform in Neo-Pentecostal directions, and Pentecostal and Neo-Charismatic features coexist in the same denomination or even congregation.

Except for the classification dilemma ("what goes where") semantic problems arise. One kind of scholarly cop-out is illustrated by the creation of neologisms by adding the "neo" prefix to terms in order to signal new developments. While this reflects awareness of religious movements' inherent dynamism, it also causes terminological issues for future labeling, as well as for precision in describing developing movements; what counts as "neo" changes continuously. Emic labels and terminologies may also cause confusion. In the Nordic countries, the Pentecostal Movement (in Finnish "Helluntaiherätys," in Norwegian "Pinsebevegelsen," and in Swedish "Pingströrelsen"), the term or terms that researchers use for referring to early revivals, is homonymous to the emic names of denomination-like structures coming out of these movements. If we apply the term "Pentecostal Movement," we not only risk conflating the emerging organizational outcome with the wider transdenominational revival, but also concealing the many other Charismatic groups and influences on alternate Christian denominations. Noting the particular emic Nordic terminology, we have chosen to use the term "Charismatic Christianity" as an umbrella term in the introduction. The term "Pentecostal" refers exclusively to organization structures that have roots in the revival of the early twentieth century. We further find the term "Charismatic Movement" useful for describing Charismatic expressions taking place in established churches, including Nordic state churches, older Baptist churches, and independent churches. "Neo-Charismatic" is used to refer to a range of traditions emerging in the post-World War II period and onwards. It includes materially oriented movements like the Faith movement, and more socially inclined and low-key movements like the Vineyard Movement. Current expressions involve a spectrum of different organizations that focus on wellbeing in the here and now, emotional healing, adoption and sacralization of popular music, and new media, and that tend to favor network structures to well-defined denominations. However, we are well aware that not all terms map perfectly on to all case studies included in the anthology. As such, we have let the authors make their own definitions in the respective chapters.

The Nordic Backdrop

The Nordic countries (Denmark, Norway, Sweden, Finland, and Iceland) have shared experiences in that they are all located in the northern hemisphere, and in relatively scarcely populated areas. They also largely share a common religious, cultural, and lingual heritage. The exception to the latter is Finland, whose native language (Finland is bilingual Finnish–Swedish) strongly differs from those of the other Nordic countries. Moreover, their individual histories are intricately intertwined with each other. For example,

Sweden and Finland formed a union up until 1809, after which Finland came under Russian rule. Norway, in turn, has been in union with both Denmark and Sweden, and Iceland a part of Denmark. Norway gained its independence in 1905 and Iceland in 1944. The histories of Christianity in the Nordic countries have also taken similar trajectories, starting with Catholic Christianization, the Protestant Reformation in the sixteenth century, and close cooperation between monarchs and Lutheran state churches. As a result of the Russian influence, Finland stands out with its two national churches: one Lutheran and one Orthodox (see Alvarsson 2011, 19). While the Reformation was implemented top-down, each of the countries have a history of Protestant grassroots revivals, like the Pietist movements in the late seventeenth century onwards. These popular movements arose and took form within the state churches. In the nineteenth century, several processes impacted the religious scene. Industrialization, urbanization, large-scale migration, and the rise of popular movements changed the religious topography. Among these, the revival movements led to the formation of a number of different Free Church (i.e., state-independent) denominations, mainly Baptist-, Methodist-, and Holiness-influenced ones. Yet, the state churches that set the agenda for religious life in the public domain did not welcome competition. Social stigmatization and legislation prevented larger religious assemblies from outside the state churches from gathering together. This led many members of emerging Baptist denominations to migrate to the United States in pursuit of religious freedom and better economic prospects (see also Martin 2002, 14–15). All these historical developments set the stage for and shaped Charismatic Christian presence in the region which, in turn, fueled religious pluralization and globalization. While the earlier revivals paved the way, the dominance of the state churches along with Nordic modern developments seem to have made the region less fertile for mission (cf. Hunt 2010, 190–191).

The Beginnings

Charismatic Christianity in the Nordic countries has relied upon and furthered global connections since the outset (Anderson 2014, 93–99; Bundy 2009, 1–3). In fact, the Pentecostal revival was introduced to Norway and Sweden only a few months after the Azusa Street revival caught on (Hunt 2010, 190). It is impossible to understand its early introduction without considering the increased contacts with the United States, and particularly the recently established migrant networks, between

Nordic countries and the United States (cf. Bloch-Hoell 1964, 65; Holm 1970, 16–17). First- and second-generation Nordic migrants, many of whom had Free Church backgrounds, obtained new influences "over there" that they recounted in letters to their families and friends in their countries of origin. Besides, a substantial number returned as missionaries. As pointed out by cultural anthropologist Jan-Åke Alvarsson, some of the first Swedish Pentecostals, like Andrew Johnson (an anglicization of Anders Johansson) and Emma Östberg, were active in William J. Seymour's prayer group (2011, 20, 2014, 23–32). Visiting New York, they also encountered another émigré whose influence would be momentous in the forming of Nordic Pentecostalism: Thomas Ball Barratt (1862–1940). A few years after returning to Norway, the latter established the independent Filadelfia Congregation in Kristiania (now Oslo). Barratt was closely connected to other Pentecostal leaders to-be. For instance, he was baptized by Swedish Pentecostal icon and colossus Lewi Pethrus (1884–1974). The ministry of Barratt and his followers was of huge importance in spreading Pentecostalism in Norway and in other Nordic countries (Anderson 2014, 76, 93–94, 84–88; Fell 1999, 288–291).

The new revival was characterized by strong emphasis on personal conversion, ecstatic practices, baptism in the Holy Spirit, and the belief that the return of Jesus was imminent. The practitioners were called "Friends of Pentecost." The movement mainly took root in the Free Church revivalist scene. On the organizational level, the enthusiasts belonged to different denominations and assemblies, and gathered around the gospel of rebirth in the Holy Spirit (cf. Nilsen 1984, 31). The early converts mainly fit the pattern that has been detected in international studies; a major part of them were women from the lower socioeconomic strata, for which the movement served as a vehicle for upward social mobility (Alvarsson 2011; Mantsinen 2014). In contrast to other parts of the world, where Pentecostalism became a chiefly urban phenomenon, Nordic Pentecostalism also developed a strong rural and small-town base (see Alvarsson 2007).

Although the new revival grew rapidly during the first decades, Pentecostalism did not become a separate movement until around 1910. At this time, tensions and conflicts within the older denominations in which it had taken root led to divisions. Both Barratt and Pethrus were excluded from their Methodist and Baptist denominations, leading the enthusiasts to form independent Pentecostal networks (Alvarsson 2011, 25, 37; Bloch-Hoell 1964, 68–71). Consequently, Pinsebevegelsen (Norway), Pingströrelsen (Sweden), and Helluntaiherätys (Finland) were formed. These movements were comparably loosely organized, avoided bureaucratization and centralization, and emphasized congregational independence (Alvarsson 2011, 37; Bloch-Hoell 1964, 71). However, over the years, they would become increasingly institutionalized and some took the form of registered denominations.

Post-World War II Nordic Contexts

Leaping forward to the postwar period, the Nordic countries underwent significant changes that affected and shaped the Pentecostal movements. Coming out of the war with different experiences, the countries began to lay the foundation for a particular brand of Nordic postwar modernity, based upon social democratic ideas and ideals. This model—a third way between capitalism and communism—was characterized by its emphasis on strong welfare states, including extensive state monopolies. The state systems were to provide healthcare and education, by means of progressive taxation, a system which would diminish gaps between rich and poor. The postwar period also saw the weakening of the Lutheran state churches, visible in legislation that ensured citizens increased religious freedom. In parallel, organized Christianity lost ground in society and the wider culture, and both state churches and many Free Church denominations lost members (Davie 2002, 5–8; cf. Stark et al. 2005).

Unlike many other Free Churches, the Pentecostal movements fared very well during World War II (see Bloch-Hoell 1964, 91). Alvarsson, referring to Bloch-Hoell, claims that Sweden in the 1950s was the country with the highest number of Pentecostals in the world. According to Bloch-Hoell (1964, 91), they numbered around 92,000. Internal dynamics had also contributed to changes within the movements. Correlated to other factors, the increased numbers of practitioners born and socialized into the movements turned Nordic Pentecostalism in a more institutionalized and societally engaged direction. This, in turn, fueled various responses and internal schisms. The churches also attained new visibility in the public sphere, including in political debate. In 1945, the Pentecostal newspaper *Dagen* ("The Day") was created in Sweden, giving voice to the movement and confronting secularization. Another such attempt was the founding of the Christian Democratic Party (Kristen demokratisk samling) in 1964 (Alvarsson 2011, 29–34). Other Charismatic movements were also established, some of which were integrated into the Pentecostal congregations. This was the case with the Jesus Movement, inspired by hippie Christians in California, which attracted many young Pentecostals. However, not everyone was happy with the current course. In the late 1950s and early 1960s, the Maranata Movement, influenced by William Branham and Oral Roberts, took the form of a protest movement in Norway and Sweden. Pentecostal pastors Aage Samuelsen and Arne Imsen joined forces with Swedish collaborators, criticizing both institutionalization and increased societal involvement, and calling on Pentecostals to return to their more expressive and less "worldly" roots. The result was a splinter movement. The 1960s also saw internal schism in Finland, as the Free Pentecostal Movement (Soumen vapaa Helluntaiherätys) broke away (Alvarsson 2011, 29–33).

As in many parts of the world, Nordic Pentecostalism continued to grow until the 1970s, particularly in Finland, Norway, and Sweden. Thereafter, the Nordic movements began to lag behind (Alvarsson 2011, 38). The presence of the full-fledged welfare states likely had a negative impact in this regard (see Zuckerman 2009). As many scholars have emphasized, Charismatic Christianity has developed into the form of mass movements in poorer, rapidly modernizing countries, while remaining marginal in richer societies (see also Marshall 2009). Philip Jenkins, for one, has called this form of Christianity "the most successful social movement of the twentieth century" (Jenkins 2007, 9). If Pentecostalism's success lies in its ability to lift people from poverty, integrate them into communities, and encourage civil discipline, Pentecostal organizations obviously met competition from welfare states, which took care of poverty, and offered free education and cheap healthcare from the cradle to the grave. Also, in the postwar period, young people in the Nordic region gained other religious options, such as various non-Christian new religions (Frisk 1998, 58, cf. Frisk and Åkerbäck 2013; Gilhus and Mikaelsson 2005).

Pentecostalism's rapid growth came to a halt in the 1970s. The same decade witnessed the emergence of Charismatic movements within Protestant and Catholic communities (cf. Csordas 1997; McGuire 1983). In Norway and Sweden, Charismatic Lutherans organized themselves in the Oasis Movement—a network above the parish level. In Norway, the movement was founded in 1977 and in Sweden in 1984 (cf. Alvarsson 2011, 33–34). Today, the network exists in Denmark, Sweden, Finland, and Norway (Svalfors 2012, 158). In the churches of Denmark and Sweden, Alpha courses spread from the Free Churches and became important for introducing Charismatic features since the 1990s (Svalfors 2012, 158–159, Thomsen 2012, 120–134).

Late Modern Developments

In the last three decades, the Nordic countries have taken new paths in terms of economy and politics, and changed culturally and religiously. As a consequence of increased global mobility, ethnic and religious pluralization has expanded. Another prominent tendency in the late twentieth century was the therapeutization of popular and religious culture, as well as their intersections (Hornborg 2012; Kivivuori 1991, 1996; Moberg 2015). Although the extent of this has varied, the once strong welfare states have been weakened, with privatizations of previous monopolies, and no longer play the same role as provider of welfare and public services. In the meantime, church attendance and membership rates have continued to drop in many churches—the Lutheran state churches as well as many Free Churches. The state and church were officially (semi-)separated in Sweden (2000) and in Norway (2012). Although this has often been interpreted as evidence of secularization, such views have been called into question by several Nordic scholars of religion who emphasize that other forms of faith are growing. Migrants from different parts of the world have brought with them their own forms of organized religion (e.g., Islam, and Catholic and Orthodox Christianity), and nonorganized spirituality is on the rise. Lisbeth Mikaelsson and Ingvild S. Gilhus have criticized images emerging from large-scale quantitative studies, such as the Pew Research Center's depiction of Scandinavia as one-dimensionally "secularized," calling attention to the prolific establishment of new religious movements and their strong influence (Gilhus and Mikaelsson 2005; Kraft et al. 2015). Similarly, a Finnish research group involving one of the contributors to this volume suggests that Finland is better described as a postsecular country, where alternative spiritualities, Charismatic Christian traditions, and migrant religiosity are transforming the religious landscape (Åbo Akademi University 2017). In fact, some scholars have gone so far as to suggest that the rise of non-Christian spiritualities in the region is a form of massive popular revival (Hammer 2010; Hornborg 2012).

Charismatic Christianity has also pluralized, changing in terms of practice, organization, and orientation, including a shift from national denominations to international networks. Several new forms of Neo-Charismatic movement have been born. In the 1980s, the international prosperity-oriented Faith Movement took root. This movement, which became equally influential and controversial, was vital for bringing about change. The result was both the emergence of new churches, and the morphing of

Pentecostal churches and congregations in the same direction. Word of Life (Livets ord) in Uppsala in Sweden, led by Ulf Ekman, a former Lutheran priest trained at Kenneth E. Hagin's Rhema Bible Center in Tulsa, Oklahoma, became the key center of the Nordic Faith Movement. The Bible school at Uppsala became particularly important for furthering the Faith Movement's theology, its new worship music, and its styles of preaching, all of which helped attract young people from all over the Nordic region, especially from Norway. These students often founded similar churches in their hometowns (Alvarsson 2011, 33–35; Coleman 2000).

The 1990s saw the establishment of several other Neo-Charismatic groups, many of which were affiliated with global megachurches or massive networks (cf. Meyer 2010), such as the Vineyard Movement. Global migration has also redrawn the Charismatic map of the region; migrants from Latin America and western and eastern Africa have been particularly important in this respect (Alvarsson 2011, 36; Malmström 2013). Since the 2000s, the Charismatic field has become increasingly heterogenic as new movements are continuing to be established. Several global churches have both integrated local groups and planted new congregations; Hillsong Church and Calvary Chapel are both examples of this. New generations of Charismatics are currently in the process of founding new communities and cooperative networks where the boundaries between various Charismatic traditions are often blurred (Hovi 2010, 41; Moberg 2013b).

Contemporary Numbers

On the global stage, Charismatics dominate the Christian landscape, together with Catholics. In the Nordic countries, however, the former remains a small minority. Attempts have been made at estimating their numbers. As a result of the diverging methods of counting and classification used, diverse figures have been presented (cf. Anderson 2014, 92). Stephen Hunt (2010, 190; cf. Anderson 2005, 92) suggests that less than 1 percent of the populations in Norway and Sweden respectively are classic Pentecostals. Anderson (2014, 92), on the other hand, claims that Finland and Norway stand out in a European-wide comparison in that they have more than 4 percent, a number that includes different forms of Charismatics. Alvarsson (2011, 38) estimates that there are 32,000 Pentecostals in Norway, and 49,000 in Finland. In Sweden, the Pentecostal Movement counted 84,700 members at the end of 2013 (Pingst—fria församlingar i samverkan 2017). According to Alvarsson's (2011, 38) assessment, the number of Pentecostals and Neo-Charismatics is lower than 100,000 in Sweden. Charismatic Christianity has never gained the same foothold in Denmark, where it makes for an even more marginal phenomenon (Anderson 2014, 96).[1] Alvarsson (2011, 38) counts fewer than 4000 Pentecostals in Iceland and around 5000 in Denmark (see also Thomsen 2012, 122). There are, however, several difficulties with such estimations, meaning that we should take them with a large pinch of salt. The first problem is that many scholars draw upon the membership statistics provided by Charismatic organizations. The second problem is that Pentecostal denominations and old networks are far more organized, and it is therefore easier to assess them than to trace Neo-Charismatic communities. Yet, reported figures for Pentecostals may also be inaccurate. For instance, people may move and leave their congregations but remain listed. In Norway and Sweden, congregations receive funding depending on their membership rates, meaning that there are economic (and status) motives for not "delisting" them. For this reason, the overall figures may need to be lowered. Still, there are many Neo-Charismatic groups that do not form part of national denominations and do not keep track of their members. Some non-organized groups fly under the radar entirely. Migrant groups in particular seem to thrive, and then fade away from view. This means that the total numbers of Charismatics must be increased. By and large, we have to rely on estimates, particularly when discussing Neo-Pentecostalism. According to Finnish scholar of religion Tuija Hovi (2010, 40), there are around 4000 members of Neo-Charismatic groups in Finland. Based on Alvarsson's (2011, 38) estimation that the total number of Charismatics was lower than 100,000 in Sweden, and the fact that the Pentecostal Movement counts 84,000 of them, there would be at most 16,000 Neo-Charismatics.

Another problem is the binary "yes-or-no" approach which is often evident in general estimations, meaning that denominations/congregations are understood as either Charismatic or non-Charismatic—Charismatics are expected to appear solely in Charismatic denominations and churches. This does not always reflect reality, and by following this principle, one misses variations within denominations, as well as the levels of Charismatic expression within them. Charismatics do exist in otherwise non-Charismatic denominations and churches, either because they were influenced by the early Pentecostal revival or by later Neo-Charismatic ones. In Sweden, such branches exist in many Free Church denominations. Moreover, Sweden is home to the Charismatic denomination Interact—the result of the fusion of three nineteenth-century Baptist denominations that were pentecostalized in the early twentieth century but did not join the formalized Pentecostal Movement. In 2013, Interact numbered 33,000 members (cf. Moberg 2013a). Charismatics are also found within the Catholic and Lutheran churches. Being listed as members of those churches, their Charismatic involvement is not statistically visible (see Svalfors 2012). Maria Thomsen (2012) claims that around 15,000 Danes are members of Charismatically inclined congregations within the Evangelical Lutheran Church (2012, 122). If this were the case, the number of Charismatics in Denmark would be three times as high in the Lutheran church as in the Pentecostal congregations. This could mean that the numbers of Charismatics in Nordic countries are higher than commonly estimated.

On the contrary, many old Pentecostal congregations have more or less ceased engaging in Charismatic practices. If one attends a service in one of the largest Pentecostal congregations in Stockholm or Gothenburg, one finds few if any indications that one is visiting a Charismatic organization. This leads us to a more philosophical question: When is the level of Charismatic expression so low that a group no longer qualifies as Charismatic? These problems demonstrate the need to heed the nuances that complicate issues of membership and Charismatic identity; there are spectrums of involvement with variable features of identification. Perhaps discouragingly, it is extremely difficult to pinpoint numbers of Charismatics based upon our current knowledge. Nevertheless, as several of the upcoming chapters indicate, Charismatic Christianity appears quite stable in the region.

This Book

Much like our topic of study, Pentecostal studies in general reaches, covers, and investigates Pentecostal-Charismatic interconnections in vast parts of the globe. Although Nordic international missions have received universal attention (Anderson 2014; Bundy 2009), the region is something of a *terra incognita* in the global field of research. Language barriers need to take their share of the blame; most studies are written in Nordic languages, proficiency in which is not particularly widespread.[2] Another reason is probably that the Nordic countries have considerably lower numbers of Charismatics than the American, African, and Asian countries, especially in the "global South" where this form of Christianity is blooming, along with Catholicism (Allen 2009, 144–145).

Against this backdrop, we deem it necessary to call for more overarching studies of Charismatic Christianity in non-Anglophone countries of the "global North." We are glad to see new interest in this matter, visible in a special issue of *Approaching Religion* (2015) dedicated to the Baltic Sea area. Until now, no efforts have been made to gather and publish Nordic case studies in a collective work, nor to discuss them in relation to processes particular to the region. As is visible from the historical overview, Charismatic Christianity has had a strong and interwoven presence in Norway, Sweden, and Finland.

The overall aim of this anthology is to shed light on diverse trajectories of Charismatic Christianity in the Nordic countries. Generally, the term "Nordic countries" also includes Denmark and Iceland, but this anthology focuses on the three countries where Charismatic Christianity has had the strongest presence: Sweden, Norway, and Finland (Anderson 2014, 92; cf. Bloch-Hoell 1964, 91). Evidently, we not only wish to fill in some of the uncharted territories on the global map, but to contribute to international research more broadly by providing case studies that further discussion on how this form of Christianity globalizes and spreads. In the Nordic countries, Charismatic Christianity has a long history, but has remained the religion of a small minority, making the region intriguing from a global perspective. In order to understand and theorize about such a complex phenomenon, it is necessary not only to study areas of massive growth, but also to include settings that have proven to be less responsive to Charismatic revivalism. In this way, the Nordic case challenges the "master narrative" of global success, contradicting the common claim that Charismatic Christianity is a form of religion that "travels easily" and adapts to various cultural circumstances (see Anderson 2010, 1). By focusing on some of the "smaller narratives" in countries that are usually neglected in studies, we gain a more complex and nuanced picture, and invite future discussion about similar groups and individuals elsewhere.

The Contributions to This Volume

The volume engages with the region's historical and contemporary landscape from different scholarly perspectives. The contributors' backgrounds involve various branches of the study of religion and cultural and social anthropology.

The anthology is divided into three thematic parts. In this way, we wish to alert readers to parallels between the three countries and their great potential for comparison. The first part addresses the early Pentecostal Movement(s) from historical perspectives; the second concerns internal dynamics in Charismatic organizations; and the closing part deals with twenty-first-century innovations. The historical chapters are based on two case studies from Norway, which illustrate the organizations' linkage to older revivalist movements, as well as contemporaneous interconnections between the Nordic countries. Scholar of religion Lisbeth Mikaelsson analyzes the early Pentecostal Movement's international missions, highlighting the role of women. Historian of religion Anne Stensvold discusses Pentecostalism's introduction to Norway in the light of pre-existing American-influenced movements that had been fueled by returning Nordic migrants. These movements paved the way for Pentecostalism, while simultaneously narrowing the scope of target groups.

Opening the second part, social anthropologist Teemu T. Mantsinen analyzes contemporary tensions within the Finnish Pentecostal Movement. Applying perspectives from Pierre Bourdieu, Mantsinen proposes that an obvious organizational dispute is only the tip of the iceberg, concealing an underlying differentiation of the Pentecostal habitus. In the following chapter, scholar of religion Jane Skjoldli sheds light upon the reconstruction of a former Faith Movement church, the Living Word Bible Center (Levende Ord Bibelsenter) as the Credo Church (Credokirken), and the accompanying transformations of charismatic authority and practices, looking at these from a Weberian perspective. Next, scholar of religion Liselotte Frisk discusses the controversial congregation Knutby Filadelfia, which hit newspaper headlines across Scandinavia in 2004 when a young female member shot and killed another member, and injured yet another. The chapter addresses the group's exclusion from the Pentecostal Movement, from a new religious movements perspective.

The third part begins with a chapter authored by scholar of religion Tuija Hovi, who examines the recent modernization of Charismatic practice and outreach implemented in and by the Healing Rooms. Hovi investigates how this originally American concept has been adapted to the Finnish milieu, pointing out how open proselytization has been abolished in the organization, and how its practices tap into therapeutic processes in Finland. Scholar of religion Jessica Moberg follows up with a study from Sweden, where Charismatic organizations are increasingly intimized, reflecting therapeutization trends in Sweden. Moberg focuses on how informalization is materialized and embodied, where hugs are standardized ritual acts, and church interiors resemble cafeterias. Cultural anthropologist Jan-Åke Alvarsson closes this part, and the volume, with a study on a recently founded Charismatic TV station, Channel 10. He illustrates how old-fashioned sermons and songs have more or less vanished from

Pentecostal churches in general, as a result of the adoption of contemporary worship music. Alvarsson analyzes the channel's success as a response to nostalgia among older Pentecostal members, who feel increasingly estranged from their own communities.

Notes

1. According to Nikolaj Christensen, the most influential early Pentecostal preachers in Denmark took the view that "every human being would in the end be reconciled to God and saved" (Christensen 2016). This presents a possible explanation for the low number of Pentecostals in Denmark, as it would render the imperative for evangelization considerably less urgent.
2. A few exceptions are Simon Colman's (2000) work on the Swedish Faith Movement, David Bundy's (2009) studies of Scandinavian Pentecostal missions, and David Thurfjell's (2013) study of the revival among the Kaale Roma in Sweden and Finland.

References

Åbo Akademi University. 2017. *Post-secular Culture and a Changing Religious Landscape in Finland*. http://web.abo.fi/fak/hf/relvet/pccr/. Accessed 30 Mar 2017.

Allen, John L., Jr. 2009. *The Future Church: How Ten Trends Are Revolutionizing the Catholic Church*. New York: Image.

Alvarsson, Jan-Åke. 2007. Pingstväckelsens etablering i Sverige: Från Azusa Street till Skövde på sju månader. In *Pingströrelsen: Verksamheter och särdrag under 1900-talet*, ed. Jan-Åke Alvarsson and Claes Waern, vol. 1, 10–45. Örebro: Libris.

———. 2011. The Development of Pentecostalism in the Scandinavian Countries. In *European Pentecostalism*, ed. William K. Kay and Anne E. Dyer, 19–39. Boston: Brill.

———. 2014. *Om Pingströrelsen: Essäer, översikter och analyser*. Skellefteå: Artos.

Anderson, Allan. 2005. Revising Pentecostal History in Global Perspective. In *Asian and Pentecostal: The Charismatic Face of Christianity in Asia*, ed. Allan Anderson and Edmond Tang, 147–173. Oxford: Regnum.

———. 2010. Introduction. In *Studying Global Pentecostalism: Theories and Methods*, ed. Allan Anderson, Michael Bergunder, André Droogers, and Cornelis van der Laan, 1–9. Berkeley: University of California Press.

Anderson, Allan H. 2014. *An Introduction to Pentecostalism: Global Charismatic Christianity*. 2nd ed. Cambridge: Cambridge University Press.

Bergunder, Michael. 2010. The Cultural Turn. In *Studying Global Pentecostalism: Theories and Methods*, ed. Allan Anderson, Michael Bergunder, André Droogers, and Cornelis van der Laan, 51–73. Berkeley: University of California Press.
Bloch-Hoell, Nils. 1964. *The Pentecostal Movement: Its Origin, Development, and Distinctive Character*. Oslo: Universitetsforlaget.
Bundy, David. 2009. *Visions of Apostolic Mission: Scandinavian Pentecostal Mission to 1935*. PhD dissertation, University of Uppsala.
Christensen, Nikolaj. 2016. *The Early Pentecostal Movement in Denmark, 1907–1919*. Paper presented at GloPent Conference in Uppsala, Sweden, June 11.
Chryssides, George. 2000. Healing and Curing: Spiritual Healing, Old and New. In *Healing and Religion*, ed. Marion Bowman, 59–68. Enfield Lock: Hisarlik Press.
Coleman, Simon. 2000. *The Globalisation of Charismatic Christianity: Spreading the Gospel of Prosperity*. Cambridge: Cambridge University Press.
Cox, Harvey. 2001. *Fire from Heaven: Pentecostalism, Spirituality, and the Reshaping of Religion in the Twenty-First Century*. Cambridge, MA: Da Capo Press.
Csordas, Thomas J. 1997. *Language Charisma, and Creativity: The Ritual Life of a Religious Movement*. Berkeley: University of California Press.
Davie, Grace. 2002. *Europe: The Exceptional Case: Parameters of Faith in the Modern World*. London: Longman and Todd.
Droogers, André. 2010. Essentialist and Normative Approaches. In *Studying Global Pentecostalism: Theories and Methods*, ed. Allan Anderson, Michael Bergunder, André Droogers, and Cornelis van der Laan, 30–50. Berkeley: University of California Press.
Fell, Michael. 1999. *And Some Fell into Good Soil: A History of Christianity in Iceland*. New York: P. Lang.
Frisk, Liselotte. 1998. *Nyreligiositet i Sverige: Ett religionsvetenskapligt perspektiv*. Nora: Nya Doxa.
Frisk, Liselotte, and Peter Åkerbäck. 2013. *Den mediterande dalahästen: Religion på nya arenor i samtidens Sverige*. Stockholm: Dialogos.
Gilhus, Ingvild S., and Lisbeth Mikaelsson. 2005. *Kulturens refortrylling: Nyreligiøsitet i moderne samfunn*. Oslo: Universitetsforlaget.
Hammer, Olav. 2010. *På spaning efter helheten. New Age: En ny folktro?* Stockholm: Dejavu.
Hollenweger, Walter J. 2005. *Pentecostalism: Origins and Developments Worldwide*. Peabody: Hendrickson Publishers.
Holm, Nils G. 1970. *Pingströrelsen i Svenskfinland 1908–1935: Från överkonfessionell pingstväckelse till autonom pingströrelse*. Åbo: Kyrkohistoriska arkivet vid Åbo akademi.
Hornborg, Anne-Christine. 2012. *Coaching och lekmannaterapi: En modern väckelse?* Stockholm: Dialogos.

Hovi, Tuija. 2010. Gender, Agency and Change in Neo-charismatic Christianity. *Aura: Tidskrift för akademiska studier av nyreligiositet* 2: 38–62.
Hunt, Stephen. 2010. Sociology of Religion. In *Studying Global Pentecostalism: Theories and Methods*, ed. Allan H. Anderson, Michael Bergunder, André Droogers, and Cornelis van der Laans, 179–201. Berkeley: University of California Press.
Jenkins, Philip. 2006. *The New Faces of Christianity: Believing the Bible in the Global South*. New York: Oxford University Press.
———. 2007. *The Next Christendom: The Coming of Global Christianity*. New York: Oxford University Press.
Kivivuori, Janne. 1991. *Psykokulttuuri: Sosiologinen näkökulma arjen psykologisoitumisen prosessiin*. Helsinki: Hanki ja jää.
———. 1996. *Psykopolitiikka: Paljastava psykologia suomalaisen yhteiskunnallisen keskustelun perinteenä*. Helsinki: Hanki ja jää.
Kraft, Siv Ellen, Trude Fonneland, and James R. Lewis. 2015. Introduction. In *Nordic Neoshamanisms*, ed. Siv Ellen Kraft, Trude Fonneland, and James R. Lewis, 1–9. New York: Palgrave Macmillan.
Lindhardt, Martin, ed. 2011. *Practicing the Faith: The Ritual Life of Pentecostal-Charismatic Christians*. New York: Berghahn Books.
———, ed. 2014. *Pentecostalism in Africa*. Leiden: Brill.
Malmström, Nils. 2013. Pentekostala invandrarkyrkor. In *Pentekostalismen i Sverige på 2000-talet: Rapport från ett forskningsprojekt på IPS 2012–2013*, ed. Jan-Åke Alvarsson, vol. 5, 75–92. Uppsala: Forskningsrapporter från Institutet för pentekostala studier.
Mantsinen, Teemu. T. 2014. *Helluntailaiset luokkakuvassa: Uskontokulttuuri ja yksilön luokka-asema Turun helluntaiseurakunnassa*. PhD dissertation, University of Turku.
Marshall, Ruth A. 2009. *Political Spiritualties: The Pentecostal Revolution in Nigeria*. Chicago: University of Chicago Press.
Martin, David. 1990. *Tongues of Fire: The Explosion of Protestantism in Latin America*. Oxford: Basil Blackwell.
———. 2002. *Pentecostalism: The World Their Parish*. Oxford: Blackwell.
McGuire, Meredith B. 1983. *Pentecostal Catholics: Power, Charisma and Order in a Religious Movement*. Philadelphia: Temple University Press.
Meyer, Birgit. 2010. Pentecostalism and Globalization. In *Studying Global Pentecostalism: Theories and Methods*, ed. Allan Anderson, Michael Bergunder, André Droogers, and Cornelis van der Laan, 113–130. Berkeley: University of California Press.
Miller, Donald E. 1997. *Reinventing American Protestantism: Christianity in the New Millennium*. Berkeley: University of California Press.
Moberg, Jessica. 2013a. *Piety, Intimacy and Mobility: A Case Study of Charismatic Christianity in Present-Day Stockholm*. PhD dissertation, Södertörn University.

———. 2013b. Pentekostal spiritualitet i Stockholms län: En kartläggning. In *Pentekostalismen i Sverige på 2000-talet: Rapport från ett forskningsprojekt på IPS 2012–2013*, ed. Jan-Åke Alvarsson, 41–73. Uppsala: Forskningsrapporter från Institutet för pentekostala studier.

———. 2015. Pentecostal Currents and Individual Mobility: Visiting Church Services in Stockholm County. *Approaching Religion* 1: 31–43.

Neitz, Mary Jo. 2012. The Charismatic Renewal and the Culture of Narcissism. In Fundamentalism and Charismatic Movements: Critical Concepts in Religious Studies volume 3, ed. Humeira Iqtidar, and David Lehmann, 225–48. London: Routledge.

Nilsen, Oddvar. 1984. *Ut i all verden. Pinsevennenes ytre misjon i 75 år*. Oslo: Filadelfiaforlaget.

Pingst – fria församlingar i samverkan. 2017. *Statistik*. http://www.pingst.se/om-pingst/fakta-och-forskning/statistik/. Accessed 30 Mar 2017.

Stark, Rodney, Eva Hamberg, and Alan S. Miller. 2005. Exploring Spirituality and Unchurched Religions in America, Sweden, and Japan. *Journal of Contemporary Religion* 20: 3–23.

Svalfors, Ulrika. 2012. Charismatic Movements Within the Church of Sweden. In *Exploring a Heritage: Evangelical Lutheran Churches in the North*, ed. Ann-Louise Eriksson, Göran Gunner, and Niclas Blåder, 156–172. Eugene: Pickwick Publications Church of Sweden Research Series.

Thomsen, Maria. 2012. Building Church on Freedom from Within: Contemporary Congregational Life in the Evangelical Lutheran Church of Denmark. In *Exploring a Heritage: Evangelical Lutheran Churches in the North*, ed. Ann-Louise Eriksson, Göran Gunner, and Niclas Blåder, 119–136. Eugene: Pickwick Publications Church of Sweden Research Series.

Thurfjell, David. 2013. *Faith and Revivalism in a Nordic Romani Community: Pentecostalism amongst the Kaale Roma of Sweden and Finland*. London: Tauris.

van der Laan, Cornelis. 2010. Historical Approaches. In Studying Global Pentecostalism: Theories and Methods, ed. Allan Anderson, Michael Bergunder, André Droogers, and Cornelis van der Laan, 202–219. Berkeley: University of California Press.

Westerlund, David, ed. 2009. *Global Pentecostalism: Encounters with Other Religious Traditions*. London: Tauris.

Woodhead, Linda, and Paul Heelas. 2000. *Religion in Modern Times: An Interpretive Anthology*. Malden, MA: Blackwell.

Zuckerman, Phil. 2009. Why Are Danes and Swedes so Irreligious? *Nordic Journal of Religion and Society* 22: 55–69.

Open Access This chapter is distributed under the terms of the Creative Commons Attribution 4.0 International License (http://creativecommons.org/licenses/by/4.0/), which permits use, duplication, adaptation, distribution and reproduction in any medium or format, as long as you give appropriate credit to the original author(s) and the source, provide a link to the Creative Commons license and indicate if changes were made.

The images or other third party material in this chapter are included in the chapter's Creative Commons license, unless indicated otherwise in a credit line to the material. If material is not included in the chapter's Creative Commons license and your intended use is not permitted by statutory regulation or exceeds the permitted use, you will need to obtain permission directly from the copyright holder.

PART 1

Historical Perspectives on the Early Pentecostal Movement

CHAPTER 2

Paving the Way for Pentecostalism: A Historical Exploration of Post-Reformation Revivals in Norway

Anne Stensvold

The first European country that was introduced to Pentecostalism was Norway. In 1906, a Methodist minister returned from a trip to the United States where he had by chance, so the story goes, become caught up in this intense new form of Christianity, a form which gave him hopes of a gigantic new revival to be shared among all Christians. The Pentecostals attracted attention through their strong millenarian expectations, but their most distinctive trait was the practice of speaking in tongues (Lie 2007; Ski 1981). On his return, the minister immediately started spreading the word, and within a few years, several thousand Norwegians had been struck by his message; Pentecostal congregations were established in almost every town in the country (Bloch-Hoell 1956; Lie 2007; Ski 1981). In this emic and biographical narrative, the triumph of Pentecostalism is accredited to the heroic efforts of one man, the former-Methodist-turned-Pentecostal pastor Thomas Ball Barratt (1862–1940). From a historical perspective, however, the arrival of Pentecostalism in Norway cannot be reduced to the story of one man's achievements. In order to make sense of the narrative, we need to understand the religious landscape in which Pentecostalism arrived.

A. Stensvold (✉)
IKOS, University of Oslo, Oslo, Norway

© The Author(s) 2018
J. Moberg, J. Skjoldli (eds.), *Charismatic Christianity in Finland, Norway, and Sweden*, Palgrave Studies in New Religions and Alternative Spiritualities, https://doi.org/10.1007/978-3-319-69614-0_2

As already mentioned, the first Pentecostal preacher in Norway was originally a Methodist minister. This is significant. The fact that he traveled to the United States in 1906 in order to ask for financial support from American Methodist congregations is also important, because it points to the strong relationships of economic dependence between congregations in the two countries. It also shows the results of earlier Norwegian–American contact, whereby American-influenced migrants had introduced Methodism five decades earlier. The financial aim of Barratt's mission was unsuccessful, as he returned without a penny; what he brought with him from America was inspiration—literally speaking—from the Pentecostal revival he had encountered "over there." In this sense, the story is emblematic because it shows how new and larger processes can be set in motion almost by chance, but it also demonstrates that the introduction of new revivals greatly depends on the history of previous movements and on social structures. Here was a Methodist pastor who unwittingly encountered Pentecostalism's different but also familiar message. We may say that Methodism provided the background that prepared Barratt for his encounter with Pentecostalism. In a similar manner, his own ministry provided a bridge to Pentecostalism for many others. When he went back to Norway to spread the "good news," he preached to Methodist congregations in which he was already known. In other words, Methodism offered an organizational network of congregations which allowed him to preach and secured him an audience across the country. More importantly, Methodism provided the theological concepts (e.g., sanctification through the Holy Spirit), looser liturgical structures, and enthusiastic preachers needed in order to make sense of the new message.

Religious change and innovation are complex processes, partly because religions often rely on exclusive notions. In a study of medieval Catholicism, Jean-Pierre Albert analyzes the process of making *new* saints. In order for a would-be saint to be recognized as holy, he argues, the new saint needs to tap into existing traditions and provide answers to present-day relevant questions, needs, and expectations. If a would-be saint fails to do so, he or she is regarded as either crazy or possessed (Albert 1997, 47–48). Inspired by Max Weber's ideal type of "the prophet," Albert points out that would-be saints pop up all the time, but only a few of them are taken seriously and become foci of devotion. For this to happen, the saint's new message must be better adapted to the existing social and emotional conditions of believers. The aspect of Albert's study that pertains to religious change is useful to the analysis in this chapter, because it helps clarify the significance of Pentecostalism in the Norwegian context, and it will thus be applied in the present analysis.

I approach the establishment of Pentecostalism in Norway as an example of religious change, paying particular attention to national revivalist history. I begin by framing Norwegian Christianity historically. Starting with a brief account of the Lutheran state church after the Reformation (1536), I take a closer look at the late nineteenth century, when the first steps towards lifting the state's religious monopoly were taken (1845), up to the first decade of the twentieth century when Pentecostalism arrived (1906). It should be noted that these developments are not unique to the Norwegian case. Although each of the Nordic countries has its own history, the sequence of main events followed similar patterns—from Lutheran state churches to the start of the dismantling of religious monopolies in the 1800s, and the arrival of Pentecostalism in the first decades of the twentieth century. In this chapter, Norway serves as an example of these developments.

The Monarch's Religious Power: The Protestant Reformation

The Protestant Reformation was introduced by the Danish-Norwegian King Christian III in 1536. Regarding himself as the protector of the true faith, the king severed ties with Rome, appropriated church property and placed the church under his own rule. This is an important reason for the radical difference between the religious context in the Nordic countries and in American society, where Pentecostalism emerged. Whereas religion in the United States was established as a domain principally independent of state interference, religion in the Nordic countries was integrated in the state. The Lutheran state churches created during the Protestant Reformation were headed by their monarchs; priests were state employees, and the population had no choice but to loyally accept the king's rule. In the Nordic countries, Protestantism was introduced top-down, and the population was quite unprepared for the transformation from Catholicism to Protestantism (Schumacher 2005). In Denmark-Norway, the transition seems to have happened smoothly in the Norwegian part of the territory, as far as the written sources can tell. Apart from an account of an iconoclastic purge under Bishop Schjelderup in Bergen in the 1550s, there are no accounts of violent iconoclasm. This is not to imply that the population accepted the new form of Christianity with enthusiasm. The existence of the many pieces of Catholic art (e.g., crucifixes and statues of Mary) that have survived down to our times suggests that Protestant iconoclasm was neither systematic nor complete. Although devotional images were banned and church buildings thoroughly stripped of decoration, much Catholic art remained unharmed, hidden away by the local population (Rasmussen and Thomassen 2002). As far as the priests (and their wives) were concerned, they seem to have been readily accepted—not just as the heirs to Catholic clergy, but also as rightful local representatives of the crown.

The power of European kings to decide the religious affiliation of their subjects was legitimised by the Augsburg Agreement (1555), which contained the principle that the king should have the authority to decide which religion his people should belong to. This royal prerogative is known as *cuius regio, eius religio,* "whose realm, his religion." It was a pragmatic arrangement that monarchs could invoke to quell religious rebellion. As a consequence of the Augsburg Principle, people of different faiths were usually allowed to leave their country. This religio-political reality endured well until the mid-nineteenth century, when democracy was introduced, and people were gradually given greater ability to choose their own religious affiliations. Put bluntly, we may say that faith was democratized as it became a matter of individual choice and responsibility. The roots of this development can be traced back to the early stages of eighteenth-century Pietism, a theological and devotional innovation associated with the German Lutheran theologians Philip Jacob Spener and August Hermann Francke (Shantz 2013). Building on the mystical tradition from Johann Arnt and Jacob Böhme, the Pietists valued personal faith over religious convention, and religious experience over liturgical participation. Eighteenth-century Pietism changed the face of European Protestantism, so much so that it has been described as the final realization of Protestantism, and a logical conclusion of its critique of Catholic ritualism and outward moralism (Amundsen 2005). Pietism has also been described as an important early part of the "individual turn" in Western culture (Tylor 2007). At first, Pietism, with its emphasis on personal piety, was a movement among the clergy and the bourgeoisie, who were attracted to its Bible study, popular mysticism, and focus on prayer. By the end of the century, Pietistic devotion had spread to broader segments of the population, and was turning into a mass movement.

Popular Pietism: Hauge and Norwegian Mainstream Religion

In the nineteenth century, Pietism spread to the lower strata of society and gave rise to new, emotional forms of Christian devotion. This form of Pietism emphasized the idea of a universal priesthood of all believers, and put it into practice by arranging religious meetings at home (i.e., in locations other than church buildings), where lay people assembled for Bible study and prayer groups. As a consequence, the state church clergy started to lose control of religion, and the authorities regarded Pietism as a threat to the existing religious order. In order to put a stop to this development, a new law was introduced in 1741, which banned unauthorized preaching—the Conventicle Act (Konventikkelplakaten). In the kingdom of Denmark-Norway, all such meetings without the presence of a state church priest were illegal, but the religious ideas associated with Pietism did not disappear; they re-emerged and gave rise to popular forms of devotion at the turn of the nineteenth century.

Popular Pietism had a distinctively collective aspect, with its closely knit study and prayer groups that would meet clandestinely in peoples' homes, now in defiance of national law. No doubt, the fear of repercussions helped turn these groups into particularly close communities. To the authorities, their activities undermined the state church, and several lay preachers were punished with prison sentences. The most important among them, lay preacher Hans Nilsen Hauge (1771–1842), was imprisoned for years, but kept in touch with his associates via letters, and secretly published books (Christoffersen 1996; Gilje 1995). For eight years (1796–1804), Hauge traveled widely across the country and preached the need for repentance, criticized state church priests for their lack of true and heartfelt faith, and elaborated on the concept of faith as total trust in the Almighty. He became a national figure through his books and letters, which were copied and secretly circulated among his followers, called "friends" (*venner*).

Hauge's "friends" comprised both women and men, and formed an informal network that spanned the country and which, until 1842, remained illegal (Amundsen 2005). Formally, they acknowledged the state church, followed its precepts, and attended church on Sundays, but their personal faith was defined by Hauge's brand of popular piety. These followers were also known as "readers" (*lesere*) for their frequent use of the Bible, and were mostly recruited from the poorer strata of the farming population. Through their participation in the movement, they received training in literacy, the importance of which should not be underestimated. In fact, some of Hauge's "friends" were industrial entrepreneurs; some of the first printing presses and weaver mills in the country were initiated by Hauge and his "friends" (Greve 2011). However, this enterprise was also one of the main reasons for the state church priests' irritation with Hauge (Gilje 1995), since it provided him and his "friends" with economic autonomy to pursue their mission and spread the Word, and challenge the religious monopoly of the state church. Hauge was imprisoned for 10 years (1804–1814) in an ineffective attempt to curb his influence. To some extent, this harsh treatment may have influenced him to speak less critically of the state church. In the last years of his mission, Hauge encouraged his followers to attend church services regularly and remain loyal to the state church. This would eventually diminish tensions between the church and the Haugian movement, which later resulted in the establishment of the Inner Mission (Indremisjonen), a gigantic attempt to "convert" the Norwegian population (99 percent of whom were members of the state church) to Hauge's brand of Protestant Christianity, an effort to which we will return later in this chapter.

The religiosity promoted by Hauge can be summed up, although somewhat crudely, as a combination of three main components: First among these are emotionally oriented elements, exemplified by Hauge's reported visions of Christ. Second is an acute sense of one's inherent sinfulness. Third is an emphasis on individual submission to God, commonly referred to as "receiving Christ." The need for repentance found expression in a severe moral code that emphasized honesty and hard labor, and banned all forms of entertainment, including dancing, card games, and alcohol consumption. Hauge's books were not only read by his followers, but were also studied by church authorities, and discussed by university theologians. Eventually, they gave rise to heated theological debates and two parallel cultures in the national church: one focusing on tradition, authority, and rituals, and the other inspired by Hauge. Socially, ritually, and intellectually, Haugian piety redefined mainstream Norwegian Christianity.

The Dismantling of Religious Monopoly and the Rise of the Inner Mission

State officials' attempts at stopping Haugian Pietism proved ineffective. After several decades of unlawful religious activities outside the state church, the law against lay preaching was abolished in 1842 (Oftestad 1998). In the same liberal vein, the Catholic Church was allowed to re-establish itself in Norway in 1843, through a special provision to cater to Catholic foreigners. This was a delicate affair in which the apostolic vicariate, Monsignor Laurentius Studach, who was closely associated with the royal family, played an active part in getting the king's support for establishing a Catholic congregation in Norway (Gran et al. 1993). It was intended exclusively as a service for foreigners, and according to the Norwegian Constitution (1814), Catholics were not allowed to conduct missionary work in Norway. This was rooted in deeply seated prejudice against Catholicism, an attitude that is amply illustrated by the fact that Jesuits were not allowed entry to the country until 1956.

Two years later, in 1845, the Dissension Act (Dissenterloven) was passed, which allowed "free" (i.e., nonstate) churches to establish themselves in Norway. The law, which made religious individualism a legal principle, allowed persons above the age of 25 (age of majority) to abandon the state church and take up membership in free Christian congregations. This was an important step towards dismantling the state monopoly on religion. It was also a decisive legal invention, which detached membership of the Norwegian state church from Norwegian citizenship (Oftestad 1998). An immediate consequence was that a number of Free Churches were founded in the following decades. Most of them were small local groups, and were comprised of between a couple of hundred to 1000 members. Most of these groups were critical of the state church, especially the subordination of religion to the power of king and state. Some criticized infant baptism, such as The Free Evangelical Congregations (De Frie Evangeliske Forsamlinger; Froholt 1993), and the centrality of the Eucharist, for example "the Lammers Movement" (Lammersbevegelsen; Øverland 1981).

However, despite this relaxation of the legislation, religious freedom was not yet realized, since only Christian and Jewish groups were allowed to establish themselves (Stensvold 2005c: 370–373). The state invested considerable resources in maintaining control. Partly inspired by Hauge and relying on his network of "friends," the Inner Mission (Indremisjonen) was established by state church priests in 1855. From the 1850s and '60s onwards, this initiative would grow into a folk movement (Gundersen 1996). The aim was to reach the entire population and create a fundamental change in folk piety; the movement involved a novel message clad in recognizable religious language. The Inner Mission's ideology and activities are significant, as they can be seen as a state response to independent revivals by the creation of local movements, by means of which it could thus exerting its own influence in shaping the state church from below.

The first generation of the Inner Mission's traveling preachers (*emissærer*) was recruited from among the "friends" (Amundsen 1995). In this way, we may say that Hauge's heritage became the basis for a form of popular piety that eventually gained state sanction and united Norwegian clergy and large segments of the population in a shared vision of Christianity. It was an emotionally charged faith, motivated by an acute awareness of inescapable sinfulness. It was solemn, meek, and morally severe, with a complete ban on "unchristian" entertainment. In short: immoral behavior was interpreted as signs of damnation, and the Inner Mission offered the route to salvation. Teetotalism and charitable work became popular in local communities as well as in towns. By the end of the century, an estimated 20 percent of the population was part of the Inner Mission. During the first decades of the twentieth century, the popularity of the movement reached a peak, marked by a massive increase in the number of local Inner Mission groups, accompanied by a significant rise in the number of "prayer houses" (*bedehus*). Although an integral part of the state church, the Inner Mission represented an alternative, austere type of religiosity, and stressed equality among its members instead of subordination to church authorities. The prayer houses were owned by the local groups, which gave the members an important sense of participation (Aagedal 1986). Here, the Inner Mission would hold meetings, also on Sundays, at which communal prayer, singing, and coffee-drinking offered popular alternatives to the state church rituals.

Migrants and Missionaries

The gradual deterioration of the religious monopoly coincided with other major changes in Norwegian society, notably industrialization, urbanization, and the migration of impoverished farmers to North America. In only three decades, from 1860 to 1890, almost one fourth of the Norwegian population emigrated. Whereas many of the first migrants were religiously motivated to seek refuge "over there"—among them Quakers and Hauge's "friends"—poverty and new opportunities for obtaining material wealth were motivational factors for the mass emigration. In the United States, the Homestead Act (1862) enabled immigrant farmers to obtain ownership by cultivating new soil, and when the Civil War (1861–1865) came to a close, mass migration from Norway began (Østrem 2006). For the "old country," the exodus was not entirely a story of a lost generation, but also had a positive effect, since it decreased the effects of overpopulation and opened up Norwegian culture to foreign influences. Books and letters provided "a wealth of practical information along with their advocacy of American conditions," which added to the interest called America-fever (Mauk 2013, 135). But most of all, letters to family and friends increased general knowledge of life "over there" and familiarized Norwegians with the religious ideas and practices that migrants encountered. As a result, North America seemed closer and thus more familiar to those left behind.

The religious landscape encountered by the migrants differed substantially from that of the Nordic countries. The United States was considerably more pluralistic; among the declarations enshrined in the First Amendment to the Constitution were freedom of religion, freedom of speech, and separation between church and state. This enabled competition between a wide variety of different churches and groups. Significantly, religious freedom was based upon an understanding of faith as an individual's relationship to God, and construed as a private privilege. Charles Taylor (2007) calls this a change in "the conditions of belief," whereby the authority of the individual reigns in religious matters.

At the time Norwegian and other Nordic immigrants arrived, the United States was ripe with fervent activity in the aftermath of the Second Great Awakening's gigantic revival meetings (ca. 1790–1830), religious ardor, and millenarian belief. Many immigrants' letters described these events. Even more important were migrants who returned to the "old country," bringing their impressions with them. Some of these migrants returned as missionaries. Focusing their activities on new industrial towns, they had easy access to the working-class population, who were more receptive to their mission; the countryside was virtually closed to them unless they knew the addresses of friends and families who could vouch for them to the local priest. Although the Dissension Act (1842) legalized lay preachers, legal and practical obstacles still limited their sphere of activity. Outdoor gatherings were not allowed, which meant that preachers of various kinds had to find other venues for meetings, usually in private homes. This placed serious practical impediments on traveling preachers, who were totally reliant on well-established personal contacts. These restrictions did not apply to the same extent in the growing cities, where strangers were not as conspicuous, and where *one* open door could suffice as a platform for starting missionary activities.

The history of Methodist missionary Ole Peter Petersen well illustrates the strong dependence on personal networks for missionary activities. Petersen started his ministry in his birthplace, Fredrikstad, a small industrial town in the southeastern part of the country, where he first contacted local people who he knew would be open to new religious ideas. Petersen focused his preaching on younger members of the working class, who were receptive to his message of personal faith, as well as his emotional style of peaching (Hassing 1981, 72). Yet the American-influenced missionaries like Petersen did not have an easy task; they were met with skepticism, and sometimes even open hostility, by official authorities. For example, in Halden, another small town in southeastern Norway, one local priest managed to stop Methodist meetings on the grounds that they collided with Sunday church services (Hassing 1981, 81). Many state church priests also reacted strongly against what they saw as the missionaries' distorted image of Christianity. In 1876, a state church priest in Bergen, whose daughter had joined the local Baptist community, initiated a smear campaign in the newspapers, targeting Baptists and charging them of attracting naïve adherents by promising salvation (Eidberg 1981, 67). The history of Mormonism, or the Church of Jesus Christ of Latter-day Saints, adds to the same story of local hostility. The Mormon Church was actually the first religious organization of United States origin established in Norway (1852), with branches in the coastal towns of Risør, Brevik, and Fredrikstad. Only a year later, these were closed on the grounds that they were not Christian because, in addition to the Bible, members recognized the Book of Mormon as a revealed and authoritative sacred scripture (Stensvold 2005b, 347).

Missionaries to Norway and a Discussion of Labels

Missionaries coming to Norway, a significant number of whom were returning Norwegian migrants, emphasized faith in Jesus and his ability to change the inner person and deliver believers from sin, thereby making them holy and restoring them to an original state of grace through the agency of the Holy Spirit. Theologically, this understanding of grace was introduced with Methodism, but with the American revival movements (the Great Awakenings) in the eighteenth and nineteenth centuries, it became an integrated characteristic of what came to be known as the Holiness Movement. The Second Great Awakening (1790–1830) also introduced a powerful new mode of assembly that came to dominate the emerging movements; mass meetings or camp meetings attracted large crowds and many formerly passive believers. These meetings centered on an enthusiastic and emotional form of preaching, designed to cater to what the preachers considered to be the needs of their largely uneducated and socially uprooted audiences (Lambert 1999).

The returning migrant missionaries were inspired by the Wesleyan idea of holiness or "Christian perfection," preaching that it was possible for people to live a life permeated by holiness: the combined result of faith, grace, and regeneration. Unlike the Inner Mission's brand of Protestant revivalism, the American-influenced preachers believed that the end of the world was imminent, giving their message a sense of urgency and this, being new and strange to some, was new and refreshing to others. Their preaching had an acute sense of haste and fear of being "left behind" when the Savior returned to save his own at the Second Coming (Harding 1993). These ideas were revolutionary to Norwegians, who had been raised in the state church tradition and taught by the local priest to respect authority, and hope for God's mercy at the Final Judgment. They were now told that the only way to salvation was to repent of their sins, contemplate the consequences of those sins, and ask God's forgiveness. There were also great differences in sermon delivery and style: whereas American and American-influenced preachers were optimistic and self-assured, Norwegian Inner Mission preachers embodied an inward-gazing kind of religiosity. They also had a different sermon style. Traveling preachers from the Inner Mission and preachers from the domestic Norwegian Free Churches (e.g., The Lamb's Revival [Lammets Vekkelse] and The Free Apostolic Christian Community [Den Frie Apostoliske Christelige Menighet]) emphasized repentance, and would typically ask their listeners to start the day by examining their conscience, cautioning them to be aware of their sinful character. Naturally, there were several other differences between the American and American-influenced preachers, but these particular features set them apart from the existing religious context in Norway.

The fact that the new missionaries belonged to churches with roots in the revivalist movements of the Great Awakenings gave United States-based Protestant Christianity a distinct character: a culture of devotion and a special brand of preaching. In scholarly literature, various terms are used to emphasize these characteristics: folk religion or lay Christianity, popular Pietism, born-again Christianity, and Evangelicalism (Hackett and Lindsay 2008). The latter term most frequently refers to theologically conservative Protestants. Mostly, "Evangelical" does not include Pentecostals, while at other times it largely overlaps with what used to be referred to as Fundamentalism (Casanova 1994). However, it is problematic to directly apply the term "Evangelical" to the Norwegian context without pointing out important differences; the term's connotations in the American context differs from those it has in the Norwegian one. The meaning of the term "Evangelical," which in Norwegian is *evangelisk*, derives from the Latin word for "gospel," *evangelium*. Rather confusingly, the Norwegian constitution contains a reference to the state church as "the Evangelical-Lutheran religion" (*Evangelisk-Luthersk religion*). In the constitution, the word signifies the Norwegian state church's Protestant identity, or more specifically its foundation on the gospel (*evangelium*).

This usage differs from *evangelikal*, a term that refers to a particular kind of revivalist church or congregation. Whereas the Norwegian distinction between *evangelisk* and *evangelikal* has no parallel in English, it is worth noting that *evangelisk* is construed in opposition to Catholic, whereas *evangelikal* refers (in Norwegian usage) to those congregations that emerged from the Great Awakenings. In this chapter, the term "American-influenced revivalism" is used to accentuate the special nature of these movements in a different cultural and regional setting. This equips us with categories that are useful for discussing similarities and differences in relation to Norwegian–United States contacts and earlier revivalist movements in the Norwegian context and, most importantly, enable us to see Pentecostalism as a part of a larger history of American-Norwegian revivals.

The First Wave: Methodists and Baptists

The relaxation of legislation in the 1840s enabled competition between state-employed priests and various independent traveling preachers. Soon thereafter, American and Norwegian returning migrants started to arrive. Over a period of 50 years, these missionaries arrived in three waves. The first—Methodists, Baptists, and Mormons—came to Norway in the 1850s and '60s. From the state church officials' point of view, they posed a serious threat, and the priests did what they could to maintain their own status as custodians of the "true religion." Yet, in spite of ridicule and practical difficulties, these missionaries were able to develop viable and lasting institutions by presenting their forms of Protestantism as attractive alternatives to that of the state church.

Methodism was first introduced in 1853, by returning migrant and former seaman Ole Peter Petersen, who had been sent on an official mission by his church in the United States—the Methodist Church of America—to establish a congregation in his hometown Fredrikstad. Petersen brought with him an optimistic and apparently appealing message: In order to achieve salvation it was enough to *want* it, to desire to believe in Christ. In 1884, 4418 Methodists were registered in Norway, more than twice the number of Baptists (2132), and Methodism formed the largest Christian body outside the state church. In his presentation of Methodism in Norway, scholar of religion Arne Hassing includes a list of members at the end of the nineteenth century, which shows a pattern shared with other American-influenced churches and denominations: In the beginning, a large majority of the recruits were young manual laborers, factory workers, day laborers, and servants (Hassing 1981, 85). Moreover, a significant part of the membership consisted of widows and unmarried young women employed in domestic work.

The Methodists placed great emphasis on diaconal efforts and they offered members the security of a tight-knit community (Hassing 1981). The social aspect was important in a cultural context rife with prejudice. In addition to hostility and mockery, people outside the state church were subjected to systematic discrimination. For example, dissidents from the state church were banned from work as state employees. The ban was lifted gradually: In 1878 dissenters could be accepted as army officers, in 1891 they could take up positions as state functionaries, and finally, in 1917, they were allowed to take up positions as teachers.

In 1857, Baptist Fredrick Ludvig Rymker (1819–1883), another former seafarer and returning migrant who had already preached in his native Denmark for seven years, decided to continue his work in Norway. Rymker converted in the First Baptist Mariners' Church in New York in 1845. When he first started his missionary work in Denmark, which he engaged in from 1850 to 1857, he received financial support from the Bethel Union in New York. He also worked as a shoemaker to support his family. In 1857 Rymker arrived in Skien, a small industrial town on the east side of the Oslo Fjord, where he conducted his first baptism, on Christmas Day 1858. The first convert was a young man, only 18 years old, and below the age required for discontinuing state church membership (the age of majority was 25 years until 1858, when it was reduced to 21 years of age). Rymker feared that it would be judged a criminal offence, but the baptism, which took place on an ice-covered river and created quite a stir, was ignored by the authorities. In 1860, Rymker established the first Baptist congregation in Skien. The majority of the converts came from a local Norwegian revivalist group, which shared the Baptist criticism of infant baptism, but otherwise was closer to the Inner Mission and Hauge's heritage.

After 10 years of missionary work, 15 Baptist congregations had been established in towns all over the country, even as far north as Tromsø. Swedish Baptists helped out with missionary work, but contacts with the United States nevertheless remained vital. The strength of connections between Baptists in Norway and the United States is clearly illustrated by the fact that a school offering formal training for Scandinavian Baptist pastors was established in Morgan Park near Chicago in 1884. This arrangement lasted until 1910, when a similar institution was opened in Oslo. Membership numbers in Baptist congregations in Norway reached a peak in the years following World War II, with 7500 members at the end of the 1940s (Eidberg 1981; Mikalsen 1993).

In the 1870s, the average age in Baptist congregations was 35 years, with a large majority of women (Eidberg 1981). Similarly to its Methodist counterpart, the female majority was mainly made up of single women working as servants, but there were also widows, and some married women whose husbands were away at sea. The rest were married men, mostly manual laborers. Economic deprivation was not the primary motive for joining the new movements; rather, it was social isolation and a need for a community of like-minded individuals. Viewed like this, this brand of American-influenced Protestantism, with its emphasis on emotional preaching and its social engagement, had much to offer. With its focus on holiness, grace, and the promise of salvation, Baptism presented an attractive alternative to the Inner Mission's call for self-criticism and seriousness.

The Second Wave: Adventists and Jehovah's Witnesses

The message of Methodists and Baptists was sometimes hard to distinguish from that of the Inner Mission, as they all stressed conversion and warned against the consequences of alcohol and extramarital sexual relationships. On the other hand, the dramatic eschatologies of Adventists and Jehovah's Witnesses were something new. The first Adventist preacher arrived in Kristiania (now Oslo) in 1879 and was of Danish origin. The eschatological aspect was not as central to Norwegian Adventists as it had been when Adventism first emerged in the United States in 1833. William Miller, a Baptist preacher in upstate New York, declared that the Second Coming and the end of the world would occur in 1844. When this prediction failed, the dominant interpretation was that Christ had indeed returned as predicted, but instead of introducing an imminent end of the world, he had initiated the process that would eventually lead to the end of our times. In the 1870s, the prediction was that the end would come on October 22, 1914. Nevertheless, Adventists in Norway were soon associated with other Adventist features such as focusing on the body as "the temple of the Holy Spirit," and with various health practices such as bathing and vegetarianism (Kvinge and Næsheim 1993).

In 1892, Norway's first missionary from the Jehovah's Witnesses, Rasmus P. Hammer, settled in Bergen. Hammer was a returning Norwegian migrant and had been a Baptist minister in North Dakota (Ringnes and

Sødal 2009). The beliefs of Jehovah's Witnesses differ from Christian mainstream theology in that they do not accept the Trinity, and argue that this dogma lacks biblical foundation. To them, Jesus Christ is the son of God and separate from, and subordinate, to the Father. On a similar note, they hold that the number of those who will be saved is a mere 144,000, the number given in the Book of Revelation (7: 3–8). Thus, they have shared the fate of the Mormons and have often not been recognized as a Christian church, even though they regard themselves as Christians and read the Bible in a particular, yet strictly literal way. Their teachings differ significantly from mainstream Lutheranism as well as from Methodism and Baptism, which are Trinitarian, and in which redemption is much less exclusive and is obtainable by everyone who has faith. The belief in predestination made the Jehovah's Witnesses appear especially severe, and in Norway they received criticism and faced outright hostility, particularly from many state church priests. Despite differing theological orientations, Adventist and Jehovah's Witnesses missionaries managed to establish congregations in Norway, and like the Methodists and Baptists, the members were mainly recruited from among the working classes in industrial towns. Although we lack official numbers for Adventists and Jehovah's Witnesses, a reasonable estimate would place their members as numbering between 1000 and 1500 at the turn of the century.

The Third Wave: Pentecostals

In 1906, the Pentecostal revival was still spreading in the United States. The very same year, this movement was introduced to Norway. Within two decades, Pentecostalism had become the largest of the American-influenced revivalist groups in the country. What made it so comparably successful? Looking at their teachings and religious practices, Pentecostals resembled the first wave of American-influenced Protestants, and shared the Adventists' eschatological expectations for Christ's second coming. However, the most distinctive trait of Pentecostalism—manifestations of the Holy Spirit in mystical and loud signs: speaking in tongues (glossolalia)—was an unknown religious practice in Norway and appeared to many as both fascinating and appalling. Although there are references to similar practices in the Bible, where it is described as a *charisma*, a "spiritual gift," speaking in tongues was promoted by Norwegian Pentecostals not just as a sign of divine presence, but as evidence of baptism in the Holy Spirit. When compared to the Inner Mission's stress on repentance and intense self-reflection, the

Pentecostal message could provide a tangible answer to religious needs for the assurance of salvation, at least for those who realized the practice. Viewed from this perspective, the attraction of the Pentecostal message comes to the fore. The emotional impact of such an experience—receiving the Holy Spirit—was central to the spread of Pentecostalism. These experiences often occurred at mass meetings, and dramatic manifestations of faith became emblematic of the Pentecostal brand of American revivalism. Such gatherings became increasingly important in all sections of civil society from the 1880s onwards, as Norway developed into a democratic country in the modern sense of the word. Political mass meetings for voting rights, teetotaler rallies, and extensive and heated debates about everything from language and dialects to the legal status of children born out of wedlock, eroded the ban on mass gatherings and preaching in public. These factors may to some extent account for the relative success of Pentecostalism in Norway, but historical circumstances also need to be considered. Pentecostalism arrived in a country where other forms of American-influenced Protestantism had prepared the way by establishing hopes of a revival soon to be realized. Pentecostalism was interpreted as that revival, which made its arrival a welcome event.

In the first decades of the twentieth century, emigration waned and the majority of emigrants were now city dwellers. Moreover, instead of entire emigrant families leaving, these emigrants were largely single men (Østrem 2006). This was a reflection of social changes that were taking place in Norway, particularly a new economic optimism, political liberation, and a significant increase in civil freedoms: Voting rights for all men regardless of economic status (1891), general suffrage for women (1913), and national independence from Swedish rule (1905) created a fervent cultural climate characterized by optimism (Sørensen 1998). Meanwhile, the state church, which still accounted for 98–99 percent of the population, struggled with passive members. These were the main features of the Norwegian historical context and religious landscape into which Pentecostalism was introduced. This was also a time of intense struggle among university theologians over the introduction of historical criticism in Bible interpretations. The struggle went far beyond academic milieus, and split the state church down the middle. However, no attempts were made to strengthen church attendance by modernizing church services or liturgical language. Instead, church representatives tried to appeal to people's sense of decency and duty as parents and responsible citizens (Klaveness 1901). At this point in time, American and American-influenced missionaries were well-known figures in Norwegian religious life, and Pentecostalism placed itself squarely within the existent contextual pattern of alternative Christianities.

Thomas Ball Barratt

The single most important agent behind the new movement was the already mentioned Methodist pastor Thomas Ball Barratt (1862–1940), who had traveled to the United States in 1906. Visiting New York, he heard rumors about a new revival that had started on Azusa Street, Los Angeles. Captivated by the vivid descriptions of speaking in tongues and encounters with the Holy Spirit, he sought these experiences for himself. On October 7, 1906, Barratt experienced a breakthrough, which he describes in the following way: "Hallelujah! It happened yesterday between 5 and 6 PM […] My soul is burning. I believe I am the happiest man in the world. Everything is made new to me" (Barratt 1941, 101, author's translation). Barratt, however, did not interpret this experience as *the* baptism in the Spirit, but as a preparatory experience that opened him to the *real* baptism in the Spirit, which took place a month later, after days of intense prayer and theological discussions with friends and acquaintances. On November 15, he received the gift of tongues, alone in his room in the middle of the night (1941, 120). He describes it as a peaceful and deeply meaningful experience of being filled with light and speaking in unknown languages all through that night. These events were relayed to Norwegian Methodists in the autumn of 1906 through the Methodist monthly publication "The City Mail" (*Byposten*), which was edited by Barratt (The Azusa revival is described in no. 22, 1906). When he returned to Norway at the end of the year, his audience was already prepared for something exceptional. That Christmas, 10 people "received baptism in the Spirit, and five of us are singing in tongues" (1941, 134). Barratt himself described these first meetings as exciting events directed entirely by the Holy Spirit, at which singing, prayer, and witnessing occurred spontaneously, intermediated by long periods of silence. When referring to the gift of "speaking in tongues" he writes "singing in tongues" (1941, 136). The next years, Barratt preached in Methodist and Baptist congregations and traveled widely across Norway and other Nordic countries. However, the exact time of birth of organized Norwegian Pentecostalism is disputed (Bloch-Hoell 1956). The first congregation—"the Tabernacle" (Tabernaklet)—was established in Skien in 1908, but it was not until 1916 that Barratt became minister of a Pentecostal congregation: Filadelfia in Oslo.

Although Barratt certainly played a key role in spreading Pentecostalism, it is difficult to identify causal factors for why it would catch on and in less than a decade have grown larger than the Methodist Church. Undoubtedly, however, it was largely due to timing. Except for its revivalist heritage, Norway in the first decade of the twentieth century was a young nation characterized by economic and social change, particularly industrialization and urbanization, as well as political optimism.

Recruits, Community, and American Dreams

Within 50 years of Barratt's return, Pentecostal congregations counted more members than the other American-influenced congregations altogether. Yet, no matter how one looks at it, Christian groups outside the state church were a relatively marginal phenomenon. The first convert to Baptist Christianity was baptized on Christmas Day in 1858, in a river filled with ice and snow. It must have been a strange sight to the freezing bystanders. The ritual was unknown to them; the place was usually associated with timber floating, and the convert, dressed in a white linen cloth, must have made a dramatic impression. But the strange ritual was emblematic of the drama that the first converts experienced. While the large majority of active Christians who sought personal transformation and religious experiences did so in the state church's Inner Mission, conversion to the American-influenced movements meant something else. Whereas a Baptist or Pentecostal conversion involved adult baptism (albeit not always on a river in midwinter), the Inner Mission's idea of conversion was a quiet, inner experience, thought to manifest itself after the spiritual event, in a moral way of life. For those who joined the new movements, conversion also involved dramatic social and organizational change. Becoming a member of one of the American-influenced congregations implied leaving the state church, making the process difficult and complicated. Until 1891, this was a humiliating experience, whereby the convert was obliged to undergo an oral examination at the office of the parish priest and account for his or her theological reasons for leaving the state church. If the priest remained unconvinced of the seriousness of the request, he would deny permission to leave (Stensvold 2005b, 348).

Why, then, did people convert? Although social stigma waned as the new congregations grew and the dominance of the state church diminished, it was still there. What attracted new members is a complex question which merits its own study, but some preliminary conclusions may be drawn. The negative impact of social contempt was largely negated by the supportive social structures offered to the converts in revivalist congregations. They promoted common moral values like temperance, strict work ethics, and education, and they would also monitor practitioners' behavior. In addition, they provided solidarity, as well as protection from the conspicuous gaze of skeptical outsiders. Like other Protestant churches, they encouraged high moral standards that, in time, contributed to social mobility and shifted the majority of its members from the working class to the functionary and *petite bourgeoisie*. Over time, this aspect may have attracted members in its own right.

American revivalist movements, Pentecostalism in particular, are often discussed in relation to social change, and as discussed in the introductory chapter, it has been argued that they have integrated and disciplined the masses of people who have moved into new industrial settings in pursuit of work. The Norwegian case fits well into this pattern. However, it is likely that the "American touch" may have been part of these movements' appeal, including Pentecostalism. In the United States, specific theologies about the role of that country had been developed. Mormonism has a uniquely explicit American angle to its eschatology, with its members' belief that the second coming of Christ will occur in America, and the New Jerusalem will be erected there. In this particular vision, the United States replaces Israel as the point of reference and is effectively established as the land of the chosen. A similar tendency, to regard the United States as an exemplary country and endow it with a certain aura of holiness, can also be found. It is questionable whether such ideas would have attracted Norwegian converts. Still, it may well be the case that accounts of religious freedom, new revivals, and pluralism that the Norwegian immigrants and visitors to the United States sent back to Norway had an appeal, and that becoming a Pentecostal (or a Baptist) meant acquiring a piece of the American dream— "the promised land," the land of plenty, a symbol of hope and a better future.

Concluding Remarks and Later Developments

In Norway today, congregations and churches rooted in American-influenced revivals count approximately 80,000–100,000 members; that is, slightly under the reported number of Catholics in Norway, and almost double the number of members of congregations that came out of domestic initiatives. Comparing their historical development, they have followed similar trajectories of success—or the lack thereof. In 1884, 10 years after it was founded, The Evangelical-Lutheran Free Church (Den Evangelisk-Lutherske Frikirke) counted 1000 members. Twenty years later, that number had grown to 3200. Today it has 20,000 members and is the largest of the churches with domestic origins (Kristiansen and Lund 1993). The Pentecostal Movement (Pinsebevegelsen) is bigger, and is the denomination that descends directly from the movement of the early twentieth century. Regardless of how one looks at it, however, the impact of nonstate Christian initiatives in Norway has been limited. There are several reasons that may account for this, but secularization and the dominant position of the state church and its Inner Mission are important factors.

Historically, the state church played a crucial role in constructing a shared world and moral universe for the Norwegian population. Through obligatory confirmation (introduced in 1736), children were taught to respect authorities—God, king, parents, priest—and literacy spread to all social strata. The introduction of obligatory elementary school—for boys as well as girls—in both cities and the countryside (where it was introduced in 1860) was an important means of creating cultural consensus. With a syllabus of reading, writing, history, and Christian ethics, the schools' main focus was on the latter, which was taught through fables and children's tales as well as psalms and rhymes. Together, the state church and the school system made the country as a whole more homogenous than would otherwise have been possible outside of small communities (Anderson 1991). The demise of the state's religious monopoly (1842 and 1845) opened Norway to new religious innovation and foreign influences. Nevertheless, the state church managed to maintain its hold on the population. When Pentecostalism arrived in 1906, 99 percent of the population were state church members. The remaining 1 percent was divided among a number of churches and congregations of local or American origins.

The Inner Mission may have smoothed the path for American revivalist traditions, but its success at a time when significant number of new missions arrived in the country may also explain those organizations' relatively meager results. In other words, the Inner Mission may be seen as a formidable competitor, which combined experience-oriented religious individualism with traditional state church membership, tapping into the changing religious climate with a less radical and more familiar kind of Christianity than the American-influenced missionaries advocated.

Ironically, it seems that the Inner Mission—originally an attempt to reform and keep people in the state church—may have contributed to further processes that later served to undermine it. In the second half of the nineteenth century—a period of religious change, and of emissaries and traveling preachers from various groups—there was also a marked tendency toward cultural secularization. A prominent sign of this change was a radical decline in participation in state church rituals. The Bishop of Trondheim reports that: "In the Trondheim diocese there were 173,200 participants in the Eucharist in 1870 [...] In 1887 there were 104,000" (Sandvik 1998, 27, author's translation). The number of converts to other churches and congregations was too small to explain the decline. Instead, the explanation seems to be a combination of secularization on the one hand and the growing influence of the Inner Mission on the other. In this particular case, the two tendencies conflated and resulted in what can be described as an identity crisis for Norwegian Christianity: On the one hand, rising individualism fed into secularization and undermined traditions such as attending church on Sundays. On the other hand, the Inner Mission's narrow definition of "true faith" implied suspicion of religious rituals, and unwittingly fueled secularizing tendencies (Sandvik 1998). This trend was also strengthened by the Inner Mission's rhetoric, which referred to regular churchgoers as "Christians by habit" (*vanekristne*) or "Christians in name only" (*navnekristne*). This way of thinking about religion in terms of conversion and strong personal faith spread to larger segments of the population, entailing te individualization of formerly collective Christian identities. To the Inner Mission, attending church rituals out of habit, or a sense of duty, was a mockery of true faith. Religious rituals were null and void unless motivated by deeply felt belief. As a result, many state church members chose to remain at home, leaving the shaping of the Norwegian religious landscape to Pentecostals and other American-influenced churches.

References

Aagedal, Olaf, ed. 1986. *Bedehuset: Rørsla, bygda, folket*. Oslo: Samlaget.
Albert, Jean-Pierre. 1997. *Le sang et le ciel*. Paris: Aubier.
Amundsen, Arne Bugge. 1995. 'En lidet forsøgt og mindre skriftlærd dreng.' Hans Nielsen Hauge. In *Arv og utfordring: Menneske og samfunn i den kristne moraltradisjon*, ed. Svein Aage Christoffersen and Trygve Wyller, 68–89. Oslo: Universitetsforlaget.
———. 2005. Mellom inderlighet og fornuft. In *Norges religionshistorie*, ed. Arne Bugge Amundsen, 243–294. Oslo: Universitetsforlaget.
Anderson, Benedict. 1991. *Imagined Communities*. New York: Verso.

Barratt, Thomas Ball. 1941. *Erindringer.* Oslo: Filadelfiaforlaget.
Bloch-Hoell, Nils. 1956. *Pinsebevegelsen.* Oslo: Universitetsforlaget.
Casanova, José. 1994. *Public Religions in the Modern World.* Chicago: University of Chicago Press.
Christoffersen, Svein Aage, ed. 1996. *Hans Nielsen Hauge og det moderne Norge.* Oslo: Norges Forskningsråd.
Eidberg, Peder A. 1981. Baptistene i Norge. In *Norske frikirker. Fremvekst og konfesjonell egenart i brytning med statskirkelighet,* ed. Per Øverland, 52–70. Trondheim: Tapir.
Froholt, Asbjørn. 1993. De Frie Evangelsike Forsamlinger. In *Kristne kirker og trossamfunn,* ed. Peder Borgen and Brynjar Haraldsø, 57–68. Trondheim: Tapir.
Gilje, Nils. 1995. Haugebevegelsen og sekulariseringens dialektikk. In *Arv og utfordring: Menneske og samfunn i den kristne moraltradisjon,* ed. Svein Aage Christoffersen and Trygve Wyller, 215–229. Oslo: Universitetsforlaget.
Gran, John W., Erik Gunnes, and Lars Roar Langset. 1993. *Den katolske krike i Norge: Fra kristningen til i dag.* Oslo: Aschehoug.
Greve, Kari. 2011. Hans Nielsen Hauges papirmøller. *Nordisk Papperhistorisk Tidskrift* 3: 3–7.
Gundersen, Knut T. 1996. Vision og vekst: Fremveksten av de frivillige kristne organisasjoner 1814–1940. *Tidsskrift for Kirke, kultur og samfunn* (1996): Appendix 3.
Hackett, Conrad, and D. Michael Lindsay. 2008. Measuring Evangelicalism: Consequences of Different Operationalization Strategies. *Journal for the Scientific Study of Religion* 47: 499–514.
Harding, Susan. 1993. Imagining the Last Days: The Politics of Apocalyptic Language. In *Accounting for Fundamentalisms,* ed. Martin E. Marty and R. Scott Appleby, 57–78. Chicago: University of Chicago Press.
Hassing, Arne. 1981. Frikirkelighet og statskirkelighet i forhold til metodismen i det nittende århundret. In *Norske frikirker: Fremvekst og konfesjonell egenart i brytning med statskirkelighet,* ed. Per Øverland, 71–92. Trondheim: Tapir.
Klaveness, Thorvald. 1901. Den moderne indifferentisme og kirken. *For kirke og kultur.* In *Norsk tro og tanke 1800–1940,* compiled by Jan Ebbestad-Hansen, 419–423. Oslo: Tano-Aschehoug.
Kristiansen, Arne, and Jon Magne Lund. 1993. Den Evangelisk-Lutherske Frikirke. In *Kristne kirker og trossamfunn,* ed. Peder Borgen and Bjynjar Haraldsø, 95–110. Trondheim: Tapir.
Kvinge, Rolf H., and Per W. Næsheim. 1993. Syvendedags-adventistsamfunnet. In *Kristne kirker og torssamfunn,* ed. Peder Borgen and Brynjar Haraldsø, 259–272. Trondheim: Tapir.
Lambert, Frank. 1999. *Inventing the "Great Awakening".* Princeton: Princeton University Press.
Lie, Geir. 2007. *Norsk pinsekristendom og karismatisk fornyelse.* Oslo: Refleks Publishing.

Mauk, David C. 2013. Norwegians and Norwegian Americans, to 1870. In *Immigrants in American History: Arrival, Adaption and Integration*, ed. Elliott Robert Barkan, vol. 1. Santa Barbara: ABC-CLIO.
Mikalsen, Tor. 1993. Baptistene. In *Kristne kirker og torssamfunn*, ed. Peder Borgen and Brynjar Haraldsø, 41–56. Trondheim: Tapir.
Oftestad, Bernt T. 1998. *Den norske statsreligion: Fra øvrighetskirke til demokratisk statskirke*. Kristiansand: Høyskoleforlaget.
Østrem, Nils Olav. 2006. *Norsk utvandringshistorie*. Oslo: Det norske samlaget.
Rasmussen, Tarad, and Einar Thomassen. 2002. *Kristendommen: En historisk innføring*. Oslo: Universitetsforlaget.
Ringnes, Hege Kristin, and Helje Kringlebotn Sødal. 2009. *Jehovas Vitner: En flerfaglig studie*. Oslo: Universitetsforlaget.
Sandvik, Bjørn. 1998. *Det store nattverdsfallet: En undersøkelse av avsperring og tilhørighet i norsk kirkeliv*. Trondheim: Tapir.
Schumacher, Jan. 2005. Kristendommen i høymiddelalderen. In *Norges religionshistorie*, ed. Arne Bugge Amundsen, 105–162. Oslo: Universitetsforlaget.
Shantz, Douglas H. 2013. *An Introduction to German Pietism: Protestant Renewal at the Dawn of Modern Europe*. Baltimore: Johns Hopkins University Press.
Ski, Martin. 1981. Pinsebevegelsen i Norge. In *Norske frikirker: Fremvekst og konfesjonell egenart i brytning med statskirkelighet*, ed. Per Øverland, 117–125. Trondheim: Tapir.
Sørensen, Øystein, ed. 1998. *Jakten på det norske: Perspektiver på utviklingen av en norsk nasjonal identitet på 1800-tallet*. Oslo: Gyldendal.
Stensvold, Anne. 2005b. Amerikansk vekkelseskristendom i Norge. In *Norges religionshistorie*, ed. Arne Bugge Amundsen, 342–355. Oslo: Universitetsforlaget.
———. 2005c. Kulturkamp–religiøs kultur og motkultur. In *Norges religionshistorie*, ed. Arne Bugge Amundsen, 356–374. Oslo: Universitetsforlaget.
Taylor, Charles. 2007. *A Secular Age*. Cambridge, MA: The Belknap Press of Harvard University Press.

Open Access This chapter is distributed under the terms of the Creative Commons Attribution 4.0 International License (http://creativecommons.org/licenses/by/4.0/), which permits use, duplication, adaptation, distribution and reproduction in any medium or format, as long as you give appropriate credit to the original author(s) and the source, provide a link to the Creative Commons license and indicate if changes were made.

The images or other third party material in this chapter are included in the chapter's Creative Commons license, unless indicated otherwise in a credit line to the material. If material is not included in the chapter's Creative Commons license and your intended use is not permitted by statutory regulation or exceeds the permitted use, you will need to obtain permission directly from the copyright holder.

CHAPTER 3

The Norwegian Pentecostal Foreign Mission: A Survey of Mission History with an Emphasis on Organization, Expansion, and Gender

Lisbeth Mikaelsson

WIN THE WORLD[1]

In December 1906, the American strand of the Pentecostal revival was brought to Norway by Methodist pastor Thomas Ball Barratt (1862–1940). He returned from New York as a burning witness of rebirth in the Holy Spirit as it was preached and experienced in the Azusa Street milieu in Los Angeles, a milieu that had guided his own intense longing for the life-shaking event. Back in Kristiania (now Oslo), his evangelist fire immediately instigated a Pentecostal revival in the city. He soon caught the attention of Christian leaders from a variety of denominations in Scandinavia and other parts of Europe. Accepting invitations to preach at meetings abroad in 1907, Barratt toured countries in Europe, the Middle East, and India over the next few months. Thus the activities of Barratt himself, the progenitor of European Pentecostalism (Alvarsson 2011, 22; Bundy 2009, 174), demonstrated a

L. Mikaelsson (✉)
University of Bergen, Bergen, Norway

© The Author(s) 2018
J. Moberg, J. Skjoldli (eds.), *Charismatic Christianity in Finland, Norway, and Sweden*, Palgrave Studies in New Religions and Alternative Spiritualities, https://doi.org/10.1007/978-3-319-69614-0_3

missionary zeal combined with a world-oriented perspective—characteristics that have marked Pentecostalism through its history in Norway and elsewhere.

This chapter sketches Norwegian Pentecostal mission history from the beginning until the present. Within the format of a single chapter, that means a strict economy of topics will be needed. Since institutionalized arrangements in the home milieu are generally essential for the social and economic support most foreign missionaries need, a main issue here is the organization of Pentecostal foreign mission in Norway. In general, Protestant mission societies constitute common frameworks for the missionaries and their supporters at home. These frameworks influence options, strategies, and activities in the field as well as securing continuity of work. Thus, to a large extent, the adoption of the Christian faith in the Third World has been both directly and indirectly influenced by the missions' organizational structures. Among the many fellow-believers at home, an interest in mission and responsibility vis-à-vis the missionaries' circumstances has been promoted by the regular streams of information coming from periodicals and other literary productions issued by the organizations. Given Norwegian Pentecostals' emphasis on individual spiritual gifts and belief in the guidance of God, a key question here is to what extent they adopted the kind of multifunctional system typical of the Protestant missionary organizations. I am conscious that this approach means that central aspects of Pentecostal foreign mission are given less attention than deserved, and I try to make amends for it by presenting a few central cases in more detail. As in other branches of Protestant mission, women have numerically dominated Norwegian Pentecostal mission, and one of the aims of this chapter has been to shed some light on gender issues and the agency of women missionaries.

Constructing a "national" account of Pentecostal foreign mission is complicated by the decentralized character of this mission in Norway. Since the 1930s, mission has mainly been based in local congregations, or in some cases, independent foundations and even individual enterprises. This means that mission history largely consists of a bunch of locally anchored accounts yet to be investigated. Nevertheless, I try to impart a bird's-eye view to mission history, which remains greatly dependent on the following Pentecostal historical works: Oddvar Johansen et al.'s "Pentecostal Mission over 100 Years" (*Pinsemisjon i 100 år*, 2010), Oddvar Nilsen's "Out into All the World: The Pentecostals' Foreign Mission in 75 Years" (*Ut i all verden: Pinsevennenes ytre misjon i 75 år*, 1984), and Martin Ski's "The Pentecostals' Foreign Mission" (*Pinsevennenes Ytre Misjon*, 1967). Additionally, the importance of the academic works of Nils Bloch-Hoell and David Bundy should be emphasized: Bloch-Hoell's *The Pentecostal Movement: Its Origin, Development and Distinctive Character* (1964) is a pioneering national and international contribution to research on Pentecostalism, which was generally ignored by scholars until the 1960s.[2] Bundy's momentous *Visions of Apostolic Mission: Scandinavian Pentecostal Mission to 1935* (2009) is a scholarly milestone in terms of the Scandinavian contribution to Pentecostal mission.

The Initial Phase

In 1909, Barratt emphasized the necessity of mission for "Pentecost friends" (*pinsevenner*) in his paper "The City Post" (*Byposten*)[3]—the Norwegian name for Pentecostals here being used for the first time (Nilsen 1984, 25–26). Yet, Barratt himself represented the group of traveling evangelists, who in 1912 were criticized by E.N. Bell, editor of *Word and Witness*,[4] for not staying with non-Christian peoples on a more permanent basis (McGee 2010, 120). However, Barratt was soon followed by Norwegian Pentecostals to the far ends of the earth, and several of them spent decades abroad. From early on in its history, foreign mission went hand in hand with the growing Pentecostal revival in Norway. In 1910 nine missionaries, five women and four men, set out to their chosen countries: India, China, Swaziland, and Argentina. By 1914, the number of missionaries had doubled (Gulbrandsen 1937, 135–136). The geographical dispersion demonstrates the aforementioned global horizon, as well as an individualist determination in the mental makeup of these pioneers. Their efforts were part of the wider Scandinavian Pentecostal missionary enterprise taking place in the first decades of the twentieth century. As argued by Bundy, Scandinavian activity has been vital for the development of global Pentecostalism, yet has been generally overlooked in scholarly studies outside Scandinavia (Bundy 2009, 1–3).

At the time, no coordinating institution in Norway existed that could influence candidates' decisions to become missionaries or where to go. Mission strategies and guidelines for the work were lacking in the new movement. Also, no arrangement securing a regular income for the missionaries had been established. In line with their own and their fellow-believers' conviction, the pioneers trusted in the providence of God and the guidance of the Holy Spirit. They belonged to different groups and assemblies, and are considered Pentecostal because they had joined the revival and preached the gospel of rebirth and baptism in the Holy Spirit—not because they represented any established congregation (Nilsen 1984, 31). Many were "Free Friends" (*Frie venner*), an independent group associated with the Holiness movement. In its first years, the center of the Pentecostal revival in Kristiania was the Free Friends' assembly at Torvgaten 7, whose leader was Erik Andersen Nordquelle. He had welcomed Barratt and the Pentecostal revival, in contrast to the Methodist Church, which had turned against him (Bloch-Hoell 1964, 67–68; Bundy 2009, 177). The initial mission period of the Pentecostals and the Free Friends coincided, but subsequent developments would later create a schism between them, which will be discussed later.

The Norwegian Mission Context

Inspired by the Pietist movement, the Danish-Norwegian monarchy supported Lutheran mission in India, Greenland, and among the Sami peoples in the north of Norway during the eighteenth century (Danbolt 1947). A fundamental change took place in the nineteenth century, when foreign mission became a major interest for the rising lay movement and was no longer an elite activity controlled by state authorities. At the time when the Pentecostals appeared, the bulk of mission activities were directed by large lay organizations related to the Church of Norway and to some extent by alliance missions and the interdenominational China Inland Mission (CIM). A decisive move had been taken in 1842, when the Norwegian Missionary Society (NMS) was founded by a triune confederacy consisting of Moravians,[5] clergy in the Lutheran state church, and lay people belonging to the revival instigated by evangelist Hans Nielsen Hauge (1771–1824). The Hauge movement had stayed within the state church, and the movement's vital role in religious, economic, and political developments in Norway is universally recognized (Aarflot 1969; Kullerud 1996; Molland 1979; Sjursen 1993 and 1997, II, III, IV). The foundation of NMS shaped the subsequent mission history of the country. This is due to the great impact of the Missionary Society itself; in addition, it functioned as a model for succeeding organizations affiliated with the Church of Norway.[6] When the Pentecostal movement arose, there was already a nationwide mission culture rooted in the running of mission organizations. Madagascar, China, and India were well-known mission fields to domestic mission supporters. All the major organizations directed their efforts to selected mission fields that were agreed to by democratic decisions in boards and conferences. Money was collected in local mission associations through gifts and bazaars. Missionaries had salaries and could ask the central administration for extra grants for special needs or projects (Jørgensen 1992; Mikaelsson 2003; Seland 2001; Slettan 1992).

This kind of orderly mission system had demonstrated its viability for decades, but the Pentecostals questioned its spiritual character: Was the system too worldly, too powerful, too little guided by the Holy Spirit through spiritually equipped messengers? Yet, personal piety was not absent in contemporary mission, deeply rooted as it was in the lay movement and its pietistic religiosity. A subjective motivation, generally understood as a personal missionary calling, was inevitable. This represented the "inner call," while an organization's acceptance of a candidate was thought of as an "outer call." Together, they constituted a fulfillment of God's commission in Matthew 28: 18–20. The organizational apparatus invited every participant to understand herself as part of the god-willed project. Thus the mission call became a "democratic" idea and a vital ingredient in the common identity nourished by the organizations: this was the ideological basis of the social and economic alliance between missionaries abroad, administrative staff at home, and the large number of common supporters meeting regularly in thousands of local auxiliary associations. The missionaries filled the role of figures of identification throughout the entire system. Their first-hand stories from the field, about charity, education, and triumphant victories over "heathenism," were told in letters, reports, magazines, travelogues, and autobiographical accounts. These were generally published by the organizations or affiliated publishers for a domestic audience intent on learning how the work was going. It was supposed that the audience would appreciate stories confirming the positive effects of mission as well as its fulfillment of divine will. Descriptions of exotic scenery and strange customs often seasoned the accounts and made for good entertainment. No wonder mission supporters at the coming of Pentecostalism belonged to the most internationally oriented part of the Norwegian public (cf. Mikaelsson 2003).

Norwegian Pentecostals were not unaffected by contemporary mission culture and its legacy from the Hauge revival. Barratt and his followers admired Hauge and looked upon him as a spiritual model; Barratt even thought that Hauge had experienced a baptism in the Holy Spirit (Bundy 2009, 34). Thus in Norway, Pentecostal self-understanding and theory of mission were not only inspired by Methodist and Holiness influences, but also by the Pietist legacy, as Bundy has argued (2009, 32–38). The conviction that other religions were "heathen" idolatry—widespread in Protestant mission—found continuity among the Pentecostals (cf. Anderson 2009).

Parallel to the situation in other Norwegian missions, literary production and emphasis on literacy became part of Pentecostal foreign mission. The periodical "The Victory of the Cross" (*Korsets Seier*) was an arena for mission-related subjects from the outset. Besides, letters were welcomed in other periodicals and local papers, and missionaries published book-length accounts of their lives and experiences.[7] If evangelism is the heart of Pentecostal mission, its biblical focus necessitates literacy. Thus alphabetization has been a major missionary task. The distribution of tracts, newsletters, and excerpts from the Bible has been a common working method.[8] Written language and translations of the Bible in vernacular languages, however, have generally been present in places where Norwegian Pentecostals have worked (Nilsen 1984, 91). The corporate leadership model developed by the main Lutheran organizations was not embraced by the Pentecostals, and history demonstrates that finding pragmatic, institutional solutions to practical problems proved to be challenging. Nor did the Pentecostals establish obligatory education for prospective missionaries. Their educational background therefore varied. Bible courses, language courses, and missionary courses abroad prepared them for the task.

Tension Between Spiritual Idealism and Practical Circumstances

A premillennialist belief in the return of Christ affected the Pentecostal understanding of the mission call and fueled the urge to bring the gospel to the "heathen world" (cf. Anderson 2009; McGee 2010). Matthew 24: 14: "This gospel shall be preached to all nations and then the end shall come," guided the Pentecostals' understanding of mission (Dyer 2011, 11). Spirit baptism accompanied by glossolalia, as well as healing and prophecy, were classical Pentecostal elements that were passed on to Third World converts. The belief that xenolalia is a means to convey the gospel's message in the listeners' native languages has been cherished in Pentecostal circles; Barratt himself expressed such notions (Bloch-Hoell 1964, 87). Dagmar Engstrøm, a Norwegian pioneer credited for bringing Pentecostalism to Germany, declares that she was appointed by Barratt to take on this task because she had spoken German in tongues without knowing the language (Engstrøm 1980, 23). The extreme idea that this gift is sufficient missionary equipment (cf. Anderson 2009, 121), making it unnecessary to learn foreign languages, does not seem to have had any significant support among Norwegian Pentecostals, however.

In any case, emphasis on the missionaries' individual calling and spirituality characterized Pentecostal foreign mission in Norway from the start. Initially, mission was primarily conceived as a relationship between the missionary and God. The individual was the immediate divine instrument, and did not need any social arrangements that could interfere with this relationship. These ideas were not unfamiliar among Free Church groups who were impacted by the Holiness movement or to supporters of inter-denominational alliance missions. The Methodist missionary William Taylor's ideal of self-supporting missions was well known (Bundy 2009, 71–73), as was the "faith principle" of the China Inland Mission. The "faith principle of support" holds that the missionary should not ask for any support except in prayers to God, trusting Hudson Taylor's famous declaration: "God's work done in God's way will not lack God's supply" (Fiedler 1994, 28). Yet, fellow-believers at home were expected to sustain the missionaries with their voluntary gifts. Thus they might function as God's instruments and partakers in the mission. Sometimes their assistance was interpreted as divine intervention in acute situations of need or distress, as my research in Norwegian mission literature has documented (Mikaelsson 2003). Generally, accounts of this kind support the conviction, not restricted to Pentecostals, that economy is a sphere where divine providence is realized in a way that makes miracles happen, creating a narrative blend of excitement and edification.

Nevertheless, lack of stable means soon led to tangible problems for the missionaries abroad. The common link between missionaries and the Pentecostals at home was the periodical "The Victory of the Cross" (*Korsets Seir*).[9] It printed accounts of gifts to the missionaries as well as letters and reports from them. Other papers publishing letters from the missionaries were "The Good News" (*Det gode budskap*), published by Nordquelle, and "The Missionary" (*Missionæren*), with Carl Magnus Seehuus as editor from 1914 (Bundy 2009, 316; Nilsen 1984, 32). Without a central institution to distribute resources, the missionaries' writing skills influenced the readers' willingness to supply their ministries with money. Yet, sporadic gifts from family, friends, and assemblies were often insufficient for catering to the missionaries' needs. Besides, the somewhat unpredictable character of the mission work itself sometimes created difficulties. This engendered tension between spiritual and practical considerations, which modified the individualized spiritual understanding of foreign mission.

When the Pentecostal Missionary Union was established in England, Barratt was invited to its first general assembly in 1909. He returned full of enthusiasm, and proposed that a similar organization in Norway should be ventured. The reception among many followers was chilly, however, bespeaking a critical approach to mission agencies that was not infrequent in early Pentecostalism. The Assemblies of God, founded in 1914 in the United States, had to tackle similar sentiments (cf. McGee 2010, 120–121, 140). Barratt's followers supported foreign mission, but insisted that the Holy Spirit should lead the work, not a human device (Ski 1967, 452).

Eventually, a Pentecostal mission organization, "Norway's Free Evangelical Heathen Mission" (Norges Frie Evangeliske Hedningemisjon), was founded during the next few years. The opposition to it did not disappear, however, and its existence was over when Barratt himself joined the opponents. The idea that foreign mission should be anchored in local congregations has since been dominant among Norwegian Pentecostals.

THE PIONEERS

Pentecostal historiographer Oddvar Nilsen names five men and 10 women who became foreign missionaries during the period 1910–1913 (Nilsen 1984, 30–31). Four of these young women married foreign missionaries and disappeared out of sight, and one of the young men died in China in 1912. Among the rest were Henrik Engstrøm and his wife Dagmar, who founded the Banda mission in India; Parley Gulbrandsen and his wife Chrissie, who established mission in China, Gulbrandsen originally representing the Tsjili Mission run by "The Norwegian Missionary Alliance" (Den Norske Misjonsallianse);[10] Laura Strand and Anna Østreng in Swaziland, where Strand founded the New Haven mission station; and in Argentina, Berger N. Johnsen, who started the Embarcación mission in the Salta Province there and took up a ministry among Indian tribes. Several of the pioneers were sustained economically by the Free Friends.

Dagmar Engstrøm (1882–1984), born Gregersen, occupies a special place in Norwegian Pentecostal history. She is recognized as the first foreign missionary along with Agnes Thelle (1876–1968), having been called to service in a way that has become part of Pentecostal lore. During a private prayer meeting in Kristiania, a woman is said to have prophetically proclaimed: "Dagmar, Dagmar, look, I will send you to the dark place of Banda,"[11] a name the young Dagmar had never heard of, but accepted as the place she was destined by God to go to. It proved to be a district in

Northern India with a population of about 1 million people (Engstrøm 1980, 16). In the centenary publication "Pentecostal Mission over 100 years" (*Pinsemisjon i 100 år*), the first article, illustrated with a large photo, is devoted to Engstrøm's missionary calling and lifelong service of the movement (Johansen et al. 2010, 4–7). Her calling and her response to it provided the mission with what might be called a mythical beginning.[12]

Engstrøm was not just a pioneer in India. With her companion Agnes Thelle, she brought the Pentecostal movement to Germany and Switzerland during the summer of 1907. Representatives of the German Gemeinschaftbewegung, a counterpart to the Lutheran Inner Mission in Norway, were interested in the revival set in motion by Barratt, and the two women were invited to Germany by Emil Meyer, leader of Hamburg Strandmission, who had visited Kristiania and been impressed by what he had witnessed. Engstrøm and Thelle first went to Hamburg, and then to Kassel. In Kassel, their public meetings in the period July 7– August 2 resulted in commotion and negative reporting in the press. The reason for this was the ecstatic experiences and extraordinary bodily phenomena that had gradually turned the meetings into apparently chaotic occurrences. The revival, called Die Kasseler Bewegung, was strongly opposed by religious and secular authorities in the region; even the German empress denounced it (Bloch-Hoell 1964, 80; Bundy 2009, 204–206; Simpson 2011, 62–63). Evangelist Heinrich Dallmeyer, who had experienced baptism in the Spirit himself when participating in the Hamburg meetings, had invited Engstrøm and Thelle to Kassel. He conducted the meetings in the city, but did not succeed in maintaining control when the ecstatic manifestations were at their strongest. Later, he joined other men in the Gemeinschaftbewegung who repudiated the Pentecostal revival and warned against the Spirit mediated by the women. The series of meetings held by Engstrøm and Thelle at this time is nevertheless acknowledged as the start of Pentecostalism in Germany (Meyer 2015, 97–101).[13] In her autobiography, Engstrøm presents her own version of these events. She applauds the fire that inflamed the meetings in Kassel, and regards the opposition as the work of Satan. Dallmeyer is dismissed as a traitor. According to Engstrøm, he had confided to her and Thelle that he abandoned the revival for fear of losing his wages if he left the Lutheran church (Engstrøm 1980, 25–34).

In 1908 the two women went to A.B. Simpson's Missionary Training Institute in New York. After finishing their education they traveled to

India together in March 1910. Some months later, Dagmar married missionary Carl Henrik Engstrøm. Faithful to the geographical specification in her calling, the couple arrived in the city of Banda in 1911 with their newborn son.[14] After her husband's early death in 1921, Dagmar continued in Banda on her own, with three children to provide for, until she finally left India and returned to Norway in 1943, during the Nazi occupation (Engstrøm 1980, 129).

Engstrøm's autobiography "Have Faith in God. All is Possible for the One Who Believes" (*Ha tro til Gud. Alt er mulig for den som tror*, 1980) was published when the author was nearly 100 years old, but the book is replete with lively memories.[15] It portrays a character with never-wavering faith, and a life abounding with spiritual experiences. At the beginning of the twentieth century, deviations from central doctrines in the Lutheran state church involved social costs; thus the author had to leave her position as a schoolteacher after being rebaptized in 1907 (1980, 19). In her description, "the dark place Banda" turns out to suffer from social want and Hindu idolatry, true to the cliché of "heathen darkness." More surprisingly, the epithet is also used to characterize the colonial racism that forbade Indians to enter the local English church in Banda (1980, 70–71). In spite of the premillennialist insistence on the priority of evangelization before the coming of Christ, the need and suffering that Pentecostal missionaries encountered in the Third World resulted in the founding of schools, orphanages, clinics, and hospitals, as they did in other missions. Engstrøm specifies that one aspect of the darkness of Banda was the karma doctrine that induced parents to abandon those children supposedly born under an unlucky star. The misery of these little ones begging in the streets soon moved the Engstrøm couple to establish an orphanage in Banda. Here, banished widows were also allowed to settle. The children were taken care of by Indian Bible women and sent to schools when they grew older (Engstrøm 1980, 91–92).[16]

The international networking among Pentecostals in the first decades of the twentieth century is illustrated in Engstrøm's work. Like Barratt before them (Barratt 2011, 180), Dagmar Engstrøm and Agnes Thelle visited Pandita Ramabai's Mukti Mission for young widows and orphans near Pune. Ramabai (1858–1922) was an exceptional Indian woman: feminist, scholar, author, educator, and social reformer. The honorific title *pandita* ("learned") was given her in Calcutta in 1873 as an acknowledgement of her Sanskrit learning (Sugirtharajah 2005, 7610). In 1905, a Pentecostal-type revival burst forth at the Mukti Mission, and hundreds of young women brought the revival to villages in the district. This female-led revival made the Mukti Mission a renowned Pentecostal center of international importance (Anderson 2015, 2).[17] Engstrøm and Thelle spent about six months at the Mukti Mission, and Engstrøm paints an enthusiastic portrait of Ramabai, representing her as a woman who believed strongly in Christ, the Bible, and God's guidance, and distanced herself from the Hindu religion. Allegedly Ramabai was deeply impressed by the mission call to Banda that had induced Engstrøm to go to India (Engstrøm 1980, 51–54). There is no trace in Engstrøm's recital of the complex figure described in other's accounts of Ramabai, and whose religious commitment, according to Sharada Sugirtharajah (2005), is not easily categorized. Neither does Engstrøm report any feminist discussions taking place during their stay at Mukti. In fact, feminist considerations have hardly any place in Engstrøm's book, except for a brief passage about veiled women wearing the *purdah* (1980, 100–101), an example of a common stereotype of women's misery in "heathen" countries (cf. Mikaelsson 2005). The import of Engstrøm's silence should not be overestimated; rather, the account of her actions and career indicates a person identifying with ideals of gender equality.

A Controversial Issue: How to Organize the Mission

Voluntary gifts were an unstable means of support. Besides, the practice entailed unequal distribution of resources among colleagues in the same field. Since there was no external control of how the means were allocated, nor of the activities individuals chose to undertake, problems of various kinds often arose. The ideal of self-supporting mission turned out to be hard to put into practice. When the Engstrøm couple was home on furlough, steps were taken to procure an administrative institution in Norway to oversee and regulate the mission work in Banda. A committee called "The Banda Mission" (Bandamisjonen) was then officially established on January 1, 1914. Barratt accepted the office of chair, his wife Laura Barratt was secretary, and Edvard Gasman treasurer (Bundy 2009, 321). From then on, gifts to the Banda Mission would be sent to the treasurer, as opposed to directly to the missionaries. Candidates for missionary work were required to produce letters of recommendation from their congregations, so that possible "adventurers" could be eliminated. A medical certificate was required, as was proficiency in the English language. No expansion in the mission work in Banda should be undertaken without the committee's permission (Bundy 2009, 321; Nilsen 1984, 33). Thus the Banda mission was organized with a set of directives that sorted out the candidates, regulated activities in the mission field, controlled its economy, and handed over the power of making vital decisions to a home administration.

Barratt and missionaries in other fields realized that the existence of some organizational structures could facilitate the work of their ministries. At a large meeting in 1914 hosted by "The Tabernacle" (Tabernaklet) in Skien, Telemark, Barratt suggested that the Pentecostals should develop "a more joint form of mission activity in Norway" (Nilsen 1984, 34). He was supported by the pastor of The Tabernacle, Carl Magnus Seehuus[18] and others, and on January 30, 1915, the organization "Norway's Free Evangelical Heathen Mission" (Norges Frie Evangeliske Hedningemisjon; NFEH)[19] was founded. The statutes laid down that NFEH was open to every Pentecostal congregation or assembly that wanted to join it, whether in Norway or in the mission fields. Every such unit had the right to be represented at the annual meeting of NFEH by its pastor or another appointed person. To take care of the associated work, a mission council with a chairman, treasurer, and secretary would be elected/re-elected at the annual meeting. The council was NFEH's executive body and had the power to make vital decisions concerning the mission work and the establishment or expansion of mission stations, as well as the acceptance and dispatch of missionaries. Several statutes give instructions to control the use of economic resources, which was seen by some as an encroachment on the spiritual freedom many valued so highly. Receipts of money were to be published in "The Victory of the Cross" or "The Missionary"; both publications had reader networks that supported the mission economically. Yet, donors could still decide which mission would receive their gifts. Barratt was elected chairman of the council, and his wife became secretary. She was one of two women in the first council. A corresponding administrative unit, that is, a missionary council with chairman, treasurer, and secretary, was to be established in every country in which NFEH missionaries worked. One of the council's tasks was to draw up a budget plan for the following year, but to be valid the budget had to be accepted by the NFEH council in Norway (Nilsen 1984, 40–42).

More cooperation, and more control of personnel and resources within a formalized leadership structure based on a democratic foundation made the NFEH more bureaucratic and less "spiritual," in other words more like other mission agencies at the time. Not unexpectedly, the establishment of what was understood as a haunting by the "ghost of organization" (Nilsen 1984, 45) was met with mixed feelings in the Pentecostal milieu. Berger

Johnsen in Argentina was one of those missionaries who worked all his life without any congregation backing or substantial economic support (Iversen 1946, 12). He seems to have had closer connections with the Free Friends than with the Pentecostals associated with Barratt and the "Victory of the Cross" network (Bundy 2009, 348). The Banda Mission had served as a model for NFEH, but to the disappointment of Barratt and others the Engstrøms chose not to join the new organization; thus the Banda Mission committee continued as before. Dagmar Engstrøm just hints at the founding of NFEH in her autobiography. At the time, she had decided that her faith in God should be her only support, she says, confirming her stance with a miracle story of the Lord supplying the mission station with money at a critical moment (Engstrøm 1980, 102–105). Bundy indicates that the Banda Mission and the Bilaspur Mission of Agnes Thelle Beckdahl refused to join NFEH because they had lucrative contacts with congregations in the United States that they did not want to be published in "The Victory of the Cross" or "The Missionary." However, the respected missionaries Gunnerius Tollefsen (Congo) and Parley Gulbrandsen (China) gave the new organization credibility by instantly joining it (Bundy 2009, 327–328).

Nonetheless, many Free Friends, including Nordquelle, were hostile towards NFEH (Froholt 1997, 3). Barratt's subsequent congregation policy further estranged him from this group, which denounced denominations and formalized congregations as 'unbiblical' and an origin of divisions between believers. In 1910, while still a member of the Methodist church, Barratt had founded an alliance assembly at Møllergaten 38 in Kristiania. In 1916 he instituted a congregational order at "Møllergaten 38," as the assembly was popularly called until it was named Filadelfia in 1921. In accordance with his vision of New Testament congregations, the Kristiania congregation should be independent and self-governed, have a pastor and a board of elders, thus realizing his understanding of the "biblical" model. Further, members should be accepted and registered, an unacceptable measure in the eyes of many Free Friends (Froholt 1997, 1). The same independent and formalized congregation structure was to be implemented in the mission fields. As a consequence of his founding this establishment, Barratt left the Methodist Church in 1916.[20] Subsequent history shows that the Filadelfia model was copied around the country and inaugurated "the era of local congregations" in Norwegian Pentecostalism. In the period 1917–1933, 130 local Pentecostal congregations were registered (Ski 1967, 457–460).[21] Many of these were originally Free Friends assemblies, and the organizing process often entailed bitterness and division between the followers of

Barratt's line and the others, who remained Free Friends. As time went by, the last-mentioned group established their own organization, "The Free Evangelical Congregations" (De Frie Evangeliske Forsamlinger).

The congregation model was fundamental to the future organization of foreign mission, and it contributed to the closing down of NFEH. It turned out that the emphasis on the independent status of each congregation was difficult to reconcile with the superior authority of the NFEH council, in spite of the organization's relative success, having as it did, 30 missionaries in the mission fields in 1929 (Barratt 2011, 216; Nilsen 1984, 60).[22] By this time Barratt had started to question the legitimacy of the organization. He decided that a mission board with the power to control the congregations' activities and resources, be it home mission or foreign mission, was unbiblical (Barratt 2011, 233). Consequently, he and his wife withdrew from the NFEH in 1930. His actions did not gain universal support at the time, and a critical period for Norwegian Pentecostalism followed (cf. Bundy 2009, 437–445). Yet, Barratt's authority was such that NFEH's fate was sealed. In 1931 the organization was closed down except for its work with the Congo mission, which was retained because the Belgian authorities in Congo demanded there be a legal entity behind the mission (Nilsen 1984, 60–64; Ski 1967a, 462).

Henceforth, local congregations took responsibility for the support of one or more missionaries. "The Victory of the Cross," which was published by the Filadelfia congregation in Oslo, became the mission's communications organ, and here mission reports and receipts for money transactions would be published. The development in Norway paralleled events taking place in Sweden, where Lewi Pethrus was instrumental in the closing down of the "Swedish Free Mission" (Svenska fria missionen) in 1929, which had been established five years earlier (Alvarsson 2011, 28). Barratt and Pethrus were close, and Barratt was probably influenced by the events in Sweden (Ski 1967, 460). Initially the rearrangement caused a variety of problems, but gradually the mission work stabilized in accordance with the new circumstances.

Development of a Lasting Organizational Structure

The 1930s were marked by a rapid Pentecostal growth both domestically and in the mission fields. When the Second World War broke out in 1939, the number of Norwegian missionaries had grown from 30 to 75. The number shrank to 60 missionaries during the war, but in 1945 more than 100 people were ready to depart for the mission fields (Johansen et al. 2010, 20; Nilsen 1984, 79). The expansion was welcomed, but difficult to handle for the congregations. No one had a general overview of the situation, and a need for administrative assistance and cooperation was felt. Thus the fear of a central organization that would affect the independence of the congregations, a fear that was still existent in many quarters, was surmounted by acute need.

The first step was to establish the position of mission secretary in the Filadelfia congregation in Oslo in 1946. The reputable Congo missionary Gunnerius Tollefsen (1888–1966) was appointed to the job.[23] He was to serve all Pentecostal congregations and groups in Norway who needed his assistance; the secretary therefore had a key role on a national level. The next stage was the emergence of conferences related to the different mission fields, such as the South America conference and the East Africa conference. They functioned as meeting places for missionaries and representatives of the cooperating congregations supporting them. The field conferences and their respective working committees were officially accepted at a national Pentecostal conference in Oslo in 1949. Common funds were allotted to each field, and missionary salaries, travel regulations, and other practical affairs were handled within this framework (Nilsen 1984, 81–82; Ski 1967a, 467–470).

The organizational structure comprising mission secretary, field conferences, and working committees was thought to combine congregational and administrative interests. With adjustments and personnel growth this model has survived to the present. The field committees were closed down in 2008 and replaced with mission country committees (Johansen et al. 2010, 104). The secretary has been promoted to general secretary, and is now assisted by a staff of eight employees, plus volunteers. Presently, the mission fields are apportioned to four main regions, Africa, America, Asia, and Europe, each with a regional secretary subordinated to the general secretary. The acronym PYM, short for De norske pinsemenigheters ytremisjon ("The Norwegian Pentecostal Congregations' Outer Mission"),[24] is generally used to refer to the organization. It is defined as a "nonprofit association" in the statutes, and functions as a coordinating office for the mission work run by affiliated congregations.[25] Well-informed readers will be familiar with the sometimes confusing use of "PYM" in Pentecostal texts: On the one hand, PYM, or its full name, may refer to the missionary activities that have been going on since 1910; in other words it is not a formal name but a denotation. On the other, PYM may be used as the name of the organizational structure that has developed since 1946. Even more confusingly,

PYM may be used to refer to both, perhaps signifying the lasting influence of anti-organizationism. The congregations still function as employers and take responsibility for sending out missionaries, thus preserving the independent, decentralized structure that has been so strongly emphasized in the above history. For now, PYM does not have a complete overview of Pentecostal mission activities. There are independent missionaries and mission foundations, some of which are private, while others are attached to local congregations (PYM 2015).[26] Thus Pentecostal foreign mission in Norway takes the form of a rather fragmented and complex conglomerate.

Summary of the Missionary Expansion

Looking at the number of missionaries, mission countries, stations, and activities from 1910 onwards, the word "expansion" can be said to sum up missionary development during this period. This growth has made PYM the third largest mission agency in Norway, with the widest geographical range. Today, PYM missionaries work in 30 different countries. In addition, PYM has partnerships with 19 more countries, and missionary activities in a number of countries details of which are kept secret for security reasons. Yet, the decrease in missionary activities that has taken place in Norway more generally has also befallen the classical Pentecostalism represented by PYM and its 293 affiliated congregations. As of 2015, the number of active missionaries who were sent from Norway is 94, including 24 retired missionaries who still work abroad or commute. This is a marked decline compared with earlier periods. It is necessary to take into account the broader picture, however. Partnerships with national Pentecostal churches have become a common mode for work, and Norwegian missionaries have to a great extent been substituted by local evangelists. The global diffusion of Pentecostalism makes financial support of homegrown projects and collaborators in many cases a preferable use of Norwegian resources. Today, the PYM leadership estimates that 300 million NOK (Norwegian crowns) are spent on mission purposes abroad.[27]

Until the Second World War, growth was concentrated in the original mission countries, India, China, Swaziland, and Argentina, supplemented with Congo, Iceland,[28] and Brazil. In Brazil, Ragna and Leonard Pettersen began their work as representatives of the Arvika congregation in Sweden, but they had additional support from various Norwegian congregations. In 1936, Paraguay received its first Norwegian missionary (Nilsen 1984, 75–76). In 1946, it was settled that Israel would become a mission country, and in the same year Thailand and the Faeroe Islands received their first Pentecostal missionaries from Norway. In 1947, Chile, Tibet, and Kenya were added. Also, three missionaries went to South Africa that year (Nilsen 1984, 88–89). The expansion continued into the 1950s, when missions were opened in Japan, Morocco, Bolivia, Basutoland, Taiwan, Nepal, and the West Indies. Further expansion took place in the 1960s, adding Tanzania, Mozambique, Peru, Pakistan, Myanmar, and Greenland to the list. From the 1970s onwards, activities were started in Honduras, Madeira, Somalia, Niger, the Philippines, and Rwanda. In addition, the 1970s saw a greater focus on Europe (Nilsen 1984, 132–133). The year 1980 seems to represent the heyday of the Norwegian Pentecostal mission; on its seventieth anniversary celebration this year, it was reported that 350 missionaries were working in 30 different countries (Johansen et al. 2010, 76). Statistics published in 2010 demonstrates that 40,4 percent of a total of about 1000 missionaries has worked in Africa, 24,6 percent in Latin America, 22,2 percent in Asia, and 12,8 percent in Europe (Johansen et al. 2010, 108). Both efforts and results vary when comparing the countries. This variation can be partly explained by the Pentecostal respect for the individual missionary vocation and its specific geographical assignment. Moreover, the large variety of countries would hardly have been probable given a more corporate and less spiritual apparatus to handle the choice of mission fields.

Before the Communist Revolution, the greatest progress had taken place in China. Parley and Chrissie Gulbrandsen had attended the inaugural meeting of NFEH in May 1915, and afterwards prepared to return to China under its aegis. Back in China in 1916, they settled in Sin-Pao-an in Chih-li Province and made it the center of their activities. The Gulbrandsens established a partnership with the capable Chinese Pentecostal David Li, and their successful ministry resulted in new congregations in nearby cities and towns under the leadership of Chinese pastors (Bundy 2009, 339). At the turn of the year 1936/37, there were eight main mission stations with many affiliated minor stations and Sunday schools. When the Communist revolution prohibited all Christian missions in 1949, it has been estimated that a total of more than 40 missionaries operated in the country and more than 1000 members of the congregations were left behind (Rudolf and Jones 1967, 483–484, see also Bundy 2009, 3). After the revolution a number of the missionaries went to Japan. Here, seven mission stations were operational in 1952.[29] In contrast to troubled China, with its crowds of refugees and robber gangs, civilized Japan proved to be a stubborn mission field. The scarce number of converts here has invited the metaphor of fishing with a fishing rod (Nilsen 1984, 98–99), as opposed to the "fishing net" success in Congo, where multitudes were "captured."

The Congo mission is considered the most successful of the Norwegian Pentecostals' missions. It goes back to 1915, when Gunnerius Tollefsen went to Congo, not under the aegis of NFEH, but of the Congo Inland Mission. This mission was founded in 1911 by the Pentecostalist Alma Doering from Ohio, backed by American Holiness Mennonites. Scandinavian Pentecostals viewed Doering's as a partner mission; however, cooperation with the Americans turned out to be frustrating for the European missionaries (Bundy 2009, 329–330). When Tollefsen returned to Norway in 1919, he advocated greater commitment among Norwegian Pentecostals for mission in Congo, and was supported by Barratt. Lewi Pethrus and other Swedish Pentecostals were also interested in opening a mission in the country. Thus an expedition led by Tollefsen on behalf of Norwegian and Swedish Pentecostals departed for eastern Congo in 1921 in order to find a suitable field. In 1922 the expedition settled in Nya Kaziba in the Kivu Province in Belgian Congo (Zaire). Here they started a ministry in cooperation with tribal leaders (Bundy 2009, 334–335). Nya Kaziba, with neighboring kingdoms Nya Luindja and Muganga, became the Norwegian field (Ski 1967a, 496–499). As early as 1923, the missionaries reported a revival comprising several hundred converts (Nilsen 1984, 50–51). In 1925, Tollefsen published "In the Interior of Africa. Experiences and Impressions from an Expedition Journey" (*I Afrikas indre. Oplevelser og inntrykk fra en ekspedisjonsreise*), a book describing the expedition and the first years of the work in Congo, also demonstrating the disastrous effects of European colonial exploitation in this part of Africa. The book has been characterized as "the first Pentecostal book-length missiological analysis of a particular mission field" (Bundy 2009, 336).

After 25 years of work, there had been significant growth in all respects: the mission staff now numbered 26 missionaries and between 70 and 80 Congolese assistants, five major mission stations and 40 affiliated minor stations were in use, between 3000 and 4000 children attended the schools, and 1000 people had been baptized (Nilsen 1984, 83). Ten years later, the number of baptized Congolese had increased to 6205. A hospital in Nya Kaziba was finished in 1958, and a Bible school started in 1956 at the mission station Muganga. Furthermore, it was reported in 1952 that 17,000 copies of Barratt's booklet "Clues in the Word of God" (*Ledetråd i Guds ord*, 1936) translated into Swahili, had been sold (Nilsen 1984, 95). The Republic of the Congo gained its independence in 1960, and the changing times were reflected in a decision by the field conference that year: henceforth the mission work would be directed by a council consisting of missionaries alongside Congolese pastors and elders. The placing of Congolese people in new leadership positions on equal terms with the missionaries was historic (Nilsen 1984, 93–96). However, political turbulence following in the wake of national independence worsened working conditions for the missionaries. As a result, in 1967 all of them had returned to Norway. The interruption proved to be short, and progress continued in spite of political unrest. In 1979, the "Norwegian" field encompassed 47 congregations, with a total of 37,559 members, while 9586 candidates were preparing for baptism (Nilsen 1984, 126).

In 1995, the national church Communauté des Eglises Libres de Pentecôte en Afrique (CELPA) was established. The Congo mission then transferred its work to that church. With the financial assistance of Norwegian authorities, specifically the Norwegian Agency for Development Cooperation (NORAD), CELPA has been able to develop an extensive network of schools and health institutions in parts of Congo. Presently, CELPA consists of 650 congregations with 300,000 members. It is a mission church with ministries in several African countries (Johansen et al. 2010, 95).

It has been maintained that the success of the long-lasting revival in Congo surpasses that of every other revival occasioned by Norwegian Pentecostal missionaries. A possible competitor might be the notable revival that took place at Gran Chaco in the 1930s, after Berger Johnsen (1888–1945) had invested 20 years of strenuous work with little result in Argentina. When he came to the Salta Province in 1914, the Indians were so hostile towards white people that it was dangerous to approach the places where they lived. Johnsen never gave up on gaining their confidence, however, and little by little he succeeded. According to his description, the revival suddenly started when he was speaking at a large meeting at which the crowd ecstatically experienced the presence of the Holy Spirit. From then on "the fire" spread among the Indians (Iversen 1946, 6–7; Johansen et al. 2010, 12–13; Nilsen 1984, 75).

The Evidence of Faith World Evangelism

A remarkable mission agency in Norwegian Pentecostalism is the independent foundation The Evidence of Faith World Evangelism (Troens Bevis Verdens Evangelisering). Its center, the "Valley of Saron" (Sarons Dal), was established in 1965. It is situated in the valley of Kvinesdal, in Vest-Agder county, southern Norway. The founder, Aril Edvardsen (1938–2008), was a renowned evangelist and one of the most innovative Christian leaders in Norway in his lifetime. Edvardsen's financial success, ecumenical profile, and openness towards the Charismatic Movement resulted in a long-lasting conflict between the Valley of Saron and central Pentecostal leaders (Alvarsson 2015, 49).[30] His mission strategy was to support local Evangelists in their native countries instead of sending missionaries from Norway; thus Edvardsen was a forerunner to a development that was common in the mission in later years, exemplified here by the Congo mission described above. Nor did he create a mission organization; summer rallies and money collections through his magazine "Evidence of Faith" (*Troens Bevis*) secured moral and financial support for Edvardsen's projects. Hundreds of Evangelists connected to local churches were funded in this way.

Since 1970, the summer rallies in the Valley of Saron have annually attracted thousands of participants. Since the 1960s, many countries, notably in Eastern Europe, have been visited by Edvardsen's meeting campaigns. From the 1990s onwards, the campaigns focused on the Muslim world, where Edvardsen established contacts with political authorities—a strategy that was criticized by fellow Christians in Norway. In addition, Edvardsen was a pioneer in mass media mission, with his radio and television programs being broadcast in many countries. Since 1997, these have been distributed by a satellite broadcaster covering the Middle East, parts of Africa, and Asia. Today, Edvardsen's son Rune Edvardsen is the leader of the Valley of Saron (Rimehaug 2010).

A Woman-Dominated Mission?

The foregrounding of Dagmar Engstrøm in the Norwegian Pentecostal Movement's centenary publication may well be interpreted as a tribute to all the "sisters" that have served the mission. "Pentecostal Mission over 100 Years" demonstrates the preponderance of women. A list included in the publication, containing the names of about 1000 people who have been engaged in foreign mission for longer or shorter periods, documents this fact (Johansen et al. 2010, 108–112). The gender distribution is neither specified nor commented on in the document, but my counting shows that about 620 of the people enlisted are or were women.[31] Aside from this numerical preponderance, it would be extravagant to consider the mission as woman-dominated. For one thing, all the mission secretaries so far have been male. Most of the well-known missionaries are men.

Yet, without these women's engagement the mission would not have developed into the important force it has proven to be. Since gender relations in the movement have not been studied in depth, a few cases will be mentioned here that indicate the multifaceted nature of the gender issue; these examples are on a global scale and occurred within a 100-year period, and vary according to time, place, the individuals involved as well as the local conditions.

Barratt's attitude was probably a decisive factor in the first decades. Dagmar Engstrøm and Agnes Thelle belonged to Barratt's following in Kristiania; their pioneering missionizing in Europe had his sympathy and support. The fact that Laura Barratt and another woman were members of the NFEH Mission Council bespeaks an open attitude to women's roles on his part. In fact, Barratt was an outspoken critic of religious and worldly patriarchy. In "The Victory of the Cross" he supported women's ministries and their right to preach (Bundy 2009, 417–418). His views are expressed in the booklet "Woman's Position in the Congregation" (*Kvinnens stilling i menigheten*, 1933). Using the New Testament, especially the Pauline letters, as an authoritative guide, Barratt argues that the apostle was the founder of women's emancipation (Barratt 1933, 7). He ascertains that women's qualifications enable them to perform all kinds of tasks in society and, called by the Holy Spirit, women are ready to fill every congregational role (Barratt 1933, 31–33).

Judging from later debates on these issues (cf. Hoaas and Tegnander 1984), Barratt's standpoint was much more radical than his successors'. This is argued in a recent study, which documents that attitudes are changing (Gunnestad 2015). According to the general secretary of PYM, today there are no formal rules preventing women's taking leadership positions.[32] Still, a recent debate in the Christian daily "Our Country" (*Vårt Land*) indicates that a number of Pentecostal women experience a male culture that impedes their seeking leadership positions and taking up preaching (cf. Aalborg 2014; Arntsen 2015; Myklebust 2014).

In the mission field, however, women have been able to preach and exercise leadership. Perhaps the most illustrious example of this tendency is Liv Haug (born 1943), a highly decorated Pentecostal missionary in the Peruvian Perené district in the Amazon jungle. Combining mission with entrepreneurial skills, Haug was elected chairman in Villa Perené (1982–1983), and Province Governor in the Perené region (1996–2002); both commissions reveal the high regard in which she is held by the local population. She arrived in Peru in 1971, and in 1973 she founded the congregation Iglesia Evangélica Filadelfia in Villa Perené, the province capital. The congregation, with 350 active members in 2010, is the basis for a large number of activities and projects. Sunday schools, Bible lessons, leader training, and radio broadcasting are all activities anchored in the congregation. More than 3000 women have been helped through the project "Women in Progress" (Kvinner i fremgang), and a sponsor system takes care of the poorest children. Starting with a bridge over Rio Perené, Haug has initiated a great number of building projects to improve the living conditions of the local population (Johansen et al. 2010, 38; Tveit 2011).

However, mission literature indicates a complex picture as to gender. Haug and a large number of devoted women remained single, thus enabling them to devote all their energy to the ministry. Berly Aarre Solvoll's "In the Hand of the Master" (*I mesterens hånd*, 1983) testifies that Pentecostal women trying to combine ministry and married life may face problems. The author claims that she was called and guided by God to become a missionary, but after marrying the well-known missionary Arnulf Solvoll, he seems to have controlled her life. Seven children (three of whom died in the mission field) made it necessary for her to concentrate on household tasks. The couple seemingly disagreed about priorities; he uncompromisingly gave preference to his own missionary concerns, while she emphasized the children's needs. After having twice submitted to his demands that the family should go on furlough, she refused to return to Japan with him after the furlough had ended because of the disruption this would cause to the children's schooling. Interestingly, the decision is described in terms of a divine intervention. In despair over how to manage on her own in Norway with the children, she was comforted by God with the declaration "Your creator is your husband"[33] (Solvoll 1983, 148). Solvoll became convinced that, in addition to supporting her revolt in this way, God had called her to take on children's work at home (1983, 146). When her husband returned, she was not prepared to accept him as head of the family any longer (1983, 153).

Presumably, Solvoll's submission is representative of many couples in the past, but her frank account of revolt and its spiritual legitimation is unusual in Norwegian mission literature. The social context at the time of publication gives a key to its frankness: The 1970s was a decade of feminist-inspired gender transformation in Norway, and by the 1980s the lives of missionary children had surfaced as a contested issue in the public sphere (Mikaelsson 2003, 184–185, see also Drønen and Skjortnes 2010). Solvoll's spiritual view of the situation indicates how empowering a subjective experience of divine support may be for a woman defying conventional gender norms.

A general comment on the above exposition is that Norwegian Pentecostal mission exhibits Protestant women's thrust towards equality and authority when they are confident that their ministries represent the will of God—all the more convincingly if God has communicated it directly to them. A second condition is a social and religious framework that accepts, or at least does not undermine, women's aspirations (cf. Fiedler 1994; Okkenhaug 2003).

Final Comments

Today, Pentecostalism is a dynamic religious current operating on a global scale, and since its earliest days Norwegians have contributed to its growth. Thomas Ball Barratt was an important harbinger of the Pentecostal message to Europe; his enthusiasm moved a number of young Norwegians to go abroad with the same message. The Norwegian Pentecostal mission grew into a significant agency that has affected religion and living conditions in a great number of countries, and still does. The question of how to organize a foreign mission has proven to be a contested spiritual issue and has not been solved once and for all. The mission as a whole is characterized by decentralization, which distinguishes it from most other mission agencies in Norway. Women have dominated numerically, but men have generally taken the leadership positions. Yet, women have been able to do "men's work" in the mission fields, holding positions of authority and leadership there that have not been open to them in Norway.

Acknowledgment I would like to thank the general secretary of PYM, Bjørn Bjørnø, for his obligingness in answering my questions and providing me with information.

Notes

1. The heading refers to a Pentecostal traveling mission exhibition "Win the World" (*Vinn Verden*) in 1965. On board the ship, M/S Sailing Fair, the exhibition visited large parts of the Norwegian coast (Nilsen 1984, 121).
2. The book is a translated and revised edition of Bloch-Hoell's doctorate thesis: *Pinsebevegelsen: En undersøkelse av pinsebevegelsens tilblivelse, utvikling og særpreg med særlig henblikk på bevegelsens utforming i Norge* (1956).
3. The paper was established in 1904, after Barratt had founded the interdenominational society "Kristiania City Mission" (Kristiania Bymisjon) in 1902. "The City Mail" (*Byposten*), renamed "The Victory of the Cross" (*Korsets Seir*) in 1909 was the first European Pentecostal periodical (Bundy 2009, 17). Later, the spelling changed to *Korsets Seier*.

4. *Word and Witness* was originally an American periodical of the Church of God in Christ related to Charles Parham's Apostolic Faith Movement. In 1914, it became an official periodical of the Assemblies of God.
5. "Moravians" is the English name of a branch of the Pietist movement. It originated in Sachsen, Germany, where Count Zinzendorf established a place of refuge, Herrnhut, for Protestant dissidents in 1722. The Moravian revival (Brødremenigheten) reached Norway in the 1730s. By the year 1800 Moravian groups existed in a number of Norwegian cities, but the movement was practically extinguished by the 1880s, according to church historian Einar Molland. The Moravians were keen supporters of foreign mission (Molland 1979, 98–105; Øverland 1987).
6. Cf. "the Santal Mission" (Santalmisjonen), founded in 1867, and "the Norwegian Lutheran Mission" (Norsk Luthersk Misjonssamband), founded in 1891.
7. The most prolific Pentecostal writer was Robert Bergsaker (1914–2009), who had a notable missionary career in India and Nepal. An obituary states that Bergsaker published 23 books besides newspaper and magazine articles (Bjøro 2009).
8. As a response to the lack of suitable reading matter in the local languages, "The Pentecostals's Literature Mission" (Pinsevennenes Litteraturmisjon) was established in 1950. The Pentecostal publishing company Filadelfiaforlaget undertook the task of providing books and papers (Nilsen 1984, 90).
9. The periodical was published in Swedish, Finnish, Spanish, and Russian editions (Bundy 2009, 18). As mentioned earlier, the spelling later became *Korsets Seier*.
10. The first Norwegian Pentecostal missionaries in China seem to have been Magna and Bernt Berntsen. According to Allan Anderson, the couple had experienced Spirit baptism on Azusa Street in 1907, and went to China in 1908 with a team of 13 missionaries to settle in Zhengding, 200 miles southeast of Beijing. In 1914 the Berntsens founded the Chinese periodical *Popular Gospel Truth*, connected with a church called Faith Union (Anderson 2009, 122–123).
11. In Norwegian: "Dagmar, Dagmar, se jeg sender deg. til det mørke sted Banda." Banda is situated 600 kilometres southeast of New Delhi in the Uttar Pradesh region.
12. The story is also told in Oddvar Nilsen's history (Nilsen 1984, 28–29).
13. In recognition of her status as the first person to proclaim the Pentecostal gospel in Germany, Engstrøm was invited as an honorable guest and speaker to a large Pentecostal anniversary congress in Hamburg in 1977 (Engstrøm 1980, 143).
14. Agnes Thelle established her own mission in Bilaspur near the Nepalese border. In 1915 she married Danish missionary Christian Beckdahl (Bundy 2009, 323; Nilsen 1984, 30).

15. Readers of the book are not informed whether Engstrøm had written diaries, letters, or published articles about her work which might have helped her memory.
16. "Biblewomen" is a term for a native female mission worker and collaborator. Biblewomen would contribute to evangelization and offer various kinds of assistance.
17. Anderson mentions the Mukti Mission's impact on Latin American Pentecostalism, particularly in Chile. This was due to the intervention of Minnie Abrams, Ramabai's right-hand assistant. Abrams wrote a booklet, *The Baptism of the Holy Ghost and Fire* (1906), which inspired Methodist churches in Valparaiso and Santiago to pray for a similar revival. This revival actually took place in 1909, and became the starting point of a movement resulting in the Chilean Pentecostal churches (Anderson 2015, 3).
18. The congregation led by Carl Magnus Seehuus (1864–1951) was originally Baptist. When news of the Welsh revival reached it, a revival including speaking in tongues arose in 1905. Seehuus and his congregation then became Pentecostal in 1908 (Bundy 2009, 317). It is counted as the first Pentecostal congregation in Norway. David Bundy describes the relationship between Barratt and Seehuus as competitive.
19. Originally the organization was named Norges Frie Evangeliske Missionsforbund, but the name was changed when an organization with a similar name, *Det Norske Misjonsforbund,* complained (Nilsen 1984, 39).
20. In 1919 "believers' baptism" (*troendedåp*) was introduced as a criterion for membership (Selbekk 2006, 157).
21. Barratt characterizes "Møllergaten 38" as the "mother congregation" of all the other Pentecostal assemblies in Norway (Barratt 2011, 213).
22. Oddvar Nilsen mentions that the total number of Pentecostal missionaries at this time was about 50—in other words 20 missionaries were not associated with NFEH (Nilsen 1984, 67).
23. Aside from his pioneering work in the Congo and office as the first mission secretary (1946–1964), Gunnerius Tollefsen was a scholar and a prolific author. During his Congo period he published ethnographic studies and wrote the first Norwegian grammar of two local languages: Kiswaheli and Chinyabongo (Ski 1967b, 953–954). Gunnerius and his wife Oddbjørg Tollefsen adopted the Greek-Egyptian boy Emanuel Minos (1925–2014), who became a legendary preacher in Swedish and Norwegian Pentecostalism.
24. The English name is The Pentecostal Foreign Mission of Norway. Formerly, Pinsevennenes Ytre Misjon seems to have been the name in common use.
25. There are at present 293 congregations according to general secretary Bjørn Bjørnø (personal communication, January 10, 2015).
26. This was also communicated to me by general secretary Bjørn Bjørnø (February 10, 2015).

27. Letter signed by general secretary Bjørn Bjørnø, February 12, 2015.
28. According to Oddvar Nilsen, Pentecostalism was brought to Iceland in 1920 by the Norwegian evangelist Erik Aasbø, who had also been present at the founding of the Pentecostal congregations in Göteborg and Örebro (Nilsen 1984, 55). David Bundy, however, referring to Petúr Petúrsson's *Från väckelse til samfund* (1990), imparts a more complex account of the early history of Pentecostalism in Iceland (Bundy 2009, 224).
29. In Kobe, Kyoto, Nagoya, Seto, Fukui-Mikuni, Katsuyama, and Takefu (Nilsen 1984, 98).
30. A discourse analysis of the condemnation of Edvardsen by these leaders in the period 1965–1978 was undertaken by Terje Hegertun in *Norsk tidsskrift for misjonsvitenskap* (2009).
31. For several reasons more accurate figures are not given here. First, because there are a few names on the list for which I was unable to be certain of the gender. Second, a reservation (cf. Johansen et al. 2010, 108) indicates that probably there have been non-registered missionaries. Third, sheer numbers are no reliable indication of the scope and significance of the missionary work carried out by the two genders. Married men have had better opportunities to spend their time on work outside the household than married women. Also, the list says nothing about how long the individual has been in the field.
32. General secretary Bjørn Bjørnø (personal communication, February 10, 2015).
33. In Norwegian: "Din skaper er din ektemann." The sentence is a citation from Isaiah 54: 5. In mission literature the deity often speaks in biblical phrasing (Mikaelsson 2010).

REFERENCES

Aalborg, Berit. 2014. Kristelige mannskulturer. *Vårt Land*, December 4.
Aarflot, Andreas. 1969. *Tro og lydighet: Hans Nielsen Hauges kristendomsforståelse*. Oslo: Universitetsforlaget.
Alvarsson, Jan-Åke. 2011. The Development of Pentecostalism in Scandinavian Countries. In *European Pentecostalism*, ed. William K. Kay and Anne E. Dyer, 19–39. Leiden/Boston: Brill.
———. 2015. En komparativ översikt av pentecostalismens historia i Norden från 1906 till i dag. In *Pentekostale perspektiver*, ed. Knut-Willy Sæther and Karl Inge Tangen, 31–16. Bergen: Fagbokforlaget.
Anderson, Allan. 2009. Pentecostalism in India and China in the Early Twentieth Century. In *Global Pentecostalism: Encounters with Other Religious Traditions*, ed. David Westerlund, 117–135. London/New York: I. B. Tauris.
———. 2015. To All Points of the Compass: The Azusa Street Revival and Global Pentecostalism. *Enrichment Journal*, 1–13. http://enrichmentjournal.ag.org/200602/200602_164_allpoints.cfm. Accessed 31 Mar 2017.

Arntsen, Ingrid Ofte. 2015. Høylydte feminister vs ydmyke kvinner? *Vårt Land*, January 8.
Barratt, T.B. 1933. *Kvinnens stilling i menigheten*. Korsets Seiers Forlag: Oslo.
Barratt, Thomas Ball. 1936. *Ledetråd i Guds ord: For ungdom og nyfrelste*. Oslo: Filadelfiaforlaget.
———. 2011 [1941]. *Erindringer*. Oslo: Filadelfiaforlaget. Edition 2011 by Ronny Ranestad Larsen.
Bjøro, Terje. 2009. Robert Bergsaker til minne. *Vårt Land*, October 5.
Bloch-Hoell, Nils. 1956. *Pinsebevegelsen: En undersøkelse av pinsebevegelsens tilblivelse, utvikling og særpreg med særlig henblikk på bevegelsens utforming i Norge*. Oslo: Universitetsforlaget.
———. 1964. *The Pentecostal Movement: Its Origin, Development and Distinctive Character*. Oslo/London: Universitetsforlaget/Allen & Unwin.
Bundy, David. 2009. Visions of Apostolic Mission: Scandinavian Pentecostal Mission to 1935. PhD dissertation. University of Uppsala.
Danbolt, Erling. 1947. *Misjonstankens gjennombrudd i Norge, vol. 1, Misjonsappellens tid 1800–1830*. Oslo: Egede-Instituttet.
Drønen, Tomas Sundnes, and Marianne Skjortnes, eds. 2010. *Med hjertet på flere steder: Om barn, misjon og flerkulturell oppvekst*. Trondheim: Tapir Akademisk Forlag.
Dyer, Anne E. 2011. Introduction. In *European Pentecostalism*, ed. William K. Kay and Anne E. Dyer, 1–15. Boston: Brill.
Engstrøm, Dagmar. 1980. *Ha tro til Gud: Alt er mulig for den som tror*. Oslo: Filadelfiaforlaget.
Fiedler, Klaus. 1994. *The Story of Faith Missions*. Oxford: Regnum Books International.
Froholt, Asbjørn. 1997. Landsmøtene i DFEF & Misjonsutvalget – 50 år. Paper presented at the Annual Meeting of De Frie Evangeliske Forsamlinger (DFEF). www.dfef.no/artikkel/57/landsmøtene. Accessed 20 Apr 2017.
Gulbrandsen, Parley. 1937. Hedningemisjonen blandt pinsevennene. In *Pinsevekkelsen i Norge gjennem 30 år 1907–1937*, ed. J. Bratlie, 133–157. Oslo: Filadelfiaforlaget.
Gunnestad, Kirsti Thuseth. 2015. Kvinner i lederskap i Pinsebevegelsen i Norge: En undersøkelse av endringer i synet på kvinner i eldste- og forstandertjeneste i Pinsebevegelsen i Norge. In *Pentekostale perspektiver*, ed. Knut-Willy Sæther and Karl Inge Tangen, 203–220. Bergen: Fagbokforlaget.
Hegertun, Terje. 2009. Pinsestrid i økumenisk og diskursteoretisk perspektiv. *Norsk tidsskrift for misjonsvitenskap/Norwegian Journal of Missiology* 3: 165–189.
Hoaas, Ole Georg, and Oddvar Tegnander. 1984. *Kvinnen—fri til tjeneste?* Oslo: Filadelfiaforlaget.

Iversen, G. 1946. *Blant indianere i 35 år: Berger N. Johnsens misjonsarbeid i Argentina*. Sarpsborg: Johansen & Larsen, Bok- og Aksidenstrykkeri.
Johansen, Oddvar, Kjell Hagen, Astrid Neema Nyen, and Paul Kolbjørnsrud. 2010. *Pinsemisjon i 100 år*. Oslo: De norske pinsemenigheters ytremisjon.
Jones, Spencer. 1967. India. In *Norsk Misjonsleksikon*, ed. Fritjov Birkeli et al., vol. 2, 335–358. Stavanger: Nomi Forlag.
Jørgensen, Torstein, ed. 1992. *I tro og tjeneste: Det Norske Misjonsselskap 1842–1992*. Vol. 1. Stavanger: Misjonshøgskolen.
Kullerud, Dag. 1996. *Hans Nielsen Hauge—mannen som vekket Norge*. Oslo: Forlaget Forum; H. Aschehoug & Co.
McGee, Gary B. 2010. *Miracles, Missions, and American Pentecostalism*. New York: Orbis Books.
Meyer, Ralph. 2015. Fra Kristiania til Kassel: Pinsebevegelsens begynnelse i Tyskland og forholdet til Gemeinschaftsbevegelsen. In *Pentekostale perspektiver*, ed. Knut-Willy Sæther and Karl Inge Tangen, 91–110. Bergen: Fagbokforlaget.
Mikaelsson, Lisbeth. 2003. *Kallets ekko: Studier i misjon og selvbiografi*. Stavanger: Høyskoleforlaget.
———. 2005. The Heathen Woman in Norwegian Missionary Writing. In *Gender, Poverty and Church Involvement: A Report from a Research Conference in Uppsala*, May 6–8, 2002, Ed. Katharina Hallencreutz, 175–80. Missio no 20, Uppsala: Swedish Institute of Mission Research.
———. 2010. Verification of the Word of God in Missionary Autobiography. In *Canon and Canonicity: The Formation and Use of Scripture*, ed. Einar Thomassen, 159–175. Copenhagen: Museum Tusculanum Press.
Molland, Einar. 1979. *Norges kirkehistorie i det 19. århundre*. Vol. 1. Oslo: Gyldendal Norsk Forlag.
Myklebust, Anders. 2014. Opprør mot mannsdominans. *Vårt Land*, December 19.
Nilsen, Oddvar. 1984. *Ut i all verden: Pinsevennenes ytre misjon i 75 år*. Oslo: Filadelfiaforlaget.
Okkenhaug, Inger Marie, ed. 2003. *Gender, Race and Religion: Nordic Missions 1860–1940*. Uppsala: Studia Missionalia Svecana XCI.
Øverland, Per. 1987. *Kortere avhandlinger om Brødremenigheten i Norge*. Trondheim: P. Øverland.
PYM. 2015. http://pymportal.com/about-us/ (2015). Accessed 15 Jan 2015.
Rimehaug, Erling. 2010. Aril Edvardsen. *Norsk biografisk leksikon*. Last modified December 28, 2010. https://nbl.snl.no/Aril_Edvardsen. Accessed 27 Jan 2015.
Rudolph, Willy, and Spencer Jones. 1967. China. In *Norsk Misjonsleksikon*, ed. Fridtjov Birkeli et al., vol. 3, 480–486. Stavanger: Nomi Forlag.

Seland, Bjørg. 2001. Religion på det frie marked. Folkelig pietisme og bedehuskultur. PhD dissertation. University of Bergen.
Selbekk, Vebjørn. 2006. *T.B. Barratt forfulgt og etterfulgt*. Skjetten: Hermon Forlag.
Simpson, Carl. 2011. The Development of Pentecostal and Charismatic Movements in the Germanic Countries. In *European Pentecostalism*, ed. William K. Kay and Anne E. Dyer, 61–83. Leiden/Boston: Brill.
Sjursen, Finn Wiig. 1993. *Den haugianske periode: En bibliografi*. Bergen: NLA-Forlaget.
———. 1997. *Den haugianske periode*. Bergen: NLA-Forlaget.
Ski, Martin. 1967a. Pinsevennenes Ytre Misjon. In *Norsk Misjonsleksikon*, ed. Fritjov Birkeli et al., vol. 3, 450–470. Stavanger: Nomi Forlag.
———. 1967b. Tollefsen, Gunnerius. In *Norsk Misjonsleksikon*, ed. Fritjov Birkeli et al., vol. 3, 953–954. Stavanger: Nomi Forlag.
Slettan, Bjørn. 1992. *"O, at jeg kunde min Jesum prise...": Folkelig religiøsitet og vekkelsesliv på Agder på 1800-tallet*. Oslo: Universitetsforlaget.
Solvoll, Berly Aarre. 1983. *I mesterens hånd: Med evangeliet til Østens folk*. Oslo: Filadelfiaforlaget.
Sugirtharajah, Sharada. 2005. Ramabai, Pandita. In *Encyclopedia of Religion*, ed. Lindsay Jones, 2nd ed., 7610–7611. Detroit: Thomson Gale.
Tollefsen, Gunnerius. 1925. *I Afrikas indre: Oplevelser og inntrykk fra en ekspedisjonsreise*. Oslo: Eget forlag.
Tveit, Terje. 2011. Misjonær Liv Haug 40 år i Peru. *Filadelfia Kristiansand*, November 23. http://filadelfiakristiansand.ekanal.com/tekst/4070/Misjoner-Liv-Haug-40-ar-i-Peru.aspx#.WPiJbE1MTL8. Accessed 20 Apr 2017.

Open Access This chapter is distributed under the terms of the Creative Commons Attribution 4.0 International License (http://creativecommons.org/licenses/by/4.0/), which permits use, duplication, adaptation, distribution and reproduction in any medium or format, as long as you give appropriate credit to the original author(s) and the source, provide a link to the Creative Commons license and indicate if changes were made.

The images or other third party material in this chapter are included in the chapter's Creative Commons license, unless indicated otherwise in a credit line to the material. If material is not included in the chapter's Creative Commons license and your intended use is not permitted by statutory regulation or exceeds the permitted use, you will need to obtain permission directly from the copyright holder.

PART 2

Internal Dynamics

CHAPTER 4

In the Wake of God's Fire: Transforming Charisma and Charismata in the Reconstruction of a Local Church

Jane Skjoldli

"We're pretty fresh out of a crisis a few years back," began Matthew. "People think we are Living Word. We are not. That church is dead. It doesn't exist anymore. We have the same address and the same building, but a lot has changed. The name is just one of those things. We still believe in the same God, but the leadership has been replaced completely. Only one of those who used to be involved in leadership still is."

Matthew is one of the respondents in an ethnographic study on a local Charismatic church in Bergen, Norway, carried out in the summer of 2013. The church was formerly known as "Living Word" (Levende Ord), and to some extent still is, despite being renamed "The Credo Church" (Credokirken) in 2009. In the quote above, Matthew points out similarities and differences between the two. To the extent that Living Word still exists, it is in the form of the Credo Church: Both churches believe in the same God and reside in the same building, he says. Nevertheless, much has changed. Among the changes he chose to draw attention to were those made to the leadership.

J. Skjoldli (✉)
University of Bergen, Bergen, Norway

© The Author(s) 2018
J. Moberg, J. Skjoldli (eds.), *Charismatic Christianity in Finland, Norway, and Sweden*, Palgrave Studies in New Religions and Alternative Spiritualities, https://doi.org/10.1007/978-3-319-69614-0_4

Through participant observation at Sunday services and other events; formal interviews and informal conversations over coffee; post-service Sunday dinners; small group meetings; and by reading news material, promotional material, and master theses on the church (Bryne 2007; Steinhovden 2006), I learned that the Credo Church's leadership involves new practices as well as new personnel, differences in structure as well as ideals. At Living Word, authority was primarily ascribed to the founder and senior pastor. Leadership at the Credo Church is also headed by a senior pastor, but it also involves a management team and a board with whom he collaborates. Moreover, leaders are accountable to a set of statutes and the church's general assembly, which includes all registered members, was established and is empowered to change church practice and policy. In Weberian terms, authority has shifted from a deeply charismatic form to a more rationalized form—a process commonly referred to as the *routinization of charisma* (Weber 1947, 363), which informs the analysis below. As terminological irony would have it, Weberian charismatic authority among Charismatics is often tied to the very practices they associate with the term Weber recruited for his conceptualization of the term, namely the *charismata*—the gifts and manifestations of the Holy Spirit. Living Word was no exception. Typically, *routinization* of charisma is regarded as a necessity following the loss of a charismatic leader. Sometimes, however, a leader's loss of charismatic authority precedes the loss of the leader himself (see e.g. Weber 1947, 359–60; Yukl 1999, 297). This appears to have been the case at Living Word. When members discontinued attributing charismatic authority to the leader, a group within the congregation created the previously nonexistent means for deposing the leader. The process began due to disagreement over leadership style, which was perceived as too authoritarian, even to the point of autocracy (Hellesund 2006). Furthermore, allocation of church funds had come under scrutiny from local authorities (Wiederstrøm 2006). As the discussion will show, however, gifts and manifestations were themselves important pieces of the puzzle regarding how charismatic authority diminished, but also how it was reconstructed.

What can the members interviewed for this study teach us about gifts and manifestations on the one hand, and the construction of charismatic authority on the other? This chapter examines that question mainly on the basis of semi-structured interviews with members of the Credo Church, who were also members of Living Word. The exploration is divided into three main sections: The first discusses the two concepts of *charisma* relevant to this study. Applying a Weberian perspective, the second section examines authority transformations as part of the congregation's reconstruction process. The third section analyzes respondents' approaches to gifts and manifestations in light of the discussion on authority transformations.

Making Sense of *Charisma*

For the purposes of the following analysis, two main concepts of *charisma* need to be addressed. The first is the Weberian concept of *charisma*—a sociological concept that constitutes an essential component of Weber's theory of the three sources of legitimate authority. Charisma in this respect underpins charismatic forms of authority, which are considered "inherently unstable and temporary" (Weber 1947, 71), as opposed to traditional and rational forms.

The second concept is perhaps best described as a cluster of Christian notions connected to the emic term *charisma*. According to Barclay M. Newman, Jr.'s Greek-English dictionary of the New Testament, *charisma* (plural: *charismata*) denotes a "*gift* as an expression of divine grace," or "a special *manifestation* of the divine presence, activity, power or glory" (1993, 197, italics added). Both are reflected in Norwegian Charismatic terms, where the word commonly used for *charismata* is "gifts of grace" (*nådegaver*) and "manifestations of the Spirit" (*Åndsmanifestasjoner*). The interviews were all conducted in Norwegian, and the transcript translations into English are my own. In order for the text to stay as close as possible to the original Norwegian responses, I have chosen to apply "gifts of grace" rather than the English idiomatic term *spiritual gifts*, which is more closely related to the Greek term anyway (see also Poloma 1997, 259).

What experiences and practices constitute the emic categories corresponding to the terms "gifts of grace" and "manifestations of the Spirit"? The question is rarely asked in Pentecostal studies, despite acknowledgment that the answers are subject to variation among practitioners (Skjoldli 2014, 95). Furthermore, the terms are sometimes used interchangeably, but may also refer to separate categories. An illustrative example is how elements ascribed to the "gifts" category tend to be referred to simply as "*the* gifts," often followed by just a few examples, implying that their boundaries are self-evident (e.g., Anderson 2015, 7–8; Coleman 2000, 21; Inbody 2015, 1; Poloma 1997, 259; Robbins 2004, 117; Singleton 2011, 384). The neglect of nuance has been acknowledged (Anderson 2010, 20) but, given the continued centrality of gifts and manifestations to defining

Pentecostal and Charismatic forms of Christianity (Anderson 2010, 2014, 6; di Giacomo 2009, 15; Robbins 2004, 117), the absence of problematization presents a paradox. When treated as separate categories, "gifts" are often catalogued by referring to 1 Corinthians: 12 as an index that includes glossolalia, interpretation of glossolalia, prophecy, healing, miracles, Words of Knowledge, Words of Wisdom, a special form of faith, and discernment of spirits (see also Anderson 2014, 19). By contrast, no Bible passage is treated similarly as an index for "manifestations." Instead, the limits of the latter category have often been contested. Examples habitually associated with the category count the widespread phenomenon of "falling in the Spirit" ("being slain in the Spirit" is not used in Norwegian); uncontrollable laughter, crying, and trembling; some kinds of exorcism; and animal imitation (Skjoldli 2014, 81; Poloma and Hoelter 1998, 261). While not central here, it should be noted that the respondents featuring in this study treat the categories in more complicated ways.

"Gifts" and "manifestations" also have important features in common: first, their origin and distribution is generally attributed to God. Second, when elaborated upon, gifts and manifestations are usually legitimized by recourse to biblical texts. Charismatics and non-Charismatics tend to differ on whether authentic gifts of grace are currently operational or even of interest (e.g., Anderson 2014, 20–39), thus contributing to disagreements between them. Among Charismatics themselves, disputes over manifestations have displayed the potential to create controversy, whilst providing paths to innovation as well as division. Such disputes have led to the establishment of new congregations, some of which have grown into new movements (Skjoldli 2014, 94). In short, understandings of gifts and manifestations are subject to dynamics of negotiation through the enacted theology of how they are and are not practiced. With these nuances in mind, we turn to authority transformations as part of the reconstruction of the Credo Church's congregation, paying particular attention to the gift of prophecy.

Prophecy: A Double-edged Sword

Living Word was originally founded as "Word of Life Bergen" (Livets Ord Bergen) by the married couple Enevald and Olga Flåten in 1992; its name bears testimony to the spread of "Word of Life" congregations and other Faith communities in Nordic countries during the 1980s and 1990s. The church was renamed "Living Word Bible Centre" (Levende Ord Bibelsenter) in 1994 in order to avoid confusion with Ulf Ekman's church at Uppsala, Sweden (Credokirken 2014), where Enevald Flåten attended Bible college twice. The second time, he was already the founder and senior pastor of the "Jæren Christian Center" (Jæren Kristne Senter) in the county of Rogaland, in southwestern Norway. At the Bible college, Flåten received a new vision from God. It is helpful to consider Flåten's own account:

> One day, I lay between the rows of seats at the Bible college. Then God's Spirit came. He touched my heart and he spoke to me, saying: "Write [this] down." And I wrote down the entire vision for the whole [process of] starting a church in Bergen. I wrote: It will be a base for mission, evangelizing, and church planting. […] It will be a place for teaching, where you will teach the people in all of God's counsel. It will be a place where God's love will be poured out. It will be a place of deliverance, healing, and restoration, and a prophetic voice to the nation. (Kanal 10 Norge 2014)

Flåten's story takes the form of a testimony that involves a revelation from God. Reference to prophecy is made both implicitly and explicitly—implicitly by way of reporting direct communication with God, explicitly regarding the mission and future of the church. Narratives that involve direct speech from God and appoint someone for a mission, giving them a vision for the future, and the conviction required to fulfill them, are all native to Charismatic discourse. George D. Chryssides and Margaret Z. Wilkins have identified such narratives as foundation myths. When applied to this case, the narrative can be seen to define the nature of Flåten's leadership as sanctioned by God and revealed through prophecy (Chryssides and Wilkins 2006, 35–36). The narrative had the potential to imbue Flåten with Weberian charisma. These very elements can be detected in one congregant's account of the service at Jæren Christian Center, where Flåten shared his message:

> There was one service during a conference where Enevald said he had something to share with us. He told [us] that he had received [a message] from God that he should start a church in Bergen. He had received a word, that "Bergen is an important city to God." There were many who approved of that idea. At the service, there were many who said they were going to move to Bergen and start the church. Many left [for Bergen] at that time.

Having proclaimed his new vision to the congregation, Flåten and a group of families from Jæren relocated to Bergen to establish the new church. We may note the openness with which congregants reportedly responded to the newly revealed vision. In the years to come, the proclamation that "Bergen is an important city to God" turned into a founding vision for the congregation, but also remained an individual vocation for Flåten (Opheim 2012).

My respondents disagreed on how prevalent prophecies had been at Living Word. While another respondent, Paula, reported that prophecies had been far more common at Living Word than in the present church, Matthew stated that "there were few prophecies, really." He was concerned with the function of prophecy in relation to conversion, explaining how, "in the Bible, it says that, if somebody brings prophetic words, they [non-Christians] would be busted!" Matthew was referring to 1 Corinthians: 14, 24–25, where Paul the apostle instructs his readers that "[i]f everybody speaks prophetically, and an unbeliever or an uninformed [person] comes in, he will be convinced by everybody, he will be convicted by everybody. And so, everything concealed in his heart is revealed. And then he will fall down on his face, and he will worship God and testify that God is truly among you" (*Bibelen: Guds Ord* 1997, author's translation).[1] In this interview, Matthew connected prophecy primarily to conversion, which challenges a conceptualization of prophecy as simply "prediction and revelation" (Anderson 2014, 20).

Paula had considered herself a Christian all her life, but recounted one specific experience she described as prophetic, motivating her to commit to her faith and remain in the congregation:

Paula: I know that something specific happened at the first service I attended here [at Living Word]. Something new happened then, where I was [allowed] to know Jesus. The pastor [Flåten] was walking around in the hall and said, "I feel so strongly that there is a [young person] here." [And then] he was able to give an account of my life prophetically. He had very concrete [messages] from God. But I did not dare to make myself known. I was terrified, because I had never experienced that kind [of thing] before—that you prophesy in that way. But I felt inside that something really loosened [up]. I knew it was [for] me.
Jane: That must have been an incredible experience.
Paula: It was. It was [a] very powerful [experience] for me. There were a lot of people around as well. You felt special, like, "Wow, God cares about *me*." There were lots of things he [the pastor] said, too, "God sees you and has seen you—what you have been through."

From Paula's story, we understand that, as the pastor spoke, she identified with the "you" addressed in the message given; to her, it was a prophetic account of her life. Through Paula's description of the experience as an encounter with Jesus, and of the message as prophetic, we learn how the pastor could function as the human mediator of that message. This made her feel acknowledged and singled out from the larger group of attendees, and ultimately influenced her to commit to her faith. She felt that she was important to God, important enough that God chose to convey a message to her rather than another. In this story, God emerges as a nurturer, a caretaker who acknowledges her personal struggles, and fulfills her need to feel recognized, and to have her pain acknowledged.

By 2004, Living Word had risen to national prominence and become Norway's largest independent church (Selbekk 2012, 2). That year, Living Word had 2549 registered members and formed a nucleus in a loose network of smaller churches (Gjestad 2012, 17). Living Word produced its own monthly magazine called "Flaming Fire" (*Flammende Ild*), published books at Levende Ord Forlag, and broadcast weekly services on the state television channel NRK2's frequency.[2] The church also ran a kindergarten, a primary school, a secondary school, a Bible college, various social activities, an international missionary network, and weekly and bi-weekly Bible study groups. Living Word was a congregation with megachurch ambitions that, hypothetically, could encapsulate one's entire life.

Meanwhile, Flåten's statements on God, gender, Islam, and homosexuality gained him attention in the public eye, which probably also served to increase public awareness of the church (Lie 2011, 516). In 2003, a documentary criticizing church members for organizing events that featured glossolalia at the primary school aired on national television (NRK 2003). The following year, controversial politician and former leader of the right-wing Progress Party Carl I. Hagen visited the church, trying to gain voters by making statements expressing support for the state of Israel and opposition to Islam (Aftenposten 2004; Honningsøy 2011). In 2005, politicians from other parties also visited (Hamre 2005). The years 2004–2005 were likely Living Word's peak period in terms of political influence, as well as member numbers and international outreach (Algrøy 2012b; Credokirken 2014). Living Word had grown into a bright feather of the Faith Movement's Nordic wing.

Discontent was growing within, however. Former members reported that channels by means of which members could express criticism and dissatisfaction, or ask questions, were lacking. As one former member put it, "if anyone chose to leave the congregation, they would risk being libeled from the pulpit. No one could leave retaining their honor, and many chose to stay because of that—for fear of 'falling outside the blessing'" (Almelid 2012b, 18). Toward the end of 2005, a breaking point was reached when two youth ministers left their posts (Algrøy 2012a, 27; b, 17; Gilje 2012, 24; Hamre 2006). Towards the end of one of the interviews, one respondent shared a brief description of prophecies connected to the crisis in 2006, when "horrible prophecies" were given to people who had been singled out as traitors to the former senior pastor. "That stuff was immensely harsh," the respondent said.

As Living Word was a high profile church, internal conflict within it was sure to catch the media's attention. Christian and non-Christian newspapers and channels covered the unfolding events. A group of members, led by the church's head of missions, Olav Rønhovde, rallied with the ambition to change the course of events. A crisis of authority and leadership ensued, but no internal mechanism or apparatus existed for replacing the senior pastor. Pastors from other churches were later called upon to help, but to no avail. A schism unfolded. Flåten went on sick leave and a new team of leaders gained control of the church, working to alter the organization's structure, implementing a set of statutes, and establishing a general assembly. Recounting the schism, one of my respondents emphasized the importance of new leaders who, guided by mentors from other churches, "[said] straight that the way in which things had been done was wrong." The mentors were founder and former senior pastor Åge Åleskjær of the Oslo Christian Center and Robert Ekh, former pastor of Word of Life at Uppsala. They found the church's forms of prophecy to be disturbing, in addition to other issues that were made public around the time Flåten left his post (Åleskjær and Ekh 2006).

Rønhovde was elected temporary pastor at first, and made permanent senior pastor in 2008, which was also the year when the church's secondary school was closed as a result of a decrease in numbers of students signing up. In 2009, "Living Word" was renamed "Credo Church." Since then, black italicized letters spelling "Credokirken" have made up the church's logo, which is displayed at the most conspicuous top corner of the church's large, brown building at Kråkenes, south of Bergen.[3] By 2012, 55 percent—around 1400—of the church members had left, some 1000 of whom seem to have abandoned church activity altogether (Selbekk 2012). When journalists from the Christian newspaper "The Day" (*Dagen*) contacted former members, it was reported that many declined requests for stories and testimonies, describing the events as still too painful to discuss (Gjestad 2013, 6). Years passed and the controversy died down, but was not entirely forgotten.

As illustrated, Flåten received and transmitted messages perceived to be from God, a practice clothed in the language of prophecy—for better or for worse. Understood as the gift of prophecy, the descriptions fit Weberian charisma well, as attributed to a person thought to possess "a certain quality of an individual personality by virtue of which he is set apart from ordinary men," on the basis of which Flåten was "treated as a leader" (Weber 1947, 358). Later, however, when authority met with opposition, prophecy was transformed into a tool for maintaining control. Prophecy acquired a dark side, a reminder of Weber's point that charisma is socially constructed and "what is alone important is how the individual is actually regarded by those subject to charismatic authority, by his 'followers'" (Weber 1947, 359; cf. Bensman and Givant 1975, 571; Wallis 1982, 26). Moving forward, processes of transforming charisma—and prophecy—would become key to re-establishing interpersonal bonds and authority structures within the congregation.

Transforming Foundations of Authority

Recent statistics reveal that the Credo Church has 1081 registered members, a few dozen fewer than in 2012 (Department of Culture 2017). Senior pastor Olav Rønhovde and the Credo Church rarely feature in the media, and in an interview from 2012, Rønhovde described the church as having become more relaxed (Almelid 2012a). In the same article, a married couple stated that one main difference between Living Word and the Credo Church is the latter's stronger emphasis on fellowship and relationships, as opposed to members becoming tied to the pastor: "Today, people can say what they feel and think. It's a constant, ongoing process, and that is essential" (Almelid 2012a, 37). In a more recent interview, Rønhovde stated that the congregation's drive has been rekindled (Gilje 2016). The church runs a Christian primary school, and reportedly hosts on average 300 attendees on Sundays, 60–70 young people at Friday youth services, a couple of hundred women at women's meetings. In addition the "Substance" Bible college (*Substans*) has 44 students and is run in collaboration with two local Pentecostal congregations (Gilje 2016).

In the beginning of this chapter, Matthew pointed out style of leadership as one of the defining differences between the Credo Church and

Living Word. Asking Matthew how pastor Rønhovde had been elected, Matthew explained that he was originally employed as a missionary and teacher at the Bible college. Matthew was himself present at the meeting where Rønhovde was elected senior pastor:

> He heard from God that God wanted to use him as pastor. He told us at a service when we were about to elect a new [pastor] [...] He asked if we accepted him as pastor and we would vote for or against. Almost everyone [voted] in favor [...] You wrote "yes" or "no" or "blank" on a note. "No" and "blank" comprised maybe around ten percent of the total votes, not much more. The "yes" was almost unison.

We learn three things from Matthew: first, that Rønhovde was already an established leader figure in the congregation. Second, that Rønhovde had "heard from God,"[4] and had shared this experience at a service prior to the election. While the initiative in this narrative is God's own, it should be noted that Rønhovde tells the story somewhat more cautiously, framing the task of becoming senior pastor as a vocation for which he had no particular desire (Almelid 2012a, 37). Third, his experience of God calling him to the post as senior pastor was not itself sufficient; the congregation's consent was sought in general assembly, which was given by means of a ballot. Rønhovde's election involved elements of charisma that are not entirely divorced from prophecy, but also involved the new rational aspect of a ballot in general assembly. Combined, these elements constitute the routinization of charisma in the Credo Church, not by replacing charismatic authority outright, but by introducing new elements to the mix.

Matthew continued to stress that "[the senior pastor] must be able to hear from God. He must be able to bring messages he receives from God to the church in such a way that you understand what he's saying." He connected the ability to receive messages from God to a leadership model that is often called the fivefold ministry, based on Ephesians 4: 11–12, which includes evangelist, teacher, pastor, prophet, and apostle. I asked Matthew whether he would call the pastor a prophet. He responded that he may be used as one, but pointed out that "[it's] not his primary function." Rather, he explained, the senior pastor bears the main *responsibility* for the church; he "carries the whole church on his shoulders—for better or worse. It can [involve] spiritual battles too [...] He has spiritual, but also practical and financial advisors, [but] he has the heaviest load with regards to decisions, both financially and spiritually." Matthew was also careful to point out that, while there are ups and downs to being a senior pastor, he has no "fringe benefits like [he might] in a company": the responsibility will gain him a greater reward from God, but also a stricter judgment.

Whereas the position of senior pastor used to have numerous benefits, it is now framed in terms of responsibility, involving heavy demands and difficult decisions. Paula was also sensitive to the burden that comes with leadership. She explained that when somebody is doing God's work, they should not be in that position for too long. She saw change as something healthy, not only to the church, but also to the person in the position of responsibility: "You shouldn't build something strongly around your own person, but be allowed to grow into new things," she said, indicating that the vocation needs not be permanent.

Per Ove Berg, who is pastor at the Credo Church along with Rønhovde, and who consented to being referred to by name, elaborated on the possibility of the senior pastor terminating his ministry. Quoting and elaborating on the statutes, he provided a normative perspective on the issue. The senior pastor can step down if he so wishes, in agreement with the management team and the board, who also suggest his successor to the church. Reading from the statutes, and commenting upon them as he went, Berg explained that a senior pastor may be removed if he engages in "inappropriate conduct incompatible with the ethic and moral norms of God's Word: such as immorality, financial default, heresy […] or if the senior pastor in other ways neglects or abuses his ministry, the other [members of the] management team and the board together will consider termination of the position." In other words, a legal-rational aspect has been added to the legitimacy of the senior pastor's authority, namely a set of statutes to which he is accountable. The senior pastor's position then, depends on a collection of elements: a vocation from God, his personal capability, the congregation's confidence, and conformity with the church's statutes. The introduction of these aspects is also reflected in the procedures established for electing a new pastor, in which case, the statutes demand that the board makes a suggestion for a new senior pastor to the congregation in general assembly. A two-thirds majority is required from the members present. Berg explained that all adult church members have the right to vote at general assemblies and that the gatherings, ordinarily held once a year, decide the contents of the statutes, to which "everyone, including the senior pastor, every organ is subordinate […] No one can go and change that."

Berg also explained how a vocation is discovered and how to proceed if, for example, several individuals were to perceive themselves as called by God to be the new senior pastor:

> There is a dynamic between the first [criterion], that God is calling [the person], which is recognized through the second [criterion]: the people, who give trust, who experience the person in question as worthy of our trust; that the person has a gift […] and a personal demeanor that qualifies him for the job. Thus viewed, human beings elect [the pastor]. You can only be a leader based on trust. Everything is built on trust. Everything is built on free will […] The dynamic is such that the person in question, naturally, must have faith and be convinced that this is right, that this is what he is supposed to do. There may also be formal qualifications, but that is not always so.

It appears that the election process contains elements of democratic process mixed with personal conviction. One could argue that there is a certain tension in this dynamic: on the one hand, there are the congregants, who may have a favorite candidate. On the other, there is always the question of whether one has interpreted God's will correctly—especially, one might imagine, on the part of the newly elected leader. However, Berg's explanation brings the two into line.

To Matthew, it was important not to forget that "a pastor, whether he leads one hundred or ten thousand, should ideally be chosen by God: [I]f Rønhovde were to quit as pastor [or] died […we] must ask God: 'Who do you want as a new pastor?' It comes down to asking him: 'What do you want?'" I asked Matthew how one would find out what God wanted: "You'd have to seek God and let God answer. You need some time, really, because God is sometimes slow on the trigger. He likes to test us, [to see] if we're serious. If you seek God, you have to wait until he responds."

In the Credo Church, leadership is also shared. There is a senior pastor, who "hears from God," as well as people with different areas of responsibility, including the board and management team, spiritual and economic advisors, cell group coordinators, missionaries, and youth ministers. The respondents seemed to appreciate these more formalized leadership structures. At the same time, in reference to leadership more generally, another respondent, Mark, emphasized the initiative of up-and-coming leaders. "It happens naturally," he explained, and continued:

> You see people who branch out, who have the interest needed and who work at it. I guess a lot of it [happens in the way that] people who take responsibility receive responsibility. It's voluntary and people rarely do it for the sake of their own gain. It's because they have the heart for it and take initiative.

I asked him to elaborate. Responding, he immediately connected the question to Living Word's leadership structure: "With regards to the pastor being fired by the church without the involvement of an elder council—no such thing existed at the time." The question, then, was who had the authority to ask the pastor to leave. He stated that the authority to depose a leader "rests with the church."

Along with the transformation of leadership structures came new understandings and practices, particularly involving gifts and manifestations. For example, prophecy is still an important gift of grace. Respondents varied in their perceptions of these changes. While Paula's view was largely positive, she was not altogether dismissive of the old ways: "In the beginning, a lot of people experienced that the pastor or other leaders received prophecies that changed people's lives," she stated, expressing a sense of nostalgia for the way prophecy had been practiced at Living Word. "There was a lot of prophecy, which I experienced," she said reminiscing, "where the pastor walks around and receives messages from God. There was a lot that was not from God, but also a lot that was from God." There is a sense of ambivalence to Paula's words: she distinguishes between true and false prophecies, emphasizing the helpfulness of the former, while also expressing reservations.

When prophecy at Living Word turned into a means for public rejection of and creating a social stigma for dissenters, what followed can be viewed through the lens of Weber's description of how a leader's charisma is likely to disappear if "he is for long unsuccessful." We have learned that prophecy was important to constructing and maintaining charismatic authority at Living Word. However, the particular way in which prophecy was applied seems to have changed over time, as it went from providing reassurance to carrying exclusion and social stigma. It seems that the shift in how prophecy was enacted robbed it of its capacity for generating charisma for the senior pastor; what had previously been a source of trust was tainted through its employment to discourage dissent. From a Weberian perspective, such a reaction to delinquency is to be expected from a charismatic leader (Weber 1947, 359). It is more noteworthy that a gift of grace that had initially been so important for establishing charismatic authority itself seems to have become corrupted, causing not only the charismatic authority it had served to support to consequently crumble, but also the very status of prophecy itself. This is coherent with the prevailing interpretation of Weberian charisma being solely in the eye of the beholder(s), as quoted earlier. In the words of David Setley and Douglas Gautsch, charisma is "based solely on the evaluation of the follower on a leader's traits, not on any absolutes or skills the leader actually has" (Setley and Gautsch 2015, 23–24). While this study's findings are consistent with that interpretation, they also show how abuse of a charisma-generating practice can turn against itself. Such an interpretation of transformations and the respondents' views on prophecy is also helpful for an understanding of how the congregation acquired a cautionary approach to prophecy. From this angle, it follows that transforming the foundations of authority was a necessary step in order to rebuild trust in the emerging leadership, as well as in wider fellowship within the church.

So far, we have seen that these transformations entailed a process of rationalization in favor of which "the *purely* personal character of leadership is eliminated" (Weber 1947, 364, italics added). The keyword here is *purely*; it is significant that the charismatic element of authority has not been replaced. Rather, it seems to have been toned down, while legal-rational elements have been added as mechanisms for guarding against the abuse that may come with a purely charismatic leadership. The language of prophecy is conspicuously absent in illustrating the reconstructed charismatic element of authority, which could mean that charisma itself has been transformed. Its previous conditions for authenticity have been replaced by new ones. Such a revamp of conditions for authority also bears on questions of authenticity, detectable in relation to other gifts and manifestations, among them "falling in the Spirit."

Falling in the Spirit and the Problem of Authenticity

Falling in the Spirit is often considered a hallmark of Charismatic Christianity (Inbody 2015, 7), and was widespread within the Faith Movement. Living Word was no exception. Berg was careful to point out that falling in the Spirit is not something that it is possible to "practice" as such, and connected a description of falling in the Spirit to a question of authenticity:

At certain times and under certain circumstances, God's power has manifested in such a way that, upon encountering it, there is a physical reaction: you fall easily, because it is a real encounter with the power of God. But the point is not falling in the Spirit. The point is that human beings have needs and God wants to meet those needs, whether it be healing or other things. And that is not something that you could construct, though there may be some who have tried, [maintaining] that "this is proof that God is doing something"—that people fall in the Spirit. It's not any kind of proof at all; it is a physical reaction—a phenomenon, but it isn't something that you could construct.

Berg's response contains a rationalistic explanation of the purpose of, and reason for occurrences of "falling in the Spirit": It is a physical reaction, a natural consequence of encounters between human beings and the power of God. Berg finds objectionable, however, the implication of human agency and involvement that, in his view, is neither wanted nor warranted. He is concerned that this is detrimental to an authentic experience as opposed to one that is "constructed." Berg connects falling in the Spirit to an understanding of God as nurturer, expressed in the normative statement that falling in the Spirit is not supposed to be an end unto itself. Rather, it is a way in which God gets involved in people's emotional lives. He further objects to the perceived notion that physical reactions to God's presence are proof of God's activity, yet remain a way in which God meets human needs. Berg's response, then, serves as an entry point to unraveling the rich complexity concealed in the phenomena of gifts of grace and manifestations of the Spirit.

Considering the contexts in which falling in the Spirit is commonly observed, I was also curious as to whether Berg considered any specific social or ritual conditions to be associated with the phenomenon. Asking whether it might be possible to facilitate such events, he responded: "Yes, perhaps you could. You can tell that maybe it happens more often at some types of services than at others, but to us: if it happens, it happens." He further explained that falling in the Spirit also occurs outside the practices of laying on of hands or intercession, "but it is often connected to it—for some reason or other." In cases where falling in the Spirit occurs frequently over a period of time, however, "it is very easy to start imitating, that you are going to 'pull this off,' and then you give a little push." Berg expressed that encouraging people to fall in this manner amounts to a human factor entering the picture in a way that is "not good." He particularly expresses reservations that, when falling in the Spirit happens frequently, people become socially conditioned to expect its occurrence. This, in turn, creates social pressures that can lead to interference whereby the phenomenon is, quite literally, pushed to occur. On the one hand, we may note an acknowledgment of a frequent connection to tactile human mediation, a practice whereby a pastor or intercessor lays hands on a person, often connected to falling in the Spirit. On the other hand, Berg rejects the idea that the two are linked by necessity; human mediation is not necessary, and falling in the Spirit may take place without it. Given Berg's reservations, it appears that a concern for authenticity is central to the new official position of the church.

Interestingly, Berg also connected authenticity to geographical location and culturally conditioned interpretation of the phenomenon. Having worked in Brazil as a missionary for several years, he recounts how falling in the Spirit was associated with "evil spiritual powers manifesting in encounters with God's power and the name of Jesus." People did not fall in the Spirit outside these particular situations, he pointed out. Despite these reservations, there are some ways in which the congregation may facilitate falling in the Spirit by being prepared just in case someone does fall. However, it is neither expected nor explicitly encouraged; this preparation is meant to create a "safe place" so as to prevent people from incurring injuries (see also Poloma 1997, 264).

Berg attributes the authenticity of falling in the Spirit to God's agency, and its dependence upon the human subject's passivity. From this perspective, any human involvement would undermine the authenticity of the experience, and consequently, the expression itself. However, as illustrated by the example from Brazil, the interpretation of falling in the Spirit is subject to cultural conditions quite apart from the question of authenticity. These nuances and reservations are important to keep in mind with regard to the reflections of respondents from among the ordinary members.

During an interview with Matthew, an insider discussion of authenticity intertwined with the topics of apologetics and personal reflections on differences between Living Word and the Credo Church. This was illustrated in a story he shared of a conversation with a presumably non-Charismatic Lutheran in which Matthew objected to the postulation of human interference—particularly physical touch:

I met a Lutheran on the street and he was on his way out to evangelize. We started talking and when I started telling [him] about physical stuff, he was so negative. I told him that I had been prayed for by some Americans. They gathered around me in a circle. Nobody touched me. They breathed on me. I fell straight down, as if the floor vanished. I noticed that this stopped one of [the Lutheran's] main arguments. He thought I was talking about pushing, but they didn't touch me. I just fell straight down. I also had [...] other experiences. Once, [when] somebody was talking to me, or laid hands on me, I knew that there was a guy behind me. I fell backwards, but didn't hit him. [...] When people breathe on me and I fall because they breathe on me, there must be a reason for it—that there is a power. That must be it. So you could ask, what power was it: God or something else?

Matthew's response involves legitimizing authenticity by rejecting the involvement of human touch. Well aware of the Lutheran's skepticism, and his suspicion that Matthew had been pushed to fall by his intercessors, we note the same objection to the necessity of human touch as expressed by Berg. The absence of touch in this case was used as an argument for authenticity. Nevertheless, Matthew situates his experience in a social context.

As Matthew elaborates on the event, he increasingly conveys his conviction that the experience of falling may indeed have been an effect of encountering God. He is rather cautious in doing so, however, and reveals doubt intermingled with his conviction. Interested in when these events had taken place, I asked whether they had occurred at Living Word or the Credo Church. He stated that, "falling backwards without hitting [the man behind me] was at Living Word, and that [episode] where people breathed on me was either at the Credo Church or at Living Word. So I've had a couple of powerful experiences, but none of them took place recently." At the Credo Church, Matthew reported, "it happens that people come forward and are prayed for, but not many fall to the ground. Whether that was mostly [people's] imagination, I don't know. It hasn't happened lately, except in a couple of cases [...] Some just sway. Others collapse before anyone touches them, and some fall when somebody touches them lightly." It is interesting to note that falling may be less frequent at the Credo Church than at Living Word, but Matthew's openness is also striking in that he includes a critical perspective with regards to the authenticity of falling. Despite having had several such experiences, and defending them in a conversation with a non-Charismatic, Matthew remains open to the possibility that such events are merely imagined or constructed.

Mark also expressed a critical perspective, this time linked to what he perceived to be a lack of correlation between gifts and manifestations on the one hand, and a Christian lifestyle on the other. Part of this perspective was linked to how manifestations were enacted at Living Word.

Mark: There has been some criticism. People who only come to Sunday services and fall to the ground, and then they live completely uncritically towards their own life and well-being during the week, not paying consideration to themselves or others in everyday life—that's not very fruitful. At the same time, I think a lot of people are strengthened by that experience.
Jane: Manifestation experiences didn't always lead people to …
Mark: No, not always. Some [people] liked the experience, but they didn't always bother to work on themselves sufficiently to change [their] lifestyle. Hopefully, that's the exception and most people let an experience like that strengthen them in everyday life [so that] they make changes to do what they feel is right and what they feel they are created [for] and motivated [to do].

Mark considers falling as a way to receive strength, but whether falling is sought for its own sake, or whether that strength is mobilized to transforms one's life, is up to the practitioner. Whatever he or she decides seems to have no bearing on the question of authenticity; what is at stake is how the authentic experience is used. To Mark, manifestations of the Spirit are supposed to have consequences for one's lifestyle, which he sees as having become more central to the Credo Church's teaching: "Reason may have gained a bigger place. We consciously build our lives for good values in society, development and not least family—how we want to live our lives." This suggests that the focus of manifestations has shifted from seeking manifestations to seeking life transformation by means of them.

GIFTS OF GRACE AND WORDS OF KNOWLEDGE

In addition to shifting the focus from seeking gifts and manifestations, the reconstruction of the congregation has also brought about adjustments to how they are enacted. One gift that has gained prominence is Words of Knowledge, as illustrated by Paula's description:

I also think it has become more like you can share words at the services—Words of Knowledge. We have one [person] who experiences that a lot, for example when somebody has a painful knee. Then he is allowed to pray for them. He gets a chance to [do so].

Paula's impression was that of an increased openness for people to share Words of Knowledge, which she reports as especially frequent with one congregant. Previously, the senior pastor was in charge of the service, and acted as mediator of the messages given. Today, Words of Knowledge are enacted by ordinary congregants, who are allowed to proclaim them at the discretion of the pastors. We may appreciate that Paula does not refer to current pastors as being involved in giving Words of Knowledge, although they maintain control of their enactment. This was also congruent with my observations at Sunday services, where one congregant came forward during a post-service intercession meeting and shared a Word of Knowledge through the microphone. I asked Paula whether practicing gifts of grace is now more evenly spread throughout the congregation. "Yes," she responded, "[but] during the services, not a lot of people are given the chance [to practice] gifts of grace at the moment." Paula also expressed regret that gifts of grace were not used more frequently at the church, but also added that they are practiced in small groups, which constitute "places for training and trying out the gifts of grace in safe environments. It's not easy," she said, explaining that the gifts are related to each individual's walk with God and the processes of maturing one's personal faith. Walking up to stand in front of several hundred people, proclaiming to have a message from God, can be a terrifying affair. "It is something that requires trust. You need to have the nerve for it and have a yearning for it," Paula elaborated. From her description, we understand that enacting gifts of grace puts a person in a vulnerable position. The need for training becomes clearer if we understand the element of self-doubt involved, an example for which we will find in one of Matthew's experiences.

Matthew was reminded of Words of Knowledge when discussing prophecy. The former is a gift thought to bring mental and bodily challenges to light, "that somebody is struggling with [certain] thoughts," and physical ills, such as "somebody having a painful shoulder." Matthew stated that God can provide comfort through Words of Knowledge which, he said, "happens sometimes" at the Credo Church. Words of Knowledge can be enacted in two ways, he explained: Either the message is given straight to the receiving person, or they can come forward for intercession. However, he also included the caveat that Words of Knowledge "can be too revealing," suggesting that this gift needs to be practiced with caution and consideration for the vulnerability of the receiving person. Matthew reported an experience that would fit the description of either prophecy or Word of Knowledge, although he refrained from using either of those terms:

> God said to me once, "Go over to [that guy] and tell him that he will become a Christian tonight." I went back and forth a little [but] eventually did it. Never before had I imagined that I would say something like that to someone. He wasn't a Christian, but he did become a Christian that evening. On the other hand, you could call it manipulation; I thought that I wanted to know whether the power is God or something else.

Matthew related this story in the context of having experienced an all-knowing power. Yet, doubt resulting from the inclusion of a critical perspective is part of Matthew's description, both of what happened during and after the event. First, he went "back and forth," before finally making the decision to carry out the perceived command, and second, he stated the possibility that the experience was a form of manipulation. Either way, the question of authenticity is at the very heart of Matthew's quest for confirmation of God's existence. In the end, it appears as if Matthew's curiosity over whether the message had really been from God or not led him to act. That the man actually became a Christian that evening gave Matthew reassurance that his interpretation was correct, but he hesitates to rule out his doubts completely.

A theme of vulnerability seems to permeate the respondents' reflections on practicing gifts of grace, as well as references to ritual restrictions placed upon their enactment, but also upon the language enveloping their enactment. Interestingly, experiences at Living Word, where the senior pastor transmitted messages from God, were labeled prophecy with apparent ease. By contrast, such practices now appear to be referred to as Words of Knowledge or not labeled "gifts of grace" at all. Reportedly, they are now more evenly distributed among the congregants rather than centered on the senior pastor, and invite critical perspectives rather than command obedience. It appears as if Weberian charisma has been redistributed and democratized, but this charisma also seems to inspire consciousness of one's own and others' vulnerability, as well as questions regarding authenticity. As indicated by Paula, another change can be seen in the decreased frequency of enacting gifts related to transmitting messages from God; this appears to reflect a wider trend, to which we now turn.

Frequency of Gifts and Manifestations

Mark notes that, compared to Living Word, "there is probably some difference" in how gifts and manifestations are practiced at the Credo Church. According to him, manifestations of the Spirit have "almost disappeared" there. Still, he emphasizes that members are not intimidated by manifestations when they do occur. Outsiders, however, may find manifestations of the Spirit to be a frightening experience. Mark adds that "services are much shorter now than they used to be":

Jane: Right, because they used to last for three hours?
Mark: Yes, it's only because of grace that people can sit [there] for that long—it's got to be something special [laughs]. Maybe it's [something that] comes in waves. It may well come back. I don't know.

Jokingly referring to the patience needed to endure three-hour services as a bit of a miracle, Mark also suggests the possibility of a cyclical waxing and waning of gifts and manifestations according to "waves." He also seems comfortable with the contemporary lower frequency of such events. "Do you miss anything from the old way of doing things?" I asked him:

> I don't know it all that well, but not really, because, especially regarding employment of gifts of grace and speaking in tongues during services—there is little culture for that here [in Norway] and it is seen as very strange [...] to people who are not used to going to church. So it can almost work against its purpose. When Paul teaches on [the subject], he says that [speaking in tongues] is for one's own composition, and not so much for use during services, or when [people] gather. That can be [a] positive [thing], making it easier to bring people along. So they don't just think, "Dear me, this right here ... If this is how you become when you become a Christian, that's freaky."

Mark gives several reasons why he considers a lower frequency to be a good thing: he considers it more in line with Pauline teaching, to attract less stigma, and to be less alienating to Norwegians and, consequently, more beneficial to mission activity. Matthew shared Mark's view on glossolalia at services: "If a non-Christian enters a church and everybody just jabbers on in tongues," explained Matthew, "the non-Christian would think: 'They've gone completely crazy!'" He elaborated a little further, stating that when glossolalia takes place in the presence of non-Christians, the point of practicing the gift must be the interpretation of the message:

> It is written [in the Bible] that if nobody can interpret, you should remain silent. There is supposed to be a maximum of three people [who speak in tongues] and it should be done systematically, and in order, so people can understand it. Apart from that, speaking in tongues is for private use. It says in different [Bible] passages that speaking in tongues is [to be kept] within; nobody [else] would understand what's going on. If the Spirit isn't in on it, you may ask if you could just laugh at the whole thing.

Like Mark, Matthew believed that glossolalia might alienate people who are unaccustomed to the phenomenon. Both frame their responses in a way that includes humor and self-deprecating humor, not just on their own behalf, but that of Charismatics in general. Obviously, they are quite aware that non-Christians and non-Charismatics may find glossolalia intimidating, and that this might possibly prevent new visitors from returning.

Not all congregants share this outlook. Asking Paula whether she misses anything from the Living Word era, she responded:

> You see with all congregations that they go through various phases. There may be times when there's a lot of speaking in tongues, you intercede for the sick at every service, invite [people] to come forward for salvation at every service, and when people receive intercession, they'll often lay strewn about because they fell in the Holy Spirit. After that came the laughter movement. There have been different trends.

Paula explained that she had experienced holy laughter herself, and described it as something that brought freedom to people. It is clear, however, that she considers various forms and frequencies of manifestations to be temporary: trends come and go. Paula described their enactment as more restricted at the Credo Church than at Living Word. "I [sometimes] miss that here now—that freedom at the services and that the Holy Spirit is allowed to work," she said, before adding that,

> I suppose it has also been important to build on the Word of God and that the preaching gets a healthy balance. [...] You get the foundation on the Word of God. Churches that only build on manifestations, glossolalia, and prophecies won't have that foundation on the Word of God. It just becomes vague/airy [*svevende*] and may ultimately fall apart, which is what we've seen [happen] here.

Despite her missing the freedom at Living Word, Paula's opinion on the current practice is somewhat mixed. Restricting the use of gifts has coincided with a stronger emphasis on the Bible, which she considers to be healthy and necessary. She interprets the collapse of Living Word as being attributable to several factors, one of them being its exclusive focus on gifts and manifestations without a foundation rooted in Bible-centered teaching. While valuing gifts and manifestations, the respondents also consider them to be potentially harmful, although in different ways. We may note the emergence of a view whereby such practices are a mixed blessing; there are benefits, but potential harm must also be taken into account.

At Living Word, gifts and manifestations used to be centered in the senior pastor, contributing to the generation of the charisma needed to support his authority. As the flow of these processes collapsed, charismatic authority crumbled, while also affecting views of and ways in which gifts and manifestations were practiced. As part of the reconstruction process, the new leaders ceased to regard them as ways of legitimizing leadership authority. This has entailed two transformations: On the one hand, the present view of gifts and manifestations has become tainted, which reinforces an ambivalence that has parallels to late modern radical doubt as discussed in Jessica Moberg's dissertation (2013, 111). On the other hand, thinking with Weber, this is part of the institutionalization of leadership legitimacy in terms of democratization. In addition to a decreased frequency, the enactment of gifts and manifestations has partially been relocated from front and center stage at Sunday services to more secluded settings such as cell groups and individual practice.

The Credo Church, it appears, has introduced elements of rationalization. However, concerns that fuel routinization in this congregation go beyond issues of institutionalization; they heed questions of authenticity as well as hedge personal vulnerability, thus partially relocating the enactment of gifts and manifestations from Sunday services to small groups.

Conclusion

This chapter has investigated two transformations in the Credo Church, the institutionalization of Weberian charisma on the one hand, and of enacting *charismata*—gifts and manifestations of the Spirit—on the other. Particular attention has been paid to prophecy, falling in the Spirit, and similar practices. From a Weberian perspective, charismatic authority can be said to have routinized by way of adding elements associated with rational authority. The transformation goes deeper than that, however; the very mechanisms by which Weberian charisma is generated have been altered because the enaction of prophecy, a primary source of charisma at Living Word, was corrupted. As such, the enaction of prophecy has itself lost some of its capacity for generating the charisma needed for upholding an exclusively charismatic form of authority. It does not, however, appear to be the case that receiving and transmitting messages from God has gone out of fashion. Rather, it has been transformed in terms of designation and distribution; the language of prophecy seems to have been replaced by a language predominated by Words of Knowledge. Communicating Words of Knowledge at the Credo Church is more widely distributed among congregants than prophecy has been, but is also subject to restrictions by the leadership. Those restrictions are not limited to the ways in which messages from God can be communicated, however, but apply to the enaction of gifts and manifestations more generally. The respondents rationalize these differences in terms of phases that "all congregations" go through; gifts and manifestations are more prevalent in some phases than others.

Respondents signal caution towards gifts and manifestations by expressing second thoughts concerning whether and to what extent God is involved in producing them, as well as their helpfulness in converting new Christians. Personal experiences, however, seem to have retained their significance in the respondents' religious lives. Furthermore, there is a strong emphasis on protecting the vulnerability of those involved.

NOTES

1. *Bibelen: Guds Ord* was first published by Bibelforlaget in 1997 and has become a favorite among Norwegian Charismatics (Walstad 2010).
2. Living Word's broadcast was terminated along with "The Family Channel" (Familiekanalen) in April 2004, reportedly due to its poor transmission quality. The decision met with some protest from Christian communities (Aalberg 2004). The church was offered a deal with the recently launched 2003 national Christian channel "Vision Norway" (Visjon Norge). Living Word's television broadcasts were eventually discontinued in 2007 (Algrøy 2012b, 16).
3. The logo it replaced was comprised of a stylized globe, a sword, an open Bible with a flame, and big black letters spelling "Living Word Bible Centre" (*Levende Ord Bibelsenter*), which strongly resembles Word of Life at Uppsala's logo.
4. The phrase "hear from God" is not prevalent in Anglophone Charismatic discourse, but is nevertheless familiar (Wallis 1982, 33).

References

Aalberg, Per Ole. 2004. *Fastlåst for kristen-TV*. http://www.dagen.no/Innenriks/Fastl%C3%A5st_for_kristen-TV-30588. Accessed 27 Nov 2017.
Åleskjær, Åge and Robert Ekh. 2006. Situasjonen på Levende Ord i Bergen. *Norge IDAG*, June 20. http://www.idag.no/aktuelt-oppslag.php3?ID=10405. Accessed 18 July 2014.
Algrøy, Eivind. 2012a. Fortellingen om Levende Ord. *Dagen*, October 27.
———. 2012b. Over tusen 'menighetsløse' etter Levende Ord. *Dagen*, October 27.
Almelid, Johanna H. 2012a. Menigheten har senket skuldrene. *Dagen*, October 27.
———. 2012b. Tiden etter Levende Ord: Sorgen, spørsmålene og tvilen. *Dagen*, October 27.
Anderson, Allan. 2010. Varieties, Taxonomies, and Definitions. In *Studying Global Pentecostalism: Theories and Methods*, ed. Allan Anderson, Michael Bergunder, André Droogers, and Cornelis van der Laan, 13–29. Berkeley: University of California Press.
Anderson, Allan H. 2014. *An Introduction to Pentecostalism: Global Charismatic Christianity*. Cambridge: Cambridge University Press.
———. 2015. *The Anthropology of Global Pentecostalism and Evangelicalism*. New York: New York University Press.
Bensman, Joseph, and Michael Givant. 1975. Charisma and Modernity: The Use and Abuse of a Concept. *Social Research* 42: 570–614.
Bibelen: Guds Ord. Trans. Norvald Yri, Ingulf Diesen, Leif Jacobsen, and Sigurd Grindheim. Nesbyen: Bibelforlaget, 1997.
Bryne, Jarle. 2007. *Pastorer i trosbevegelsen: En studie av to norske pastorer sin autoritetsforståelse og rolleforståelse*. MA dissertation, University of Agder
"Carl I. Hagen til angrep på islam." Aftenposten, July 13, 2004. http://www.aftenposten.no/norge/Carl-I-Hagen-til-angrep-pa-islam-498746b.html http://www.aftenposten.no/nyheter/iriks/Carl-I-Hagen-til-angrep-pa-islam-6310042.html. Accessed 4 Apr 2017
Chryssides, George D., and Margareth Z. Wilkins. 2006. *A Reader in New Religious Movements*. New York: Continuum.
Coleman, Simon. 2000. *The Globalisation of Charismatic Christianity: Spreading the Gospel of Prosperity*. Cambridge: Cambridge University Press.
Credokirken. 2014. Historikk. http://www.levendeord.no/index.php?n=80. Accessed 23 July 2014.
Department of Culture. 2017. *Oversikt over antall tilskuddstellende medlemmer i tros- og livssynssamfunn*. https://www.regjeringen.no/no/tema/religion-og-livssyn/tros-og-livssynssamfunn/innsiktsartikler/antall-tilskuddsberettigede-medlemmer-i-/id631507/. Accessed 11 Feb 2016.
di Giacomo, Michael. 2009. Pentecostal and Charismatic Christianity in Canada: Its Origins, Development, and Distinct Culture. In *Canadian Pentecostalism: Transition and Transformation*, ed. Michael Wilkinson, 15–38. Montreal: McGill-Queen's University Press.

Gilje, Tarjei. 2012. Jeg hadde ønsket å fortsette. *Dagen*, October 27.
———. 2016. Ny giv ti år etter krisen. *Dagen*, February 6. http://www.dagen.no/dagensdebatt/kristenliv/kommentar/Ny-giv-ti-%C3%A5r-etter-krisen-303437. Accessed 10 Feb 2016.
Gjestad, Fred C. 2012. Over tusen personer 'menighetsløse' etter Levende Ord kollaps. *Dagen*, October 27. http://www.dagen.no/Kristenliv/Over_tusen_personer_«menighetsløse»_etter_Levende_Ord-kollaps-55672. Accessed 21 Feb 2016.
———. 2013. Metoderapport: 'Levende Ord-kollapsen.' In *Levende ord-kollapsen: Velsignet helg: Bruddet som knekte troen*, ed. Johanna H. Almelid, Eivind Algrøy, et al, ii–vi. http://www.skup.no/metoderapporter/2012/2012-4_Levende_ord_kollapsen.pdf. Accessed 21 Feb 2016.
Hamre, Sigurd. 2005. Levende Ord mot Jens. *NRK*, July 6. http://www.nrk.no/hordaland/levende-ord-mot-jens-1.206833. Accessed 10 Feb 2016.
———. 2006. Flåten anklages – styreleder går. *NRK*, June 21. http://www.nrk.no/hordaland/flaten-anklages---styreleder-gar-1.627429. Accessed 31 Aug 2014.
Hellesund, Dag. 2006. Overlater Levende Ord til brite. *Bergensavisen*, April 24. http://www.bt.no/nyheter/lokalt/Flaten-venn-trekker-seg-1806811.html. Accessed 9 Feb 2016.
Honningsøy, Kirsti H. 2011. Grotesk utsagn fra Hagen. *NRK*, August 14. http://www.nrk.no/norge/_-grotesk-utsagn-fra-hagen-1.7749407. Accessed 9 Feb 2016.
Inbody, Joel. 2015. Sensing God: Bodily Manifestations and Their Interpretation in Pentecostal Rituals and Everyday Life. *Sociology of Religion* 76: 1–19.
Kanal 10 Norge. 2014. Enevald Flåten startet og ledet Norges største menighet i Bergen. *Kristen TV i Norge A/S*. http://www.kanal10.no/aktuelt/2014/07/19/enevald-flaten-startet-og-ledet-norges-storste-menighet-i-bergen. Accessed 30 Aug 2014.
Lie, Geir. 2011. *Fra amerikansk hellighetsbevegelse til norsk karismatikk: Et historisk overblikk*. Oslo: Akademia forlag.
Moberg, Jessica. 2013. Piety, Intimacy and Mobility: A Case Study of Charismatic Christianity in Present-Day Stockholm. PhD dissertstion, Södertörn University.
Newman, Barclay M., Jr. 1993. *A Concise Greek-English Dictionary of the New Testament*. Stuttgart: German Bible Society.
NRK. 2003. Brennpunkt: På barnetro skal landet bygges. Last modified November 25, 2003.http://www.nrk.no/nett-tv/klipp/23504/. Accessed 24 July 2014
Opheim, Birgit. 2012. Flåten melder Bergen-retur på Facebook. *Dagen*, October 24. http://www.dagen.no/Kristenliv/Fl%C3%A5ten_melder_Bergen-retur_p%C3%A5_Facebook-55664. Accessed 10 Feb 2016.
Poloma, Margaret M. 1997. The 'Toronto Blessing': Charisma, Institutionalization, and Revival. *Journal for the Scientific Study of Religion* 36: 257–271.
Poloma, Margaret M., and Lynette F. Hoelter. 1998. The 'Toronto Blessing': A Holistic Model of Healing. *Journal for the Scientific Study of Religion* 37: 257–272.

Robbins, Joel. 2004. The Globalization of Pentecostal and Charismatic Christianity. *Annual Review of Anthropology* 33: 117–143.
Selbekk, Vebjørn. 2012. Hvor er det blitt av dem? *Dagen*, October 27. http://www.dagen.no/Leder/Hvor_har_det_blitt_av_dem-4278. Accessed 30 July 2014.
Setley, David M., and Douglas Gautsch. 2015. Leadership and the Church: The Impact of Shifting Leadership Constructs. *International Journal of Business and Social Research* 5: 15–25.
Singleton, Andrew. 2011. The Rise and Fall of the Pentecostals: The Role and Significance of the Body in Pentecostal Spirituality. *Scripta Instituti Donneriani Aboensis* 23: 381–399.
Skjoldli, Jane. 2014. Charismatic Controversies in the Jesus People, Calvary Chapel, and Vineyard Movements. In *Controversial New Religions*, ed. James R. Lewis and Jesper A. Petersen, 2nd ed., 81–100. New York: Oxford University Press.
Steinhovden, Tor Magne. 2006. 'Vi leker ikke menighet': Menigheten Levende ord: Visjoner fra Gud og ambisjoner for samfunnet. MA dissertation, University of Bergen.
Wallis, Roy. 1982. The Social Construction of Charisma. *Social Compass* 29: 25–39.
Walstad, Kristin. 2010. Populær bibeloversettelse full av feil. *Forskning.no*, December 30. http://forskning.no/kristendom-boker/2010/12/populaer-bibeloversettelse-full-av-feil. Accessed 21 Feb 2016.
Weber, Max. 1947. *The Theory of Social and Economic Organization*. New York: The Free Press.
Wiederstrøm, Gunnar. 2006. Fylkesmannen reagerte på eksklusiv bilordning. *Bergens Tidende*, June 6. http://www.bt.no/nyheter/lokalt/Fylkesmannen-reagerte-pa-eksklusiv-bilordning-1805161.html. Accessed 11 Feb 2016.
Yukl, Gary. 1999. An Evaluation of Conceptual Weaknesses in Transformational and Charismatic Leadership Theories. *Leadership Quarterly* 10: 285–305.

Open Access This chapter is distributed under the terms of the Creative Commons Attribution 4.0 International License (http://creativecommons.org/licenses/by/4.0/), which permits use, duplication, adaptation, distribution and reproduction in any medium or format, as long as you give appropriate credit to the original author(s) and the source, provide a link to the Creative Commons license and indicate if changes were made.

The images or other third party material in this chapter are included in the chapter's Creative Commons license, unless indicated otherwise in a credit line to the material. If material is not included in the chapter's Creative Commons license and your intended use is not permitted by statutory regulation or exceeds the permitted use, you will need to obtain permission directly from the copyright holder.

CHAPTER 5

The Finnish Pentecostal Movement: An Analysis of Internal Struggle as a Process of Habitual Division

Teemu T. Mantsinen

The Finnish Pentecostal Movement (Helluntaiherätys, or HH) is a century-old religious movement with nearly 50,000 baptized members. The HH is the major Pentecostal group in Finland; other groups are substantially smaller. It is also the largest Christian body outside the two former national churches: the Finnish Evangelical-Lutheran Church (Suomen evankelis-luterilainen kirkko) and the Finnish Orthodox Church (Suomen ortodoksinen kirkko). Among the internal struggles the Pentecostal movement in Finland has encountered in the past, the present one is the most severe. Traditionally favoring the independence of local congregations, the movement risks being divided by a dispute, namely as to whether or not it should develop from a loose network into a registered denomination. Today, the HH faces pressure from two camps: On the one hand, there are people who want to transform the movement, including its organizational basis. On the other, there are those who defend the traditional culture.

Historically, the Finnish Freedom of Religion Act has allowed the HH to remain unregistered without conflicts with the state, unlike in some other neighboring countries, like Russia (e.g., Löfstedt 2009, 158–159).

T.T. Mantsinen (✉)
University of Turku, Turku, Finland

Instead, Pentecostal congregations have used the Association Act, for nonprofit associations, to manage their resources (including property). While many Pentecostals consider the rights granted by the legislation to be sufficient, a growing number believe that remaining unregistered is not enough. It not only restricts them from obtaining the rights granted to other religious bodies, like the right to officiate marriages; many also believe that remaining unregistered gives an unfavorable impression of the movement. To the latter group, the question of registration is merely an organizational technicality, whereas for the former, registration poses a threat to the integrity of Pentecostal identity and to the assumed doctrinal purity. The division is most evident in the creation of two opposing organizational structures: the state-registered Pentecostal Church of Finland (Suomen helluntaikirkko, SHK) and an association of Pentecostal People (Helluntaikansa, HK). These groups coexist within, or on the borders of, the same movement (HH), but have opposing views on issues like cultural practices, leadership, and organization, as well the movement's future. In this chapter, I address and analyze the current conflict and the factors behind the disruption from sociological perspectives. The main argument is that the organizational dispute is part of a deeper cultural division, resulting in different forms of social transformation within the movement. This process has brought about two different forms of Pentecostal habitus. In order to pinpoint and scrutinize these developments, I draw upon two different theoretical perspectives: Bourdieuan perspectives on identity, and transformational processes regarding religious movements.

Movement Transformation

From a sociological perspective, the question at the organizational level can be understood in terms of development from sect to denomination, or moderation of a revivalist movement and its consequences. In order to analyze the developments in the HH, I draw upon the work of several sociologists who have discussed the matter. Max Weber saw "systematization of external conduct of life," "routinization of charisma," and "institutionalization of mundane systems" as natural developments in organizations that transformed in this way (Weber 1947, 358–373; 1956, 177–183). Weber also defines three types of authority involved: charismatic, traditional, and legal. The same categorization corresponds to styles of leadership: charismatic, patriarchal, and bureaucratic. With the idea of the routinization of charisma, Weber describes how a social group changes after the loss of a charismatic leader. In some cases, the search for a new charismatic leader is successful, whereas in other cases the group dissolves or undergoes institutionalization (1964, 328–386).

Thomas O'Dea describes the development from Charismatic-led movements to institutionalized communities in a slightly different way. He focuses on particular dilemmas that may emerge. Such dilemmas can be connected to motivation, inclusion/exclusion, or administration, as well as difficulties connected to how religious symbols and interpretations should be limited. This also includes issues of power and authority, and possible problems connected to different modes of conversion (O'Dea 1961). Richard H. Niebuhr took particular interest in the generational aspects of transformation, claiming that a sect may survive for one generation, after which it is prone to change (1957, 181–182). Similarly, Rodney Stark and William Sims Bainbridge have underlined differences between converted and socialized members, arguing that socialized generations of members are crucial to the transformation of a sect into a church. If the new generations obtain higher socioeconomic status, are religiously more moderate than their parents, and gain central positions in the hierarchy, the sect is likely to transform into a mainline church (Stark and Bainbridge 1985, 149–167). In the following, these theories are used as points of departure, but in order to nuance and conceptualize the transformations, I also employ the work of scholars more interested in cultural aspects.

Pentecostal Identity as Habitus

Religion is a multifaceted phenomenon that cannot be reduced to one particular dimension. It does not include only institutions, doctrines or rituals, but also lifestyles. According to Heinz Streib "religious styles are distinct modi of practical-interactive (ritual), psychodynamic (symbolic), and cognitive (narrative) reconstruction and appropriation of religion, that originate in relation to life history and life world," and are subjected to social change (Streib 2011, 149). The factors that shape such cultural preferences and expressions are of particular interest to the present analysis. Several scholars have noted how social class informs such expressions, and that class preferences may cut across whole movements. One example is Lawrence Mamiya's study of Black American Muslims, where he notes how differences between middle-class, moderate styles of expression and the more radical practices of the lower class divided the movement (1982). The relationships between class and preferences, or "taste," have been systematically elaborated on by Pierre Bourdieu (2010, see also Köhrsen 2008). Bourdieu portrays a *habitus* as a durable disposition, a system produced by structural conditions, and as a historical product (1990, 53–54). The habitus more or less determines how a person or group presents itself, its taste, behavior, and performance, in order to produce a coherent image and an acceptable disposition of experience. Finnish sociologist J.P. Roos strongly relates *habitus* with lifestyle; a habitus is a general approach to life, and a lifestyle is the enactment of that approach with living practices (1988, 30–33).

For Bourdieu, a habitus is not the result of subjective intention but of socialization. It is motivated by the intention to belong to something; in order to be included in a group, one has to learn and present a habitus compatible with the group (Bourdieu 1990, 62; 2000, 100; 2010, 166–167, 174). He furthermore makes a distinction between class habitus and individual habitus. While the individual habitus may be informed by multiple groups, a class habitus is shared by a socioeconomic segment of people (Bourdieu 1990, 60). Class cultures are cultivated in structural conditions, which means they are subject to change over time, and shaped by the participants' needs and resources, possibilities and identification (Bourdieu 2010, 373–393; see also Mantsinen 2014, 42–47). In my view, no group or class habitus fully determines a person's individual habitus, as individuals may draw upon different habituses in different situations. This may result from conscious decisions or underlying rationales dependent upon socializations. Relationships between individual agency and habitus can be illustrated by looking at how individuals mobilize different habituses in different contexts, in order to position themselves in webs of power present in various groups (cf. Bourdieu 1990, 53–56; Mahmood 2005, 26–27; Vanberg 1993, 189–191).

Habitual Transformation

Some scholars have criticized Bourdieu for disregarding the dynamic nature of habituses (Moberg 2013, 36). In any group, the habitus incorporates what aspects, practices, and styles can be included, performed, and tolerated in the cultural milieu. Knowledge of a group habitus enables members to employ this knowledge in the social network of roles and tastes. This empowers them to justify and rationalize practices influenced by their individual habituses and incorporate them into the group habitus (Mantsinen 2014, 152–155; cf. Bourdieu 1977, 87–89). If the expressions introduced are accepted, they may result in transformation of the entire group habitus.

Such transformations may include changes in ritualized practices, even the appropriation of new goals and preferences, as Jessica Moberg has shown in her dissertation (Moberg 2013, 220). Rather than being passive victims of history, both groups and individuals are constantly engaged in negotiating and renegotiating elements of their habitus. Such processes are permeated with constant competition over the power to control and define practices, preferences, and styles included in the habitus, and thus its normative aspects. In this competition, certain classified and classifying tastes and lifestyles become dominant in the group's culture (Bourdieu 2010, 167).

Relating these theoretical perspectives to the field of Pentecostal studies, various attempts have been made to distinguish between different forms of Pentecostal-Charismatic habitus. One common approach has been to construct categories of Pentecostals according to their practices, for example the famous distinction between "Classic Pentecostals" and "Neo-Pentecostals" (Anderson 2014, 1–7). In this chapter, I do not apply this distinction, as I consider it more useful as an insider category than an analytical concept. The division of Pentecostalism into different "waves" is strongly influenced by theological understandings of history (see Barnett 1973; Hollenweger 1972). The concept of Neo-Pentecostalism is, in my view, also an Americentric and selective understanding of Pentecostal religiosity and its development (see Freston 1999; Hunt 2002, 1–2). Moreover, it does not correspond well with the history of the Finnish Pentecostal movement. This is despite the fact that some new Pentecostal groups that might be described as Neo-Pentecostal have adopted or developed new practices and rejected old Pentecostal traditions. Many of those that might be named Classical Pentecostal groups have done the same—making the concept context-specific.

Instead, I prefer to discuss transformation in the HH by relating it to developments in Finnish society at large. Analyzing two habituses, traditionalist and postmodernist Pentecostalism, I apply concepts of traditionalism, modernism, and postmodernism that describe general ways of thinking and approaches to life and to the surrounding world. Zygmunt Bauman sees postmodernity as "fully developed modernity," with "institutionalized pluralism, variety, contingency and ambivalence," in which individual identity is guarded in an uncertain world. This stands in contrast to modernity, with its struggle for "universality, homogeneity, monotony and clarity" and failed mission to capture the world (Bauman 1992, 187–188; 1998, 57, 66–69). Martin describes postmodernity in

terms of a fluid "vision of culture, [where] all the walls and boundaries are collapsed," with the fragmentation of information resulting in free-floating signifiers (Martin 1998, 103; cf. Bauman 2000; Lyotard 1984, 40–41). In a sense, postmodernism differs from both traditionalism and modernism.
Modernism and postmodernism can be seen as rivals to religious traditionalism. I will use the term *traditionalism* to describe a tradition-based habitus in the HH. *Traditional* is a concept used by one wing of HH practitioners who draw on it in order to legitimize their practices as old and authentic, sometimes expressed in the labeling of practices as "biblical." Despite this, I find the concept useful to describe a habitus shared by those who oppose modernist and postmodernist tendencies. In addition, a rival habitus that manifests the tendencies described by Bauman is referred to by the term *postmodern Pentecostal habitus*. As illustrated by Raymond L.M. Lee, these two trajectories need not be mutually exclusive, but may coexist in the same group (2005, 75–76).

The Finnish Pentecostal Movement Up to the 1970s

The Finnish Pentecostal Movement dates back to a revival in the 1910s. Rather than a denomination, it can be described as a loose network of congregations. To some extent, Lutheran revival movements dating back to Pietism in the seventeenth and eighteenth centuries, as well as Baptism, Methodism, and Adventism in the nineteenth century, paved the way for Pentecostalism. All these movements favored the idea of exclusive communities of committed believers, free from state control and influence from the perceived secular world. This stood in sharp contrast to the traditional inclusive view of the Lutheran Church, where membership was obtained by infant baptism. Particularly important for creating precedence was the Laestadian movement, famous for its combination of strict moral teachings like abstinence from alcohol with ecstatic expressions such as speaking in tongues (Mantsinen 2014; Ruohomäki 2009). A further incentive for the revival was provided by expectations of a new era of Christian flourishing, interpreted as having been heralded by the preceding movements.

A group of middle-class Lutherans were the key figures who enabled the movement to catch on. In 1911, Hanna Castrén, founder and headmistress of a middle school (*oppikoulu*), Sörnäisten yhteiskoulu, and Pietari Brofeldt, former editor of Lutheran journal *Kotimaa* and soon-to-be Pentecostal journal "The Star of Hope" (*Toivon tähti*) teamed up with a few other middle-class Christians. They organized a Pentecostal revival tour together with the Norwegian Methodist-turned-Pentecostal preacher Thomas B. Barratt. The tour, and the groups sprouting from it, resulted in a nationwide network of communities with a common involvement in Pentecostal religiosity (Mantsinen 2014; Ruohomäki 2009, 2014).

Pentecostals were officially rejected by the Lutheran Church, especially when they advocated a Baptist view of baptism. The Pentecostals, in turn, rejected the Lutheran Church. The schism created a focal point of Pentecostal identity: the clear distinction between "the Church" on the one hand, and perceived "authentic Christianity," on the other, which they claimed to represent. However, in comparison with other Nordic countries, the Finnish Pentecostals had greater legal opportunities. In 1923, six years after Finland gained independence from Russia, a law of religious freedom was ratified. The law permitted the official registration of all religious movements, giving them legal status within the country, as well as the right for people to freely choose their religion. However, since the Pentecostals were critical of "church-like" organizations, the movement was not registered at the time (Ahonen 1994, 89–105, 169–173). Some Pentecostals went as far as to reject any kind of organization, including local congregations. These people—commonly called "Pentecostal Friends" (Helluntaiystävät)—did not become members of the newly founded Pentecostal congregations, although they could still participate in the same activities. The Pentecostal Friends remained a loose network until the 1980s, and traces of their tradition can still be detected in one or two places in Finland, like Pentecostal meetings in Multia (Ahonen 1994, 127–132; Mantsinen 2014).

In their first decades, HH groups attracted members mainly from the lower classes. Pentecostal culture and identity saw increased polarization internally as well, and featured a distinct class structure, although it was still shaped by earlier, mainly Lutheran revivals. Pentecostal culture was characterized by a popular and folkish preaching style; it was emotionally expressive and members upheld strict mental and social boundaries between them and the outside world. The first decades can be described as having been characterized by Weberian charismatic leadership. When the movement grew and traditions were shaped, the leadership moved in a patriarchal direction, with male elders leading the congregations (Mantsinen 2014).

Since its establishment, the HH has witnessed both internal conflicts and schisms. The most serious historical conflict, which resulted in a division of the HH, developed between 1960 and the early 1980s. In 1960, Vilho Soininen, one of the leading Charismatic figures in the movement—was ousted due to accusations of immoral conduct. As a consequence, he and his Siion congregation in Helsinki formed a new Pentecostal network: "The Free Pentecostal Movement of Finland" (Suomen vapaa Helluntaiherätys). This alternative Pentecostal network was able to unite a few congregations involved in local disputes and numbered a total of 3000 members at most. Over the next 20 years, however, many of them returned to the HH, including the Siion congregation, and the new movement was dissolved. Although this was a dramatic incident, it only had temporary and local implications (Ahonen 1994, 316–317; *Ristin Voitto* 1985; Seila 1970), and with Soininen as one of the leading figures of the HH, it is possible to imagine a scenario where the division would have been more permanent.

Post-World War II developments also posed challenges for the HH: Finland was increasingly bureaucratized, institutionalized, and had been transformed into a welfare state, where educational reforms enabled social upward mobility. The traditional affective sermon styles were no longer intellectually appealing to new generations of educated Finns. Moreover, the formerly widespread Lutheran-influenced understanding of Christian culture and morality has, since the 1960s, slowly been undermined by increased pluralization (Haastettu Kirkko 2012, 24–28). In the HH, adoption of new practices, musical expressions, and forms of outreach also created tension within the movement. By the 1960s, acoustic guitar, accordion, and brass instruments, widely employed in outreach missions and services, had become an integral part of HH culture. The emergence of rock music and culture challenged the HH both from outside and from within. Some regarded them as "worldly" while others accepted and included them (Mantsinen 2014, 149–155).

A short-lived (1977–1981) Charismatic revival led by Pentecostal preacher Niilo Yli-Vainio was also important for introducing change into the HH. This revival generated enthusiasm and visibility for Pentecostal religiosity. Even after the sudden death of Yli-Vainio, his legacy continued to inspire a range of religious practices. Additionally, new practices emerged, such as casting out demons of sickness. On the one hand, the new revival energized the HH, while on the other it resulted in doctrinal disputes and local schisms. The casting out of demons in particular divided the Pentecostals. As new Charismatic leaders tried to imitate Yli-Vainio, they were sometimes expelled from the HH, and founded new, independent, congregations. The ministry of Yli-Vainio also strengthened the Lutheran Charismatic movement, extending Pentecostal practice outside the HH. Prior to the 1970s, relations between the Evangelical

Lutheran Church of Finland and the Pentecostal Movement were mainly antagonistic. The Charismatic Movement within the church, as well as the ministry of Yli-Vainio, contributed to bring the Lutheran Church and the HH closer together and diminish tensions. In the 1980s, a dialogue was initiated, and the parties reached several agreements concerning basic rules and conduct. For example, the issue of burial ceremonies for people who were both members of the Lutheran Church and Pentecostal congregations was finally settled (Päätösasiakirja 1989).

At the same time, though, the improved relations undermined one of the cornerstones of Pentecostal identity: the dichotomy between the "dead religion" represented by the Lutheran Church, and the "true faith" represented by the Pentecostal Movement. Even though this way of thinking had already started fading, there was even less ground for nurturing division after the dialogue had commenced. Yet, not all were happy with these developments; some saw them as yielding the "true calling", and as a dangerous dalliance with liberal theologians and "ungodly priests." Nevertheless, for many it was a necessary step towards more balanced relations with other Finnish Christians (Ahonen 1994; Mantsinen 2016).

Looking outside the HH, new Pentecostal groups have continued to form since the 1980s. Still, the Pentecostal Movement has remained strong, partly because its traditions had already been established, and partly because controversial phenomena, like casting out demons, were avoided. Today, Pentecostal groups outside the HH remain small; currently, the largest non-HH Pentecostal group has ca. 500 members, and the largest non-HH Pentecostal movement encompasses about 1300 members (Ahonen 1994, 341–364; Seurakuntien 2015).

Diversification of the Pentecostal Movement: The 1980s Onward

Since the 1970s, the HH has continued to transform: The movement has become multigenerational and Pentecostal culture has changed and diversified. In the late 1980s, tent meetings with hymns, and rock concerts with popular bands like *Heureka*, presented two very different expressions of HH Pentecostalism. The movement had also grown substantially, making it difficult to manage its many missions and organizational bodies. Some of these developments brought questions of Pentecostal identity to the fore, leading to intense debate.

Growth has resulted in calls for a united voice along with increased institutionalization, and support for an overarching denominational structure. The question has been a heated topic in the HH's most authoritative forum for discussion and cooperation: "Winter Days" (Talvipäivät)—currently "Autumn Days" (Syyspäivät), as at the forum is held at different times of the year. It resembles a synod, but is less rigid, and its authority is limited. At the Winter Days gathering in 1980, Valtter Luoto, the editor of Pentecostal journal *Ristin Voitto*, wrote an editorial about the importance of increased organizational cooperation. He deemed it remarkable that the HH as a loose network could work properly as a united movement, anticipating a need for an organization such as the Assemblies of God in the United States. At this point, the movement encompassed around 40,000 members, spread among 200 congregations. Its many projects and operations on national and international levels were impossible to realize without coordinated efforts. By then, the HH had established a publishing company, a missionary association, a Bible school, and multiple outreach organizations, including media (radio, and later also TV) ministries. These organizations demanded structure, leadership, and trained professionals. As the editorial illustrates, many Pentecostals wished for a national organization that would gather the movement around a common vision and give it a unified voice (Luoto 1980). The debate on organizational developments underlined the fact that the HH culture was not homogenous, contrary to what many thought.

Overall, the 1980s involved several turning points in the movement. New places to meet and assemble emerged in concert with new practices and evangelizing methods. For instance, worship music began to take root, with both domestic and international influences, exemplified by both the involvement of choirs at revival meetings (like in Yli-Vainio's ministry), and the use of translated, imported Anglo-American songs. The decade also witnessed a huge demographical shift. The number of converts declined, but the new generations of children—raised by Pentecostal parents—stabilized the number of baptized members at 45,000–50,000. Unlike their convert parents, the Pentecostal identity of the socialized members has been one of cultural continuity rather than disruption. They have never had to distance themselves from either "past life" or a "secular (Lutheran) church." In many cases, the previously strong stories of division between "the world" and the Pentecostal community have not necessarily coincided with the experiences of this new generation, leading them to question their social understanding of the boundary between sacred and secular. Perhaps unsurprisingly, it has been easier for them to accept and include expressions and practices from mainstream society, such as contemporary music and fashion. They also employ mainstream language rather than traditional "Pentecostal language" filled with biblical references and symbols. Moreover, they have a tendency to develop and appreciate theologies that focus on wellbeing in contemporary life rather than in the future and for eternity. The socialized members also differ from the older generations of Pentecostals in that they are mainly middle class. Although the class structure of Finnish society as a whole has moved in a middle-class direction, the shift in the HH is still significant. In contrast, of those few who converted during the 1980s and later, the majority come from lower strata in society (Mantsinen 2014, 2015b). As a consequence, the contemporary HH is comprised by two different categories of people: the older, converted Pentecostals of working-class origin, and the younger, socialized middle-class members. The diversification of the Pentecostal movement and its cultural modi have been vital to the emergence of the two different Pentecostal habituses, as described below.

Diversification of the HH has continued, and is visible in practices, services, media use, education systems, and leadership. Congregations have been founded in new types of locations, such as inside shopping malls. Some of them have been designed with specific groups in mind, such as Finnish youth or disadvantaged people. As the Internet expanded in the 1990s and the Finnish television channels were digitized in 2000s, the HH started employing these new media. Services and ministries have also been transformed, drawing on pop-cultural forms such as stand-up comedy, lifestyle sermons, and other entertaining types of service and outreach. At the same time, traditional Pentecostal practices and services have seen a drastic decline. For example, tent meetings are rare, traditional revival meetings scarce, and old forms of worship and prayer have been replaced by or coexist with new styles. For example, kneeling during services used to be commonplace, while now it is more common to stand up with lifted hands. Furthermore, traditional gender roles are questioned, and sometimes abandoned, which is visible in the gradual introduction of female pastors and elders (Mantsinen 2014).

The HH's education system has also changed in the last decades with the development of the Bible school. For a long time, it had relied on a curricular structure based upon one four-month course that could be taken by anyone, and, which also served as a basic training ground for preachers. The common understanding used to be that the Holy Spirit would inform and equip the preacher, and that reading the Bible was all that was required from the preacher himself. This ideal remained strong until the 1990s, when the level of education among younger members increased. As a result, social calls for higher quality preaching and ministry led to an overhaul of the education system. In the 1990s, the Bible school was transformed into a three-year, seminar-like institution, which offered a wide variety of courses and diplomas. Although formal education is still not required from a Pentecostal preacher in Finland, the pressure is mounting for this to change.

As for leadership, the charismatic authority type can still be found, although it no longer occupies the previous central position. In fact, all of the Weberian leadership and authority types are visible in the contemporary movement, but the emphasis has shifted over the years, somewhat as Weber described, through the routinization of charisma. The authority and popularity of charismatic leaders are still measured by their skills and ability to prove their uniqueness in the HH. But within the congregations, they have to submit to local patriarchal authority, and to cultural Finnish norms and increased organizational structures.

Pluralization has changed the face of the HH. It is no longer possible to speak of one common Pentecostal habitus. It makes more sense to speak of different habituses, where the focal points of Pentecostal identity differ between generations, and between converted and socialized members. Not all of these developments have met with approval; some have sparked controversies. New practices and styles of sermons have led to heated debates over their legitimacy. In the past decades, Pentecostals created new practices with evangelization and expansion in mind, and in order to tackle routinization, which was seen as an indication of stagnation and "dead religion." The emphasis on outreach made such introductions easier to legitimize in the Pentecostal logic. Since many of today's innovations are not directly focused on outreach, but have been created to meet the preferences of the members, they are harder to legitimize according to the old cultural system. In fact, some Pentecostals, particularly the older generations, fear that the incorporation of contemporary mainstream culture will destroy the movement from within, bringing in "the world" rather than leading to expansion.

Contemporary Disputes

At the turn of the millennium, all of the aforementioned changes and conflicts coalesced and culminated in one dispute that challenged the HH more than any other in the past decades had done. The dividing point was the registration of the Pentecostal Church of Finland (SHK) as a religious Finnish community. The decision was made on September 15, 2001, at a special meeting at which leaders or delegates from 131 of the HH's 230 congregations were present. The question, however, had older roots; the debate about and inquiry into registration had lasted for a decade. Not all congregations supported the registration and only 25 had made up their minds beforehand. Therefore, it was decided that those willing to form the registered church could do so. Others would not be forced to join. It was decided that the unity of the HH should be preserved and that the Winter Days would remain the collective forum for the whole of the HH, regardless of the decisions in local congregations. Officially, the SHK was founded in January 2002. By September 10, 2014, 41 congregations and 8011 members had joined the church (Ketoja 2001; Kuosmanen 2001; SHK 2015; Sopanen 2002).

However, the registration processes were confusing and unsettling for many. They were already spurring debate at the Winter Days forum in 2002. Obscurities and differing views as to whether or not this type of organization was "biblical" led some to suggest a suspension of the process. However, a majority decided that 10 years of discussions and the previous year's decision had been enough. Comments from the opposing side were sometimes contradictory; one could advocate a common organizational structure, only to reject it if the word "church" was mentioned. Another concern that was expressed was that the SHK organization and its leaders would speak on behalf of the whole movement, without consulting all congregations (Kättö 2002a, b). Yet, up to that point, the largest congregation (Helsinki Saalem) and the publishing company's weekly (*Ristin Voitto*) editor had in fact already spoken on behalf of HH as a whole. Looking at the arguments, those who supported the SHK thought that the result would be a better organized movement, with one voice and an improved public image. Those who rejected the development saw the SHK as a fertile ground for the rise of religious dictatorship. In the most extreme cases, SHK was viewed as a dangerous ecumenical road leading to the apocalyptical church of the Harlot in the Book of Revelation. One female Pentecostal explained to me that she did not want to belong to "the Harlot Church," and therefore opposed the SHK (Fieldnotes 2014; Mantsinen 2016).

After the SHK was founded, some of the older Pentecostal leaders felt the need for another network for those who opposed the course the HH had taken. Their plans were further fueled by their experiences of exclusion and dismissal from the registration debate. In their opinion, opposition to the SHK did not gain enough attention either in the HH, or in its journal *Ristin Voitto* (Helluntaikansa 2014; Mantsinen 2014). This experience of exclusion was the result of a number of other factors, foremost among which were educational and generational divisions. At the beginning of the millennium, younger and well-educated members had gained many positions of power, as pastors, organizational managers, and in *Ristin Voitto*. In cases where the journal seemingly favored the SHK, opponents interpreted editorial decisions to exclude their writings as pro-SHK action. From an outsider's perspective, however, editorial decisions seem to be based on common editorial standards of language, and perhaps a wish to avoid controversial topics and open condemnation. Differences in educational levels manifested themselves in differing abilities in terms of articulation and eloquence. In other words, differences in education and writing skills influenced the debate.

The opposition established "The Pentecostal People" association (Helluntaikansa, HK) on June 28, 2003. They started publishing their own journal, "People of the Cross" (*Ristin Kansa, RK*), in 2005. Later, a conference facility, Mertiöranta and three independent congregations, called "Traditional Pentecostal Churches" (Perinteinen helluntaiseurakunta, PHS), were founded. The creation of these PHS congregations had resulted from local disputes. Usually, such congregations were established in response to the founding of local SHK-congregations. Turning to the contents of the two journals, *Ristin Kansa* (*RK*) issues consist of devotional articles, traditional interpretations of the Bible, news from the missionary fields and from like-minded congregations, and biographies of previous Pentecostal leaders. Compared to *Ristin Voitto* (*RV*), the editorial guidelines are more oriented towards evangelization. The language and biblical interpretations are more uniform than in the *RV*, which offers a wider scope of news, and invites some discussion on doctrinal issues and new interpretations of the Bible. Whereas the *RK* depicts "the world" as hostile and "the end" as an imminent goal for the community of believers, *RV* discourse is characterized by more individualistic goals and depicts "the end" in the relative long term.

The current schism has also resulted in alternative forums of practice, discourse, and power. The HH Bible school was founded in 1952, and has trained the majority of HH's preachers, missionaries, evangelists, and active members (Ahonen 1994, 302–307). Since the 1980s, the Bible school organization has also hosted the HH's major summer events. The remodeling of the Bible school as a new institution named Iso Kirja ("Big

Book") in 1992 brought about strong reactions: some criticized, others applauded the shift towards more systematic teaching and thinking. The critique was intensified as some Pentecostals felt that the school was strongly pro-SHK. This contributed to the HK's decision to found another conference facility, named Mertiöranta (on the shore of Lake Mertiö), in 2012 (Helluntaiherätys 2014; Helluntaikansa 2014).

Iso Kirja and Mertiöranta can be seen as competitors, but may also be viewed as occupying different niches. They do not necessarily serve the same functions; their events, practices, and styles are obviously distinct, yet many Pentecostals visit both. Nevertheless, they are viewed as opposite bodies within the HH. Both train Pentecostals, and host conferences. Rather than competing by engaging in the same practices, however, they distinguish themselves rhetorically, educationally, musically, organizationally, and ideologically, as well as ritually (Havupalo 2014; Kuokkanen 2014). For example, Iso Kirja employs contemporary didactic and technological gadgets, like videos, whereas Mertiöranta lectures are more sermon-like and visual representation is minimal or absent. Their differences may be described in terms of postmodern (Iso Kirja) and traditional (Mertiöranta) habituses, manifested in their approaches to learning, thinking, and life in general. It is worth noting that the criticism of Iso Kirja is not limited to the HK, but also voiced by traditional-oriented Pentecostals in general, who have expressed concern about changes, particularly in theological interpretations.

Another issue that divides the HH concerns leadership, not only how it should be defined and practiced, but also what titles should be used. For example, the naming of ministry workers divides opinions. The traditional titles "preacher" (*saarnaaja*) and "shepherd" (*paimen*) have lost some of their appeal. Many younger Pentecostals consider them old-fashioned and difficult to understand. Instead, "pastor" (*pastori*) and "leader" (*johtaja*) have emerged as new titles. Many traditional Pentecostals find it difficult to accept the title "pastor", since it reminds them of the Lutheran title "priest," indicating institutionalization and loss of the "flame of the Spirit" (Helluntaikansa 2014). The divide within the HH also runs along the lines of leadership style and gender attitudes. On the HK side, leaders are regular preachers in the community, with concentrated authority according to traditional Pentecostal models. On the SHK side, the leadership is delegated to different individuals and specialists. In the HH, traditional patriarchal leadership has included clear gender division, and the highest positions have been reserved for men. A pastor in one of the PHS congregations explained to me that they have "a traditional view" on leadership, meaning that only men are eligible to be congregational elders, preachers, and teachers. As mentioned briefly, some women have been elected as pastors in the twenty-first century, and a few have gained positions as elders. Usually, HK Pentecostals see this development as a sign of secularization of the movement, and as a step away from the rightful biblical tradition (Kuokkanen 2014; Fieldnotes 2014).

Among the loudest critics are a small number of older Pentecostal preachers, whose authority is based upon Weberian charisma and appeal amongst the older generations. Even though they have now officially retired, they have continued to play a crucial role in the creation of the HK and its particular brand of Pentecostal culture. These elderly leaders tend to interpret the trajectory of the HH in terms of decline. One of them described the current situation the following way: "What the fathers built, the sons dissolved (Lahti 2006)." In contrast, the younger generations do not necessarily understand what the fuss is all about, since they lack the experiences that formed Pentecostal identity among former generations. For them, the HH is in need of change in order to appeal to future generations both inside and outside the movement (Helluntaikansa 2014).

The conflict is not only played out in the Pentecostal press and larger organizational bodies, but on the local congregational level as well. In local conflicts, both sides fiercely defend their views, practices, and territory. In one such setting, the transformation of a traditional Pentecostal Association (the legal subject of the congregation) into a formal SHK congregation led to a lawsuit. The case concerned the ownership of the group's possessions, such as buildings and bank accounts. In the case "Järvinen v Pori Pentecostal Mission Registered Association" (*Järvinen v Porin Helluntailähetys ry* 2012), the civil court ruled the case in favor of the plaintiff, and the establishment of the SHK congregation was postponed. Local disputes concerning PHS congregations further contribute to the deepening of conflicts. Due to ongoing quarrels, PHS congregations are not currently recognized as a part of the HH. This has led to situations where people who wish to switch from an SHK to a PHS congregation have not been granted the usual transfer documents, since the founding of the PHS was not mutually agreed. Mostly a symbolic gesture, this rejection still denies the PHS emotional ties to Pentecostal roots and identity. Ongoing disputes divide the movement further, as the older Pentecostal group can withhold HH status from newly established groups.

The authority of the old forums is also being questioned, such as the Winter Days, and the SHK has not been able to gain recognition as the unifying voice of the Pentecostal Movement.

This is important, because it means that there is no organizational body or authority to unite the movement. Furthermore, the traditional schismatic public image of the HH has resulted in the founding of a couple of new and independent Pentecostal churches in the 2010s. The founders of these groups grew up in the HH, but do not want to be associated with it (Fieldnotes 2014).

Within the HK, there is a fear that a church-like system of organization would bring about an authoritarian leader. This fear has its origins in past experiences in the HH, as power struggles used to be common. Even though the SHK has limited the board member terms and distributed power throughout the organization, the fear has persisted (Havupalo 2014; Kuokkanen 2014; Seila 1970).

Two Different Habituses

Many Pentecostals view these divisions and disputes as the result of organizational developments aimed at obtaining juridical church status and different interpretations of that process. In my own research, I have found that the tensions within the movement have to do with larger sociocultural shifts in Finnish society and Pentecostal reactions to them, rather than doctrinal issues. The transformations so far discussed have produced two different Pentecostal habituses. For each, claims of a "true doctrine" primarily constitute a discursive strategy to legitimize one's own particular habitus as "biblical" and "truly Christian." With this strategy, Pentecostals also assert their opinion of the world outside the HH, and its changing culture, as further illustrated below. In theoretical terms, they evaluate modern and postmodern influences and embrace or reject them, thereby drawing and redrawing boundaries between what, in scholarly terms, is often understood as the sacred and the profane.

An illustrative example comes from a retired couple in one of the PHS congregations. They explained to me that what they felt alienated them from the local Pentecostal congregation was its style of worship. They rejected not only the music, but also the entire culture that had developed around it, including the use of lighting effects and dress codes, all of which can be seen as pieces of the group's habitus. Therefore, they sought another group that better suited their preferences. As elucidated in this case,

Pentecostal congregations and new PHS congregations do not necessarily compete for the same people, but fulfill the needs of people embodying different habituses. For many Pentecostals, these matters revolve around taste rather than doctrine. In this specific case, the couple brought up a doctrinal division only later, when the topic was broached. Doctrinal discourse is here a way to legitimize taste and habitus (Field Notes 2014).

Also pointing in this direction is a Sunday service in an older Pentecostal SHK church in the same locality as the PHS congregation I visited. The service included contemporary music with jazz influences. There was an orderly fashion to the structure and peoples' conduct, and the sermon was clear and systematic, dealing with people's daily problems. In contrast, the PHS service had a small choir that led the congregation through the traditional hymns. As the participants greeted one another, they employed old-fashioned Pentecostal words and phrases, and the small talk was filled with symbolic biblical language. In the same vein, the sermon consisted of a traditional, excited proclamation of the "Word," filled with emotion and exhortations (Fieldnotes 2014). During a discussion with the male elders of this PHS congregation, they briefly commented on secularization. For them, this was the main influence at work in the development of the HH. For instance, they identified the new features described above, particularly the music, lighting effects, and new sermon content as signs of "worldliness." Complaints about "worldliness" may be seen as a response to disruption between traditional and familiar Pentecostal culture, and contemporary developments. In scholarly terms, this is an example of what was mentioned earlier: that for these men, the boundaries between the sacred and the profane had been breached. What further strengthens the importance of this example is that their responses are representative of wider segments of the contemporary HH (Fieldnotes 2014).

Although understandings of what constitutes "worldliness"—and the fear thereof—have been a common concern for Christians throughout history, such concerns have been accentuated in specific situations. In light of the current demographical and cultural changes on the one hand, as well as accusations of transgressions by preachers, and minimal or absent growth in the HH, it is not surprising that such concerns have been aired by many Pentecostals, fueling concerns about worldliness. Also, Pentecostal adoption of practices from mainstream Finnish culture has doubtless undermined some of the traditional features central to historical Pentecostal culture. Since these developments have progressed rapidly, older generations in particular see them as threatening, and as undermining the perceived uniqueness of the HH. Perhaps unsurprisingly, concerns with worldliness are more widespread at the HK end of the HH spectrum than at the SHK end. People on the SHK side also voice their opinion on their opposition, but their critique revolves around other matters. From a researcher's perspective, each group's accusations of the other—of worldliness on the one hand, and of old-fashioned stagnation on the other—may be understood as a rejection of the preferences of the opposing camp. Using this rhetoric and line of reasoning, both sides define themselves and their relation to the other group, rather than describe that group; they create a distinction between good and bad taste. Sociologist Stephanie Lawler analyzes how people describe themselves by expressing disgust over styles and practices they do not appreciate, and do not want to be associated with. She uses the concept of *disgusted subjects* to refer to such identification processes (Lawler 2005). Similarly, Pentecostals' disgust over "worldliness" and "stagnation" respectively may be seen as ways of establishing their own habitus while distancing themselves from the alternative side (Mantsinen 2014; Fieldnotes 2014).

Key Characteristics of the Habituses

Presently, members leaning to either side represent two different forms of Pentecostal habitus, each formed by the members' background and generational experiences. In the following section, I describe a few key characteristics that demonstrate their different foci. The central standing of these features does not mean that the other side lacks such attributes; I merely want to illustrate the dominant directions in each of the camps.

Individual relationships to God are emphasized across the spectrum. However, on the SHK side these relationships are expected to develop in personalized ways, while on the HK side, they are expected to develop according to shared doctrine. For SHK members, individual relationships to God are open to discussion and new interpretations. Among HK members, this is less the case; established interpretations in general are rarely subject to serious discussion. The two sides also differ in terms of leadership structure. The SHK has a stronger inclination towards bureaucratic features, while the HK is mainly patriarchally led. Although charismatic authority exists in both camps, this feature is more predominant in the HK.

Another divide can be seen in regard to rituals and service practices, mainly between intellectual and affectional forms. The more educated SHK Pentecostals prefer intellectual, well-structured rituals, and practices like sermons, and favor calmer emotional expressions. A rising trend among SHK Pentecostals is lifestyle sermons, familiar from international figures such as Joyce Meyer and Joel Osteen. HK sermons, by contrast, are typically more emotionally expressive; a standard HK sermon would utilize personal and folk stories, and would include references to biblical stories to greater extent (Mantsinen 2015a). The approach to religious experiences further divides the HH. An important part of the traditional Pentecostal habitus was strong emotional experiences, which were not to be disputed. Today, the discourse of "freedom of the Spirit" has a stronger foothold in HK congregations than it has in the considerably more bureaucratic SHK organizations. A good example of the more orderly approach in the latter is the management of speaking in tongues, which has developed from a public expression into a private devotional routine (Mantsinen 2014, 124; cf. Cartledge 1998). In the SHK, Charismatic gifts and Charismatic preachers are usually subject to stricter control and critique than in the HK groups.

The employment of different discourses of legitimization also perpetuates division. I have found that HK Pentecostals are more prone to using biblical stories and interpretations in order to legitimize their arguments. This practice has declined radically amongst the new generations of socialized SHK members, whose debates are more intellectual and often lack direct biblical references. This ties into how each side has a distinct way of evangelizing. To SHK Pentecostals, reflective dialogue is key, whereas HK Pentecostals see proclamation as the appropriate way to go. Thus, SHK Pentecostals would engage in discussion with an outsider, while HK Pentecostals would proclaim the "correct" established message.

Attitudes to attendance and participation constitute another dividing line. Since the 1980s, attendance has declined dramatically in the HH. The most important reasons for this are lack of interest in general and in high levels of social commitment, combined with increased acceptance of more "fluid", commitment-less, religious participation. Historically, participation has been the norm, and it still remains a strong sign of religiousness for the "traditional" HK wing (Mantsinen 2014). In contrast, new attitudes, widespread among younger generations, are more individualistic and do not demand steady church visits; one may instead practice at home.

If the habitus is conditioned by structural factors (Bourdieu 1990, 53–54), what has changed? It is obvious that Finnish society has changed dramatically since the 1950s, and that new generations of Pentecostals have been affected. The combined factors of the movement's internal developments and the increase in numbers of socialized members have produced a shift in habituses. Upward social mobility has created new circumstances, leading to different lifestyles and preferences. Class divisions are visible in both HK and SHK habituses. To say that the HK side would be completely in line with working-class culture would be misleading; some working-class features, such as social and political radicalism, are opposed by the vast majority of Finnish Pentecostals. Historically, Pentecostal culture in the HH has been more appealing to working-class taste, as is evident in its unrehearsed, folksy, immediate, and more direct expressions. While such elements still exist in SHK congregations, they have lost their appeal to middle-class Pentecostals, who prefer professional, carefully prepared, and intellectually stimulating elements. The HK side of the HH might consider these practices tending to favor expression at the expense of substance. The points of division between HK and SHK, as sketched here, run parallel to divisions of social strata, which means that social differences have placed their mark on Finnish Pentecostal habituses.

As demonstrated earlier, SHK and HK approaches to modern societal developments differ considerably. On the SHK side, we can see an attempt to offer responses to modernization by means of integrating popular culture. Conversely, the HK distances itself from these developments, offering an alternative. Generally, the traditionally popular features distinguish the HK side, whereas the SHK side is more elaborated and intellectualized. Moreover, postmodern emphases on loose boundaries, combined with openness to negotiating identities and participation, characterize a new Pentecostal habitus embodied by the SHK. The traditional Pentecostal habitus, embodied by the HK, concentrates on community, established interpretations, and strict boundaries between "us" and "the world."

A Struggle for the Future of Finnish Pentecostalism

Change is inevitable in religious communities, since the members constantly interpret and reproduce the elements of their tradition (cf. Bloch 2001; Sperber 1996, 70–74). If development is slow, people usually have time to adjust to the changes taking place. Controversies are likely to arise with fast-paced major and visible changes that transform the structure and culture substantially. If the leaders of a Charismatic sect are still active when a structured organization is built, the shift may feel like a home invasion or an intrusion into their identity for them.

The dynamics of Pentecostal religiosity pose a challenge for analysis. Donald E. Miller has used the concept *postmodern primitivism* to describe Pentecostalism. By this, he means that this mode of Christianity contains both primitive forms and postmodern tendencies. For example, it combines sometimes erratic experiences, discourses of self-improvement, speaking in tongues, and intellectually oriented sermons (Miller 1997, 22–24; Miller and Yamamori 2007, 142–44, 216–219). Historically, most Pentecostal movements have balanced on the edge between traditional and postmodern. This can explain some of the success of Pentecostalism in many countries. While offering something familiar and traditional, it also brings new and sometimes liberating ideas of individuality and social improvement. Such ideas include individual relationships with God and emancipation from poverty, as well as new forms of embodied practices and experiences (Robbins 2009, 62–63; Vasquez 2009).

The ambiguity and complexity inherent to Pentecostalism points to something important: The processes of division between traditional and postmodern within Finnish Pentecostalism have led to their separation and mutual opposition. The division of the HH into two opposite camps or habituses can be seen as a struggle between traditional and postmodern religion, whereby both sides have strong concerns about the future of Finnish Pentecostalism.

The ways in which these concerns are expressed very much resemble what O'Dea has listed as dilemmas of institutionalization. Especially relevant is the dilemma of delimitation: How should a religion be described and legitimized (O'Dea 1961)? Central to the dilemma are generational and socioeconomical differences between socialized and converted members. Generational conflicts are not new to the HH; as early as the 1960s, the different experiences of succeeding generations caused tensions in local congregations. The cultural boundaries between Pentecostals and the rest of society were guarded zealously at the time, and those who had called for faster progress usually resigned (Lindell 1991, 67–68). What distinguishes the present situation is that the movement has become relatively moderate towards society, and the number of converts has declined while the number of socialized members has increased; in other words, the situation has reversed. It is no longer common for "liberal" Pentecostals to leave the movement, never mind be expelled. Consequently, the HH has faced a dilemma of mixed motivation (O'Dea 1961), whereby the challenge has been to meet the needs of different groups. The ways in which these adjustments have been materialized has been problematic and a concern for those who support conserving the traditional Pentecostal habitus.

This social development and differing experiences have led to both a new habitus and identity. Moderate conversion experiences, middle-class lifestyles, and postmodern tendencies have created a position where traditional Pentecostal culture is distant to many. When a new cultural position is introduced by a new habitus with new cultural practices, it challenges the social field and supporters of old positions. The traditional identity of exclusion and authenticity was a strong part of a shared habitus, and still is for the HK side of the HH. As this position is threatened, traditional Pentecostals are feeling insecure and defend their identity and habitus (Bourdieu 1977, 80–81; 1983, 313; Mantsinen 2015b; Poloma and Green 2010, 61–83). Younger generations and well-educated Pentecostals deem traditional practices and styles as outdated and ineffective in the current social and societal context. By rejecting and labeling the opposite side, they actively describe their own preferences and habituses. This distinction between "proper" and "outdated" is primarily a way to present one's own identity. The act of describing the other side actually portrays more of their own sphere than the opposite side. Presenting the other habitus as unwanted (cf. Lawler 2005) or "unbiblical" is a strategy of limiting the acceptable cultural sphere, deeming one's own preferences as legitimate. Other discourses are used as well: While the HK side seeks "authenticity" for the HH and Pentecostalism, the SHK side questions this version of "authenticity."

While speculating on the future of these trajectories, it is possible to present some preliminary prognoses concerning the different camps. The division may become irrelevant if the other side shrinks in popularity and size, as has happened before. It seems that the future of the HK will largely depend on how many new members, and foremost younger members, it will be able to attract in the future. The foremost threat against the future of the HK is the old age of the leading Charismatic figures. The authority of leading Charismatic figures has been a stabilizing force, and without new Charismatic leaders of this variety, the HK may face its demise.

Finally, the wider dispute between SHK and HK eclipses other challenges for the HH, such as the disaffiliation of many socialized Pentecostal members, manifested in the creation of independent Pentecostal congregations. These new groups have resulted from their members' desire to differentiate their habitus from the established Pentecostal habituses within HH. Usually founded by socialized Pentecostals, the new groups originated from the HH. For them, the HH has not changed fast enough to accommodate their needs and visions—in analytical terms, it fails to accommodate the habitus they are seeking. The desired habitus includes a more individualistic and dynamic approach, open to contemporary fashion and music styles, as well as discussion of values and theologies.

Conclusions

The Finnish Pentecostal Movement has tried to foster an idea of a nationwide religious movement with a homogenous culture, and has failed. This is visible in the split that took place as SHK became a registered denomination and the HK network emerged as a response. In this chapter, I have argued that the split is the result of a larger differentiation within the HH, embodied in two different Pentecostal habituses. The resulting main argument is that the Finnish Pentecostal Movement faces its greatest challenges from within, in terms of the said differentiation of traditional and postmodern Pentecostal habituses. These are the results of a wide variety of factors both internal and external to the movement. One of the key developments has been a demographical shift in the HH, meaning that experiences vary between generations. The traditional Pentecostal habitus has been shaped by conversion, and strong distancing from mainstream society and the Lutheran state church in particular. The preferences inherent to this habitus also reflect the members' working-class background. With the relaxation of relations with mainstream Finnish society and Lutheran religion, the state church no serves as a threatening "other" to the same extent that it used to.

The emergence of a new, socialized, generation of Pentecostals has entailed a new habitus, lacking the old experiences of exclusion and separation; it constitutes a middle-class group of postmodern worshipers with more relaxed attitudes to mainstream society and practices. This group has grown to become influential in the HH. Moreover, its preferences have influenced the whole movement: its members appreciate intellectual sermons that address individual needs, new embodied routines like worship music, organizational order, and decentralized authority. The construction of the new habitus has resulted in reactions from traditionalists. The latter camp sees innovations as "worldly," while the postmodern Pentecostals depict the traditionals as outdated and old-fashioned. Hence, the current organizational split can be viewed as a manifestation of this deeper divide.

It remains to be seen how the HH will develop in the future. Currently, Pentecostals from both camps find the contemporary culture of the HH alienating. There are plenty of socialized members who want to change the movement further, although the more traditional older generations have been the most vocal. One option is that the HH might allow two opposing groups to coexist in the same city or town, or even in the same congregation. It is also possible that the HK and other factions opposing the SHK might fail to attract long-term interest among younger Pentecostals, in which case the HK would slowly vanish. Yet another possibility would be to dissolve the HH, but this seems unlikely in the near future, as it is not currently a viable option. In the long run, the movement's survival depends on the realization that groups with different religious habituses need their own spaces in which to practice Pentecostalism, and Pentecostal lifestyles that accommodate their own cultural tastes and preferences.

REFERENCES

Ahonen, Lauri K. 1994. *Suomen helluntaiheräytyksen historia*. Vantaa: Ristin Voitto.
Anderson, Allan H. 2014. *An Introduction to Pentecostalism*. 2nd ed. Cambridge: Cambridge University Press.
Barnett, Pual. 1973. *The Quest for Power: Neo-Pentecostals and the New Testament*. Sydney: Anzea Publishers.
Bauman, Zygmunt. 1992. *Intimations of Postmodernity*. London: Routledge.
———. 1998. Postmodern Religion? In *Religion, Modernity and Postmodernity*, ed. Paul Heelas, 55–78. Oxford: Blackwell Publishers.
———. 2000. *Liquid Modernity*. Cambridge: Polity.
Bourdieu, Pierre. 1977. *Outline of a Theory of Practice*. Cambridge: Cambridge University Press. [1972].
———. 1983. The Field of Cultural Production, or: The Economic World Reversed. *Poetics* 12: 311–356.
———. 1990. *The Logics of Practice*. Cambridge: Polity Press.
———. 2000. *Pascalian Meditations*. Stanford: Stanford University Press.
———. 2010. *Distinction: A Social Critique of the Judgement of Taste*. London: Routledge. [1979].
Bloch, Maurice. 2001. A Well-Disposed Social Anthropologist's Problems with Memes. In *Darwinizing Culture: The Status of Memetics as a Science*, ed. Robert Aunger, 189–203. Oxford: Oxford University Press.
Cartledge, Mark J. 1998. The Future of Glossolalia: Fundamentalist or Experientialist? *Religion* 28: 233–244.
Freston, Paul. 1999. Neo-Pentecostalism. In *Archives des Sciences Sociales des Religions*, ed. Brazil: Problems of Definition and the Struggle for Hegemony, vol. 105, 145–162.

Helluntaiherätys. 2014. Finnish Pentecostal Movement. http://www.helluntaiheratys.fi. Accessed 25 June 2014.
Helluntaikansa. 2014. Pentecostal People Organization. http://www.helluntaikansa.fi. Accessed 25 June 2014.
Hollenweger, Walter. 1972. *The Pentecostals*. Minneapolis: Augsburg Publishing House.
Hunt, Steven J. 2002. Deprivation and Western Pentecostalism Revisited: Neo-Pentecostalism. *Pentecostudies* 1: 1–29.
Järvinen v. Porin Helluntaiherätys ry. 2012. Järvinen v Pori Pentecostal Mission Registered Association. Satakunnan käräjäoikeus L11/2531, verdict 12/17013 2012.
Kättö, Outi. M. 2002a. Rekisteröinti puhutti talvipäivillä. *Ristin Voitto*, Januari 23.
———. 2002b. Rekisteröimättömyys aiheuttaa epävarmuutta. *Ristin Voitto*, January 30.
Ketoja, Kari. 2001. Päättämisen vaikeus ja oikeus. *Ristin Voitto*, September 26.
Kirkko, Haastettu. 2012. *Suomen Evankelis-luterilainen kirkko vuosina 2008–2011*. Tampere: Kirkon tutkimuskeskus.
Köhrsen, Jens. 2008. *Religious Taste: Explaining Religious Choices by the Concept of Religious Taste*. Paper Presented at the Annual Meeting of the SSSR, Louisville Kentucky, October 17, 2008.
Kuosmanen, Jorma. 2001. Valtakunnallinen neuvottelukokous päätti perustaa uskonnollisen yhdyskunnan. *Ristin Voitto*, September 26.
Lahti, Heikki. 2006. *Pojasta tuli pappi: Heikki Lahti muistelee*. Self-published.
Lawler, Stephanie. 2005. Disgusted Subjects: The Making of Middle-Class Identities. *The Sociological Review* 53: 429–446.
Lee, Raymond L.M. 2005. Bauman, Liquid Modernity and Dilemmas of Development. *Thesis Eleven* 83: 61–77.
Lindell, Liisa. 1991. *Työväen korttelista kaikkien maailmaan: Tampereen helluntaiseurakunta 1921–1991*. Tampere: Tampereen rukoushuoneyhdistys Saalem ry.
Löfstedt, Torsten. 2009. From Sect to Denomination: The Russian Church of Evangelical Christians. In *Global Pentecostalism: Encounters with Other Religious Traditions*, ed. David Westerlund, 157–178. London: I. B. Tauris.
Luoto, Valtter. 1980. Laajenevan herätysliikkeen ongelmat. *Ristin Voitto*, January 17.
Lyotard, Jean-François. 1984. *The Postmodern Condition: A Report on Knowledge*. Manchester: Manchester University Press. [1979].
Mahmood, Saba. 2005. *Politics of Piety: The Islamic Revival and the Feminist Subject*. Princeton: Princeton University Press.
Mamiya, Lawrence. 1982. From Black Muslim to Bilalian: The Evolution of a Movement. *Journal for the Scientific Study of Religion* 21: 138–152.
Mantsinen, Teemu T. 2014. *Helluntailaiset luokkakuvassa. Uskontokulttuuri ja yksilön luokka-asema Turun helluntaiseurakunnassa*. PhD dissertation, University of Turku, 2014.

———. 2015a. Postmoderni primitivismi: Helluntailaisuus ja uushenkisyys perinteisissä liikkeissä. In *Näkyvä ja näkymätön uskonto*, ed. Jaana Kouri, 128–140. Turku: University of Turku.
———. 2015b. Conversion and Transformation of Culture in the Finnish Pentecostal Movement. *Approaching Religion* 5: 44–56.
———. 2016. Suomen evankelis-luterilaisen kirkon ja helluntaiherätyksen muuttuneet suhteet työntekijöiden näkökulmasta. *Teologinen Aikakauskirja*, 120 (4): 337–351.
Martin, Bernard. 1998. From Pre- to Postmodernity in Latin America: The Case of Pentecostalism. In *Religion, Modernity and Postmodernity*, ed. Paul Heelas, 102–146. Oxford: Blackwell Publishers.
Miller, Daniel E. 1997. *Reinventing American Protestantism: Christianity in the New Millennium*. Berkeley: University of California Press.
Miller, Daniel E., and Tetsunao Yamamori. 2007. *Global Pentecostalism: The New Face of Christian Social Engagement*. Berkeley: University of California Press.
Moberg, Jessica. 2013. Piety, Intimacy and Mobility: A Case Study of Charismatic Christianity in Present-Day Stockholm. PhD dissertation, Södertörn University.
Niebuhr, Richard H. 1957. *The Social Sources of Denominationalism*. New York: Meridian. [1929].
O'Dea, Thomas. 1961. Five Dilemmas in the Institutionalization of Religion. *Journal for the Scientific Study of Religion* 1: 30–39.
Päätösasiakirja. 1989. *Päätösasiakirja: Suomen evankelisluterilaisen kirkon ja Suomen helluntaiherätyksen viralliset neuvottelut 1987–1989*. Ristin Voitto ry.
Poloma, Margaret M., and John C. Green. 2010. *Assemblies of God: Godly Love and the Revitalization of American Pentecostalism*. New York: New York University Press.
Ristin Voitto. 1985. Helsingin Siion liitettiin helluntaiherätykseen. January 24.
Robbins, Joel. 2009. Pentecostal Networks and the Spirit of Globalization: On the Social Productivity of Ritual Forms. *Social Analysis* 53: 55–66.
Roos, J.P. 1988. *Elämäntavasta elämäkertaan*. Helsinki: Tutkijaliitto.
Ruohomäki, J. 2009. *Karismaattisuuden kutsu: Karismaattisen kristillisyyden historiallinen kehitys helluntailiikkeeksi*. Keuruu: Aikamedia.
Ruohomäki, Jouko. 2014. *Suomen helluntailiikkeen synty, leviäminen ja yhteisönmuodostus 1907–1922*. Keuruu: Aikamedia.
Seila, Taito. 1970. *Mitä todella tapahtui*. Helsinki: Ristin Sanoma ry.
Seurakuntien yhteys. 2015. Seurakuntien yhteys ry. http://seurakuntienyhteys.fi/historia. Accessed 4 May 2015.
Sopanen, Tapio. 2002. Uskonnollinen yhdyskunta perustettiin. *Ristin Voitto*, January 23.
Sperber, Dan. 1996. *Explaining Culture: A Naturalistic Approach*. Oxford: Blackwell Publishers.
Stark, Rodney, and William Sims Bainbridge. 1985. *The Future of Religion: Secularization, Revival, and Cult Formation*. Berkeley: University of California Press.

Streib, Heintz. 2011. Faith Development Theory Revisited: The Religious Styles Perspective. *The International Journal for the Psychology of Religion* 11: 143–158.
Suomen helluntaikirkko. 2015. *Suomen Helluntaikirkon*. http://www.suomenhelluntaikirkko.fi. Accessed 7 May 2015.
Vanberg, Viktor J. 1993. Rational Choice, Rule-Following and Institutions: An Evolutionary Perspective. In *Rationality, Institutions, and Economic Methodology*, ed. Christian Knudsen, Gustafsson Bo, and Uskali Mäki, 171–200. London: Routledge.
Vasquez, Manuel A. 2009. The Global Portability of Pneumatic Christianity: Comparing African and Latin American Pentecostalisms. *African Studies* 68: 273–286.
Weber, Max. 1947 [1925]. *The Theory of Social and Economic Organization*. London: Collier-Macmillan Limited.
———. 1956 [1922]. *The Sociology of Religion*. Boston: Beacon Press.
———. 1964 [1947]. *The Theory of Social and Economic Organization*. London: Collier-Macmillan.

Ethnographic Material

Field Notes from an Ethnographic Study of the Pirkanmaa Traditional Pentecostal Church in Tampere, Finland. February 23 February, 2014.
Interview with M. Kuokkanen from Pirkanmaa Traditional Pentecostal Church, February 23, 2014.
Interview with P. Havupalo from the Finnish Pentecostal Church, March 26, 2014.

Open Access This chapter is distributed under the terms of the Creative Commons Attribution 4.0 International License (http://creativecommons.org/licenses/by/4.0/), which permits use, duplication, adaptation, distribution and reproduction in any medium or format, as long as you give appropriate credit to the original author(s) and the source, provide a link to the Creative Commons license and indicate if changes were made.

The images or other third party material in this chapter are included in the chapter's Creative Commons license, unless indicated otherwise in a credit line to the material. If material is not included in the chapter's Creative Commons license and your intended use is not permitted by statutory regulation or exceeds the permitted use, you will need to obtain permission directly from the copyright holder.

CHAPTER 6

Knutby Filadelfia: A Schismatic New Religious Movement Within the Pentecostal Context

Liselotte Frisk

Knutby Filadelfia, situated in Knutby just outside Uppsala, Sweden, is a small religious community with roots in the Pentecostal Movement of the early twentieth century.[1] As of 2014, it had 96 members. The congregation was structurally part of the national network the Pentecostal Movement (Pingströrelsen) until 2004, when it was expelled on the grounds that its beliefs were "unorthodox."

In January 2004, a tragic crime put this small religious community in the spotlight of media attention, which entailed the public exposure of its unique beliefs and lifestyle, including its interpretation of the Christian symbol of the Bride of Christ as a human being: Åsa Waldau. Alexandra Fossmo, the young wife of one of its pastors, Helge Fossmo, was killed by gunshot, and a young male member was seriously wounded. Pastor Fossmo was found guilty of conspiracy to murder and sentenced to life in prison.[2] The investigation revealed that the man who had been shot was the husband of one of the pastor's mistresses. A young member, Sara Svensson, was convicted as the perpetrator of the shootings. She, too, had been having a romantic relationship with the pastor. The court, however,

L. Frisk (✉)
Dalarna University, Falun, Sweden

ruled that Svensson had performed the crimes while heavily under the influence of the pastor, who had been sending anonymous text messages to her cell phone, urging her to perform the deed—messages she believed came directly from God. Svensson was committed to a psychiatric ward.

This study initially portrays the history, religious beliefs, and lifestyle of Knutby Filadelfia. The community is described and analyzed from a sociological perspective on new religious movements, and the theological and organizational boundaries of the Pentecostal Movement and the phenomenon of schism and expulsion will be discussed. At the end of the chapter, a lifeworld approach will be explored as an analytical perspective on the crimes in 2004.

Knutby Filadelfia has received very little scholarly attention, despite the high levels of media publicity and speculation. Sociologist Eva Lundgren wrote a book in 2008, mainly mirroring the former pastor Helge Fossmo's perspective on the events in Knutby Filadelfia. There is also a short summary of the events written by historian of religion Jonathan Peste, based mainly on journalistic accounts. Finally, Frisk and Palmer have written a paper (2015) using narrative analysis on the story of Helge Fossmo, based on an interview with the former pastor. Thus, this chapter may be said to be the first fieldwork-based portrayal of this religious group from an academic perspective. The material consists of interviews and informal conversations with members, pastors, representatives, and ex-members of Knutby Filadelfia, as well as material gathered from participant observation at Sunday services and social events, such as dinners and the Friday night coffee meeting—all conducted between the years 2011 and 2015. The first part of the chapter describes Waldau's own story of her journey to Knutby Filadelfia, based mainly on an interview with her and a book she authored.

History and Development

Knutby Filadelfia was founded in the village of Knutby outside Uppsala in 1921 as a Pentecostal congregation (Peste 2011, 218). It remained a fairly orthodox Pentecostal organization for the first few decades. In 1985, Kim Wincent, who had attended the Bible school at Word of Life (Livets ord), became the head pastor (Lundgren 2008, 54–56). Like in many other Pentecostal congregations at the time, several of the members of Knutby Filadelfia had been in contact with the Word of Life to various degrees—a development that continued during the 1990s. There was never, however, any formal collaboration between the two groups.

In 1992, Åsa Waldau moved to the village from Uppsala, and from that time on put her unique mark on the community. Waldau was born in 1965. She was born into a secular home, but her grandfather, Willis Säwe, with whom she had close and positive contact during her childhood, was an important figure of leadership in the early Swedish Pentecostal Movement. Waldau recalls that she had a salvation experience at the age of 16, when she accompanied a friend to a teenage camp in the Sanctification Union (Helgelseförbundet), one of the Swedish free churches.[3] A little later, in the Pentecostal Movement, she discovered what she now considers to be most important to her: an emphasis on the individual's personal experience of and relationship to God, as well as closeness to Jesus. Waldau also found the Pentecostal teachings to be consistent with what was written in the Bible. Another aspect she found important was their emphasis on love and fellowship between followers. Waldau says that she had always been more attracted to the teaching to do good to one another, to create the community Jesus preached, than to the charismatic aspects of looking for "signs and miracles." Additionally, these egalitarian values were important for Waldau, the putting into practice of the idea that God's will is sought by the community as a whole, as well as the idea that everyone could find his or her own way to serve God (Interview 1).

Waldau was baptized in 1983, and after that worked with different projects within Pentecostal congregations in, for example, Laxå and Uppsala. She worked a lot with children and teenagers, but also with music, and after some time she started to teach and evangelize. Her musical style could be described as prayers to God set to music, with some similarities to the devotional songs expressed in Neo-Pentecostal contexts. Waldau says that she met some resistance in the Pentecostal Movement. According to her, it was a problem for some that too many people came to listen to her, and that too many people asked her to come and talk. Some considered her popularity a threat, and also thought her way of speaking was too direct, meaning—according to herself—her habit of being very clear about what she considered to be right and wrong, based on the Bible. When she moved to Uppsala in 1990, she started working as a children's pastor. This ended in 1992, when Waldau's husband left her for one of her best friends, resulting in a divorce. According to Waldau, the divorce prevented her from continuing as a pastor in the Pentecostal Movement in Uppsala. Additionally, she says she could not cooperate with a younger male coworker, who wanted to decide what she should do, just because she was a woman. Waldau also expresses that she was disappointed by the hypocrisy and power struggles she saw in the Pentecostal Movement (Interview 1). The problems between Waldau and the Pentecostal Movement are confirmed by other sources; however, these often blame Waldau for the problems (Lundgren 2008, 67).

At this point, Waldau was invited to stay in Knutby for a while, as some of her friends, who were members of Knutby Filadelfia (and were the parents of her future husband), thought that this was what God wanted her to do. After some time, she was asked to stay and work there on a continual basis. This request was to some extent influenced by a prophetic message that Knutby Filadelfia should open its doors to a female servant of the Lord who had experienced a great crisis (Interview 1). This message was allegedly received by a priest in the Church of Sweden who was visiting Knutby for a meeting (Interview 4). Hearing this, Waldau also thought it was God's will that she should stay in Knutby (Interview 1).

The congregation had 40 members in 1991 (Lundgren 2008, 55). Waldau largely had the freedom to work in the ways she thought best, and immediately started working with children and music. This was, according to Waldau, a great success. In 1994 she married Patrik Waldau who, like his parents, had belonged to the community for a long time.[4] He was also one of the young people she had met at Uppsala. They had two children together (Interview 1).

During the 1990s, Åsa Waldau served as a traveling evangelist within the Pentecostal Movement, venturing all over Sweden. Many of the people she met moved to Knutby after some time and developed close relationships with her. Among these new members were Helge Fossmo and Sara Svensson. In 1997, Knutby Filadelfia started a Bible school, which still exists but now has fewer participants. At that time, the Bible school consisted of one course that lasted for three months and was held annually. Participants stayed in private homes, which led some people to take such a liking to the way of life in Knutby Filadelfia that they decided to stay. Within a few years, the membership had doubled to about 100 members (Interview 1). Some of the older members did not like Åsa Waldau's new spiritual authority and left the congregation (Lundgren 2008, 68). The new community consisted mainly of young and enthusiastic people, many of whose family backgrounds were in the Pentecostal Movement (Lundgren 2008, 59).

Around the year 2000 there was a strong expectation shared by the Knutby pastors and members that Jesus would return to usher in the millennium very soon. A belief developed concerning Knutby Filadelfia's important role in the coming global events: God had a special purpose for this particular congregation, and a specific role for Åsa Waldau. The group waited for the return of Jesus (Informal Conversations 2). The members of Knutby Filadelfia prayed for this to happen, and they talked in this context about "coming home" and "be[ing] taken home." The concept of "coming home," used by the community in this manner, has been criticized as possibly referring to death, contributing to the notion of death as something positive, and thereby providing a context of rationalization for the later murder and murder attempts (Peste 2011, 217).

Informal conversations with members point to the death of Helge Fossmo's first wife, Heléne Fossmo, in 1999, as an event which, at least retrospectively, changed many aspects of the community's thinking (Informal Conversations 1). Heléne Fossmo was found dead in the bathtub in her own house. At the time, her death was concluded to be a tragic accident,[5] but it would become important for the development of the congregation's teachings on death. The members were all relatively young, and many have since expressed that they had not thought much about death before. Now, it seemed so much closer as it had happened unexpectedly to a young person in their midst. Some thought that God's kingdom would soon come and that they would meet Heléne again, and many people in the congregation had a strong longing for this to happen. Additionally, Fossmo expressed that he had received a vision that God would take Åsa Waldau home soon, which she took seriously for some time (Interview 1).

Prophecies, visions, and demons have at times played a major role in the community's theology, as they sometimes have in Pentecostal congregations (Lundgren 2008, 61–63; Peste 2011, 219). Åsa Waldau says, however, that she resisted the excesses of searching for signs and miracles, and that the love and fellowship in the community, as well as the search for Jesus were much more central to her (Interview 1). Pastor Peter Gembäck remarks that these phenomena were especially significant at the time of Helge Fossmo's pastorship (Informal Conversations 2).

The Knutby case received a tremendous amount of media attention (Norman 2007). The congregation was criticized by all corners of society, religious as well as secular. The Pentecostal Movement was quick to denounce Knutby Filadelfia. The congregation was expelled in 2004 and is not part of any network today. Åsa Waldau has expressed disappointment, because she feels that no one from the Pentecostal Movement stood up for her and Knutby Filadelfia when the media storms ensued (Interview 1). On the contrary, the spokesman for the Pentecostal Movement, Sten-Gunnar

Hedin, was very clear that Knutby Filadelfia deviated from the Pentecostal Movement, and had nothing to do with it (Norman 2007, 28).

Åsa Waldau is no longer a pastor, but she remains a member of Knutby Filadelfia. Since 2008, she has withdrawn from leadership and lives in seclusion from the community. Waldau appeared frequently in the headlines and also live on various radio and television channels during the first few years after the event. The pressure from the events of and media storms after 2004 finally became too much, and Waldau says today that she needed to create distance between herself and people who needed her help. She also expresses disappointment in certain ex-members who have been very critical of her in the media and whom, she says, she has been prepared to give her life for. Today, she works as an artist, musician, and designer, and she says that also in these actions she aims at surrendering to God and being able to do his work (Interview 1). Although Waldau is no longer present in the everyday life of the community, her charisma is still evident in many ways. Her paintings are everywhere, as is her music, and she remains an inspiration and spiritual guide for many members.

The community has undergone significant demographic changes recently, as the number of children has increased markedly since 2004. Most children are younger than 10 years old. About 10 members have left over the last few years, some of them previously having belonged to the "inner core," such as the parents of Patrik Waldau (Informal Conversations 2).

Leadership and Authority

Knutby Filadelfia is organized as a nonprofit organization with a board chosen by the members. The board consists of 10 elders. In 2015, all the elders were men, but a few women have also held board positions, Åsa Waldau among them. As of 2015, there are three pastors, all of whom are members of the board. The organization is democratic in the formal sense (Interview 4). However, some leaders, especially Åsa Waldau, have had informal authority, which has led some to criticize the community as undemocratic.

To an observer of the community, the influence of Waldau on Knutby Filadelfia is very clear historically but also in the present. Many of the current members have moved to Knutby because they encountered her and what they describe as her spiritual power (Informal Conversations 1). Although Waldau has a unique position in the community, there are also other strong charismatic leaders. For the teenagers, important role models include some of the older men, for instance Waldau's husband Patrik and the current leader Pastor Peter Gembäck (Interviews 3).

Waldau's power and authority, as well as the presumed lack of democracy, have been criticized by ex-members (Lundgren 2008, 68), and by representatives of the Pentecostal Movement (Salomonsson 2005) among others. Some of the critics have suggested that Waldau was the real destructive force in Knutby Filadelfia, and that there is a kind of "systematic error" in the structure of the group that made the crimes possible (see for example Robèrt 2005a). Regarding Waldau, it has been claimed that she has even controlled who should marry whom in the community (Lundgren 2008, 67). Waldau confirms that many people, both historically but also today, have asked her for advice regarding many different kinds of questions in life, and have also been given advice (Interview 1).

Waldau has also been criticized for statements that have been perceived as judgmental and insulting (see for instance Lundgren 2008, 88, 125). She says today that there have been things she wishes she had never said, but that she did what she felt was right at the time. She says that, like all teachers, she has had the experience of sometimes saying the wrong thing, but that this experience is part of the development on the road to becoming more mature. According to Waldau, as a teacher one needs to be brave and clearly communicate what is right and wrong. Waldau says that, during her time in the Pentecostal Movement, she sometimes had to make decisions that were not popular with everyone, as some people were more interested in their own opinions than in God. Waldau sees her own life as an attempt to live "in spirit and truth,"[6] and to the degree that she succeeds in surrendering to God, she thinks that he is able to act through her and her words; God works through the human conscience and the inner urge to act and talk. The human interpretation, however, can be wrong sometimes, which is later shown "by the fruit" (Interview 1). It is clear that Waldau perceives herself, as do her followers, as an instrument of God and, although today there are no formal structures for her authority, her advice seems to be often sought, albeit in informal ways.

Beliefs

The main part of Knutby Filadelfia's theology conforms to classic Pentecostal and Charismatic currents in the latter part of the twentieth century. During this time, a fertile Christian milieu was significant, with influences from several orientations. In his book *The Globalisation of*

Charismatic Christianity, Simon Coleman (2000) describes this as a globalized scene with Neo-Pentecostal as well as fundamentalist currents. Significant orientations were the Faith Movement and the Toronto Blessing (Coleman 2000, 23–28). In Sweden, as elsewhere, the 1960s and 1970s were times of Charismatic revival within older churches. The Swedish Faith Movement could be seen as part of the wider Pentecostal-Charismatic landscape, with elements from Neo-Pentecostal groups in the United States, but also built on earlier revivals. The Word of Life, the most important Faith Movement church in Sweden, was established in 1983 by the former state church priest Ulf Ekman. There were also other Charismatic groups and currents at play in Sweden, which had emerged in the 1960s and 1970s. Two examples are the Maranata Movement (Maranatarörelsen), which came out of a minor Pentecostal revival, and the Jesus Movement (Coleman 2000, 89–90). In the broader Pentecostal-Charismatic context, neither the imminent return of Christ, nor God giving humans very concrete signs, were alien ideas.

However, Knutby Filadelfia also has some unique traits. A distinct characteristic is its continuous re-evaluation of previous theological positions where the members bring up subjects for discussion, study the scriptures in search for what the Bible "says," and formulate new theologies. In this way, their doctrine is dynamic and sometimes changes.

Knutby Filadelfia's most original, heterodox teaching is the idea of Åsa Waldau as the Bride of Christ.[7] This belief originated in an issue brought up for discussion during the late 1990s, namely of whether the Bride of Christ really should be interpreted as the Church—the Body of Christ—as most Christians see it, or if it might be a human woman, an otherwise very unusual interpretation. Pastor Helge Fossmo's statement to Waldau is now quite famous: "If the bride of Christ is a woman, then it must be you." Today, Waldau says she considered it her duty to look within her if there could be any truth to this suggestion and that she did reflect upon this matter for a while. She points out, however, that the whole idea came from Helge Fossmo and not from her (Waldau 2007, 237–244). The fact that she tried this belief for a while also had the effect that she withdrew from the daily tasks of the community for some time. It seems that the notion of Waldau as the Bride of Christ was unknown to the main body of the congregation, and known only to the closest group, comprised of less than a dozen people (Informal Conversations 2). Others may have heard rumors and hints, and drawn their own conclusions. Considering the negative attention this idea has received in Swedish media, it is unsurprising that the community now seeks to downplay the importance of this belief.

Between 2008 and 2009, another theological question came up for discussion and reassessment: the Trinity. Pastor Peter Gembäck explains that Knutby Filadelfia has opened up regarding the question of the humanity of Jesus. He thinks Jesus may make more sense as a human being, as a role model and example, than as a distant God. In the Christian context, this question is explosive, and Knutby Filadelfia has not taken any formal stand. The pastors and members continue to reflect on the true significance of the Trinity (Interview 4). It may be noted that humanization of Jesus goes well together with the process of reflecting on whether or not the Bride of Christ might be a human individual.

Knutby Filadelfia has also taken another stand that distinguishes it from the traditional Pentecostal churches and denominations regarding a lifestyle issue: wine drinking. In accordance with most other Christian orientations, the practitioners believe that it is not a sin to have one or two glasses of wine now and then, which most of them also do. In their view, there is nothing in the Bible indicating that wine consumption should be forbidden (Informal Conversations 2).

Lifestyle

Knutby Filadelfia is a very tight-knit community. Its foundation according to Åsa Waldau is, she says, the love and fellowship between Christian brothers and sisters, and worshiping God (Interview 1). Although families mostly live in their own houses, they often have meals together, spend time at each other's houses, and help each other with various tasks. Children sometimes sleep over in other houses than that of their parents, and single members sometimes share house with a family. These relatively close relationships between members has been criticized by psychiatrist Rigmor Robèrt, who interprets this semi-communalism as artificial intimacy and an insidious strategy for social control (Robèrt 2004). These close relations also create a tight community with boundaries dividing it from mainstream society, some of which are geographic, and others social.

The gender roles in the community generally conform to conservative, traditional Christian norms: The man should have the ultimate responsibility for and authority in the family, the woman should be cared for and provided for by the man. In the words of Åsa Waldau: the man should be "male" and the woman "female" (Waldau 2007, 187–191). This, however, has not affected the members' professional lives. Women in the community work outside the household to about the same extent as their counterparts in mainstream society. Regarding sexuality, the group has a positive approach to sexuality within marriage, but prohibits all forms of pre- and extramarital relations. There have, however, been examples of extramarital relations in the group, as seen in the case of Helge Fossmo. Fossmo himself motivated this by divine revelation and considered his relationship to Svensson to have spiritual meaning; their sexual relations were part of a form of "spiritual warfare" they were engaged in together (Lundgren 2008, 150–152).

As mentioned, there are many small children in the congregation today, and the children are often encouraged to develop close bonds to several adults beside their parents. Critics have highlighted possible negative consequences for the children, saying for example that this is part of a broader pattern of cultivation of artificial closeness among the members, and that physical and psychological abuse is common. Robèrt writes that a kind of exorcism is carried out, during which leaders discipline the children (Robèrt undated-a, b; 2005b).[8] Following the events of 2004, there have also been social investigations involving families in the community. In one case, during a custody conflict, a husband who was still a member of the group was reported to the police by his ex-wife, who had left the group, who had left the group, for physical abuse of their child. However, he was found not guilty. Three families have furthermore been reported to the local authorities for mistreating their children—among them Åsa Waldau's own family. The families were investigated and no evidence of abuse was found.[9]

In another case, two members who worked as teacher and assistant at the public school in Knutby were convicted on charges of physical violence towards their pupils. One was for pinning a child to the ground, the other for throwing snow at a child. According to an interview with the teacher involved in one of the cases, the boy held down had severe problems and was aggressively violent, and there was no other way to handle him (Interview 2). At the time of the crime, there were eight people from Knutby Filadelfia working at the school in different roles. All of them lost their jobs at the time, but were later exonerated, and some returned to jobs under the same municipal employer, albeit in other schools (Interview 2; Interview 4).

The Boundaries of the Pentecostal Movement

Before May 2004, the Pentecostal Movement in Sweden consisted of a network of independent but cooperating congregations. In that year, however, the movement transformed into a judicially religious denomination (*trossamfund*): Pingst—Fria församlingar i samverkan (PFFS) (Wahlström

2007, 316), in English, The Pentecostal Alliance of Independent Churches (PAIC). This development from network to denomination may have been partly influenced by the violent events in Knutby Filadelfia earlier the same year, although the development towards a national organization started earlier, and has parallels in the other Nordic countries, as discussed by Teemu T. Mantsinen in this volume. Two of the arguments in favor of a defined denomination were that the Pentecostal Movement would be in a stronger position to communicate with mainstream society, and that it would be clear who and which congregations represented the community. Moreover, it would be possible to ostracize "deviating" congregations (Wahlström 2007, 314). Before this, there was no formal procedure for accepting or ostracizing congregations in the network; it was more of an informal process. Lewi Pethrus himself, one of the most prominent leaders in the early Pentecostal Movement, had been disinclined to organize a denomination (Carlsson 2008, 71). The ideal of the Pentecostal Movement from the very beginning was that there should be no central organization and that the local congregations should be free and independent, but united through collaboration (Carlsson 2008, 71; Lindberg 1991, 263). On PAIC's website (2014), it says that it is necessary to encourage and give space to the life, integrity, uniqueness, and development of each local congregation, thus allowing room for certain differences between the congregations.

The Pentecostal Movement's "Marriage Committee" (Vigselnämnden) is an institution that has played a critical role in determining which local bodies should be perceived as Pentecostal congregations. This special committee determines whether local pastors should be given the right to perform juridically valid wedding ceremonies (Interview 5; Lindberg 1991, 274–276).[10] Besides, the list of congregations published each year in the Pentecostal Movement's yearbook was the go-to reference work for finding out congregations were seen as parts of the Movement. It is evident that Knutby Filadelfia, prior to 2004, was one of many Pentecostal congregations included in the yearbook's list, and the Marriage Committee had granted Pastor Helge Fossmo the right to perform wedding ceremonies.

An article published in the Pentecostal Movement's 2005 yearbook, written by the Pentecostal director in Uppsala, Dan Salomonsson, points out that there had been tensions and questions around the congregation in Knutby for a few years. He refers to its isolation, mentioning that the pastors from Knutby did not participate in collective events, and that a group of concerned relatives had contacted the Pentecostal Movement about the difficulties of keeping in contact with the members in Knutby

Filadelfia. Representatives of the Pentecostal Movement had also noticed that some of the older members of Knutby Filadelfia had left the group, due to the changed leadership style introduced with Åsa Waldau. Thus, even before the murder, representatives of the Pentecostal Movement had expressed and voiced concerns for Knutby Filadelfia (Salomonsson 2005). A contributing component was probably that Waldau had left the congregation in Uppsala under turbulent circumstances. Later in the article, Salomonsson states that in 2004, other evidence surfaced, showing that Knutby Filadelfia deviated from the "natural orientation" of a Christian (i.e., Pentecostal) congregation. Salomonsson cites amongst these the belief that the Bride of Christ could be a human being, materialized as Åsa Waldau; promiscuity in the community; alcohol consumption; the members' way of bringing up children;[11] the congregation's lack of openness towards the wider community; and the absence of a democratic structure (2005).

As part of the exclusion process, the Pentecostal Movement withdrew the right to perform marriages from Fossmo in June 2004 (Salomonsson 2005). Since then, Knutby Filadelfia has no longer been mentioned in the Pentecostal yearbook—an act of exclusion that could be interpreted as approximate to expulsion, since the Pentecostal Movement at that time lacked a formal mechanism of either affiliation or expulsion. This was not the first time the Pentecostal Movement had distanced itself from local religious bodies, and the exclusion of Knutby Filadelfia follows historical patterns. Alf Lindberg mentions a few examples from the 1950s, and the case of Södermalm's Free Congregation (Södermalms Fria Församling) in 1988.[12] Lindberg gives no specific reasons for the conflicts, except that in 1958 the pastor in Trollhättan had collaborated with pastors with whom there were "doctrinal disagreements." The Marriage Committee stated that Södermalm's Free Congregation and its pastors had shown in word and deed that they did not wish to be part of the Pentecostal Movement (Lindberg 1991, 276–283). The words and deeds corresponded to conformity with Word of Life ideals, and Ulf Ekman had also been invited to preach there (Coleman 2000, 91, 220). According to an article in the 1989 yearbook, the congregation also arranged competing conferences that were scheduled to take place at the same time as the significant Pentecostal conferences (Pingströrelsens årsbok 1989, 6). As with Knutby Filadelfia, the Marriage Committee played a central role in withdrawing the grant to perform marriages from certain pastors, and these local congregations were wiped out of the yearbook (Lindberg 1991, 276–283).

Tradition Versus Novelty, Schisms, and "Sects"

Religion tends to be expressed in traditional, as well as new and creative ways. An often emphasized component in religious innovation is the charismatic leader or charismatic authority (Barker 2004). The leading thinker on charismatic authority, Max Weber, also introduced the sociologist church/sect typology (1978, 1164), later developed by other sociologists, as discussed below. Weber considered charismatic leaders to be potential carriers of creativity, and as key to cultural and social change—religiously, politically, and economically. Charismatic authority is therefore a challenge to existing institutions, as it tends to change, undermine, and destroy them. It may thus also lead to derangement and deviance (Weber 1968, xix–xx). Concerning the case of Knutby Filadelfia, it is clear that Åsa Waldau holds charismatic authority in the Weberian sense. In Weber's terms, she is considered by the followers to possess "a certain quality of an individual personality by virtue of which [s]he is set apart from ordinary men and treated as endowed with supernatural, superhuman, or at least specifically exceptional qualities" (Weber 1964, 358). Waldau is also the initiator of the creative theological elements that developed in Knutby Filadelfia. An important exception is the Bride of Christ doctrine, which was reportedly initiated by Helge Fossmo, but revolves around the charisma of Waldau. The institutionalized Pentecostal Movement considers the doctrine unorthodox.

American sociologists Rodney Stark and William Sims Bainbridge, as well as British sociologist Eileen Barker, have taken interest in innovation in religious organizations. Barker discusses tradition versus novelty in the article "What Are We Studying? A Sociological Case for Keeping the 'Nova'" (2004). While religious creativity mostly has roots in older traditions, what Barker calls "new religious movements", or first-generation movements,[13] also exhibit characteristics that could in some sense be viewed as "new." Barker lists some of them as charismatic authority, external antagonism, atypical membership (attracting members from one strata of the population, for example, of a particular age or class), and rapid change. Knutby Filadelfia may be said to conform to several of these. Rarely has such a small religious group in Sweden been subjected to a level of external antagonism close to that of Knutby Filadelfia, which featured in media headlines daily or weekly for several years.

Living in a highly demanding religious community with a strong sense of communal identity naturally generates identification of one's group as being special compared to mainstream society, and a certain degree of separation between "us" and "them." For many of the members, it seems that the media attention has strengthened their identification with the community. Also, the members moving to, and settling in, Knutby Filadelfia were demographically in the same phase of life, mostly between 20 and 30 years of age. Several of them were second- or third-generation members of well-known Pentecostal families in Sweden, which may also have contributed to the antagonism demonstrated towards the group by some of their parents. Atypical membership-related practices are also demonstrated in the recent trend of having children in the community, as the next phase in life. Lastly, the congregation has changed rapidly in the last few years, changes rooted in its charismatic leadership structure, but also in the tragic events of 2004. Additionally, Barker identifies several elements as typical of new religious movements: enthusiasm, a strong sense of taking religion seriously, a common expectancy of dramatic changes in the future, as well as social or geographical boundaries created to keep the members separate from the world outside. To a certain extent, all these characteristics seem to apply to Knutby Filadelfia: The lifestyle of the community, which is geographically separated from the rest of society, requires deep religious commitment and high levels of participation, the combination of which results in a strong sense of community that generates social boundaries. Prior to the turn of the millennium, there was considerable expectation that Jesus would return very soon, although this characteristic is less prominent today.

Other aspects of Barker's work are less obviously applicable. Barker uses the phrase "first-generation movements," a concept that cannot be unequivocally applied to Knutby Filadelfia: The members who moved to Knutby after having met Waldau did not conceive of themselves as "converting to a new religion." At the time, Knutby Filadelfia was part of the Pentecostal Movement. The members' own understanding of their lifestyle was, and generally remains, that it was an imitation of that of the first Christians, which is not uncommon in Pentecostal groups. The case of Knutby Filadelfia and the Pentecostal Movement could better be described as a schism that happened gradually with the involvement of Åsa Waldau, and came to a final break in 2004. Barker writes that charismatic leadership is often especially important in those new religious movements that are created as an effect of schism (Barker 2004), and this seems to correspond to the developments in Knutby Filadelfia as well.

In several of their works, Stark and Bainbridge discuss religious novelty from a different perspective than Barker's, using the traditional sociological terms "sect" and "cult." Schismatic groups are key phenomena in their conceptualization. According to Stark and Bainbridge, sects, like cults, are in a state of relatively high tension with their surrounding sociocultural environment, but have prior ties to another religious organization. Furthermore, they are founded by persons who have left another religious body for the purpose of establishing the sect. They apply the term sect, therefore, only to schismatic movements (Stark and Bainbridge 1985, 25). Waldau's criticism of the Pentecostal Movement is typical of sectarian deviation: corruption, hypocrisy, and deviance from "true" religion. According to Stark and Bainbridge's conceptualization, Knutby Filadelfia is a typical case of sectarian religious revival.

The stance taken by the Pentecostal Movement regarding Knutby Filadelfia helps it distinguish itself from the crimes happening in Knutby, as well as affirming its law-abiding identity. Even before the crimes in 2004, however, there had been doubts and hesitations about some of Knutby Filadelfia's characteristics. The reaction to the crimes from the Pentecostal Movement thus also served the purpose of reaffirming its boundaries and of branding unacceptable theological traits and lifestyles as non-Pentecostal.

The Crimes in Knutby Filadelfia According to a Lifeworld Perspective

Globally, there have been several incidents connecting religion and violence in recent years, in some unfortunate cases leading to both murder and collective suicide (see Lewis 2011). In several cases, violence has been conducted by one or a few individuals, not involving the whole group, and in some of them the members have been involved to different degrees. Like in Knutby Filadelfia, religious motives may also coincide with either personal motives or, as elsewhere, with political motives.

One important question is to what extent the theology or the religious group as a whole is to blame for violent events, the answer to which certainly varies between individual cases. In the case of Knutby Filadelfia, there have been some attempts to hold the entire group responsible for the crimes. In particular, the narrative created by Fossmo in collaboration with his psychotherapist (Frisk and Palmer 2015), and recapitulated by Eva Lundgren (2008), creates a picture of Åsa Waldau as the malicious driving force, and of the theology and lifestyle of Knutby Filadelfia as a blueprint for the crimes. This picture, which has been widely spread in Swedish media, exhibits many similarities to common anticult representations of new religious movements, thus drawing on larger cultural narratives.[14] Helena Norman, investigating the media reports on the Knutby case, has found that in the media, (especially tabloid papers) the crimes were linked to the congregational milieu and the religion, rather than to individuals (2007, 17). The individuals involved in the events were represented in accordance with stereotypic narrative roles or cultural archetypes, whereby Waldau ("Bride of Christ") occupies the role as the mysterious "witch," Fossmo (often referred to as "the Sex Pastor") as the "villain," and Svensson ("the Babysitter") as the innocent and manipulated "victim"—all of whom are described with different attributes that correspond to their respective archetypical roles (Norman 2007, 37–65). Norman also writes about the "sect discourse," a dominant and favored discourse in the media reports about Knutby Filadelfia, and how it was constructed by means of statements from "sect experts," defectors, the Pentecostal Movement, and the media's own voices (Norman 2007, 68).

A more fruitful approach would take into account both individual perspectives and the broader religious context. Individuals construct, experience, and interpret their lives in different ways, as part of mutual relationships with other people and the broader social group, as well as in the wider societal context. An analytical concept that may be useful for this approach is that of the "lifeworld."[15] Originating in Husserl's phenomenological perspective, it was further developed in different directions by, for example, Alfred Schütz and Jürgen Habermas (Lotz 2001, 74–75). The lifeworld is, in short, our socially constructed, lived world. Different people may, however construct a variety of individual lifeworlds. Lifeworlds then, are both shared and individual. Dahlberg et al. write that our behavior, personal actions, and individual ways of being result from our own personal space in the world, which can be described as one's own entry to a common and shared world (2008, 39). Didactics researcher Cecilia Nielsen describes humans as active subjects in their lifeworld, experiencing and interpreting objects, events, and relations in various ways and giving them different kinds of meaning and significance. Each individual constructs, perceives, and experiences his or her own lifeworld, although this is also based on corporeality, space, time, and intersubjectivity. In other words, our comprehension is spatially and temporally bound. Human beings are parts of contexts, natural as well as cultural, in which their experiences and actions become meaningful. As the world is intersubjective, we are continuously in relation with and dependent on other people who also contribute to shaping those contexts (Nielsen 2013, 29–36).

In a small group like Knutby Filadelfia, different individuals construct and perceive the world through slightly different lifeworlds; these undoubtedly share many features but diverge on others. In all religious groups, there are several layers and levels of participation. This opens up spaces for the existence of different lifeworlds relating to each respective subgroup, even within the same community. From this perspective, it is only natural that the separate subgroups of Knutby Filadelfia embraced realities that diverged from each other to some extent. The members closest to Åsa Waldau, for example, may have taken part in the teaching of the Bride of Christ doctrine, while members in the outer circle of the community remained unfamiliar with it. A promiscuous lifestyle, usually categorized as sinful in Pentecostal and many other Christian groups, was legitimized as divinely sanctioned and may have been a natural component of the lifeworlds of Helge Fossmo and some of the women close to him before 2004. Meanwhile, other members may have been ignorant of this feature. As for Sara Svensson, her closeness to, and shared lifeworld with Helge Fossmo, were combined with the significance given to prophecies and signs in the congregation at the time. This combination may have made it seem natural to her that God would communicate with her via text messages on her cell phone, asking her to sacrifice people, with the Old Testament narratives as cultural models.

It seems probable that the crimes committed by Fossmo and Svensson could only have been committed in a very specific context, here provided by the religious group that both of them belonged to. Supporting influences in this context could, for example, have been the story from the Old Testament of God asking Abraham to sacrifice his son Isaac (Genesis 22).[16] The conjunction of this with several other beliefs may have reinforced this lifeworld: for example, the belief that God communicates with human beings through dreams or prophecies; and the belief in charismatic leaders, which provided fuel for the destructive pattern of the relationship between Fossmo and Svensson. In combination with the theological space in the community given to death after the demise of Fossmo's first wife, these factors are likely to have paved the way for the destructive relationship between Fossmo and Svensson. The notion of "coming home" may, for Svensson in co-construction with Fossmo, possibly have made sense when interpreted as death, thus contributing to the tragedy. For other members however, the meaning of those words would have been completely different.

Thus, the combination of the two individuals Fossmo and Svensson, as well as the reality they constructed together, on the basis of cultural elements current in their religious community, were certainly necessary factors in the crimes. More research is needed on the history and theology of Knutby, but based on what is currently known, it can be argued that the tragic crimes emerged out of a *folie à deux* relationship that developed between Helge Fossmo and Sara Svensson, and their idiosyncratic interpretations of the social and religious reality constructions of Knutby Filadelfia.

Conclusion

The Pentecostal Movement has distanced itself from local congregations several times during its history. An early example was in the 1950s, when a congregation in Trollhättan was excluded. In the 1980s, Södermalm's Free Congregation, with its connection to the Faith Movement, was the target, and in 2004 it was Knutby Filadelfia—the focus of this study. There has obviously been a continuous need to keep up boundaries as to what should or should not be considered part of the Pentecostal Movement. With its historical loose structure, however, there have been difficulties in expelling local congregations that do not live up to the movement's standards. The only means available to do this have been to withdraw the rights of local pastors to conduct marriages, and exclude congregations from the list of Pentecostal congregations provided in yearbooks. In the case of Knutby Filadelfia, both means were employed.

Even before the crimes of 2004, tensions were apparent in the Pentecostal Movement. Standard components of religious novelty, such as charismatic authority, external antagonism, atypical membership, rapid change, strong enthusiasm, an expectation of dramatic changes in the future, and boundaries to keep the members separate, all conform to the practices of Knutby Filadelfia. As such, this case is not unique, but a textbook example of a new religious movement or, in a sociological and non-pejorative sense, a sect, and a manifestation of how religious innovation is ordinarily constructed and expressed. As such, Knutby Filadelfia, with its unique belief system and lifestyle, can be considered as originating from a sectarian schism with the Pentecostal Movement, under the charismatic leadership of Åsa Waldau.

As for the crimes, there are no indications that they should be attributed to the religious group per se. Rather, the crimes seem connected to the unique lifeworld created by the two persons involved in the crimes—a lifeworld that also featured components from their wider religious context. The tragic outcome then, can be considered as the result of two specific individuals' co-construction of a destructive reality in their particular interpretations of specific, but not uncommon, religious components.

NOTES

1. Since autumn 2016, Knutby Filadelfia has been rapidly changing. The charismatic leader Åsa Waldau has left the group.
2. The Swedish term is *anstiftan till mord*, which means that someone persuades or forces another person to kill (incitement to murder). The closest equivalent in the English legal vocabulary is "conspiracy to murder."
3. The free churches in Sweden are a group of religious organizations outside the (former) state church, which have roots in revivalist currents from the nineteenth and twentieth centuries. The Pentecostal Movement is one of the free churches, and until 1994 "The Sanctification Union" (Helgelseförbundet) used to be another one—since 1997 this has been part of Interact (Evangeliska Frikyrkan).
4. Patrik Waldau is ten years younger than his wife, and was 18 at the time of the wedding. This fact has caused a lot of criticism and speculations (see for example Lundgren 2008, 67). However, cultural gender expectations need to be taken into consideration concerning this criticism. The opposite situation, a woman ten years younger than the man, would hardly cause any reactions in Swedish culture. The couple are still married after 20 years.
5. In 2004, Helge Fossmo was also tried for the murder of his first wife, but was not convicted. The judge decided that there was not sufficient evidence (Peste 2011, 218).
6. John 4: 24: this expression is often used in Pentecostal contexts.
7. See 2 Corinthians 11: 2 and Revelation 21: 9–27.
8. This is forcefully denied by representatives and members of Knutby Filadelfia, and also by some ex-members.
9. This information was provided by Pastor Peter Gembäck and I have seen the written record of formal decision taken by social authorities regarding one of the families.
10. Concerning the other free churches, it is the denomination as such which is granted such rights, and it thereafter grants this right to pastors in the congregations. As the Pentecostal Movement was not organized as a denomination institutionally speaking, a special office, "the Marriage Committee" (Vigselnämnden), was created within the Pentecostal Movement, with the mission to grant individual pastors the right to perform marriages (Lindberg 1991, 274).

11. Salomonsson does not specify what he means by this, but it is probably the lifestyle of closeness between the members which means that the children are sometimes taken care of by other adults than the parents (to a greater extent than in mainstream society), and the alleged physical and psychological abuse referred to earlier in the chapter.
12. This congregation has since been readmitted to PAIC.
13. Barker discusses first-generation movements in general, but most of her research concerns new religious movements that became prominent in the 1960s and 1970s, such as the Unification Church (The Family Federation), ISKCON, the Church of Scientology, and the Children of God (The Family International).
14. A report from the National Board of Forensic Medicine suggests that Fossmo needs to develop insights about his personality deficiencies and nuance the picture he maintains of being a victim of "sect disease" (Rättsmedicinalverket, June 17, 2014).
15. There are many elaborations and historical contextualizations of this concept. See for instance Lotz (2001) for a brief summary.
16. This is a reflection Svensson herself seems to have made (Cristiansson 2004, 20–21).

References

Barker, Eileen. 2004. What Are We Studying? A Sociological Case for Keeping the 'Nova'. *Nova Religio* 8: 88–102.
Carlsson, Bertil. 2008. Organisationer och beslutsprocesser inom Pingströrelsen. Skrifter utgivna av Insamlingsstiftelsen för pingstforskning, no. 1.
Coleman, Simon. 2000. *The Globalisation of Charismatic Christianity: Spreading the Gospel of Prosperity*. Cambridge: Cambridge University Press.
Cristiansson, Terese. 2004. *Himmel och helvete: Mord i Knutby*. Stockholm: Bokförlaget DN.
Dahlberg, Karin, Helena Dahlberg, and Maria Nyström. 2008. *Reflective Lifeworld Research*. 2nd ed. Stockholm: Studentlitteratur.
Frisk, Liselotte, and Susan Palmer. 2015. The Life Story of Helge Fossmo, Former Pastor of Knutby Filadelfia, as Told in Prison: A Narrative Analysis Approach. *International Journal for the Study of New Religions* 6 (1): 51–73.
Lewis, James R., ed. 2011. *Violence and New Religious Movements*. Oxford/New York: Oxford University Press.
Lindberg, Alf. 1991. *Förkunnarna och deras utbildning: Utbildningsfrågan inom Pingströrelsen, Lewi Pethrus ideologiska roll och de kvinnliga förkunnarnas situation*. Lund: Lund University Press.
Lotz, Thomas A. 2001. 'Lifeworld': A Philosophical Concept and Its Relevance for Religious Education. In *Towards Religious Competence: Diversity as a Challenge*

for Education in Europe, ed. Hans-Günther Heimbrock, Christoph Th. Scheilke, and Peter Schreiner, 78–84. New Brunswick/London: Transaction Publishers.
Lundgren, Eva. 2008. *Knutbykoden*. Stockholm: Modernista.
Nielsen, Cecilia. 2013. Att forska om människors levda värld—en livsvärldsansats. In *Barn- och ungdomsforskning: Metoder och arbetssätt*, ed. Soly Erlandsson and Lena Sjöberg, 29–46. Lund: Studentlitteratur.
Norman, Helena. 2007. *Religion som medieberättelse: Expressens rapportering om Knutbyfallet*. Uppsala: Uppsala Universitet, religionshistoriska avdelningen.
Peste, Jonathan. 2011. Murder in Knutby: Charisma, Eroticism, and Violence in a Swedish Pentecostal Community. In *Violence and New Religious Movements*, ed. James R. Lewis, 217–229. Oxford: Oxford University Press.
Pingst - Fria församlingar i samverkan 2014. http://www.pingst.se/. Accessed 5 Sept 2014.
Rättsmedicinalverket. 2014. rapport 2014-06-17, dnr G 2014-Y0005.
Robèrt, Rigmor. 2004. Kristi brud bör träda fram. *Expressen*, April 8.
———. 2005a. Kristi bruds hemliga profetia ger förklaringar till mordet i Knutby. *Dagens medicin*, November 23. http://www.dagensmedicin.se/artiklar/2005/11/23/kristi-bruds-hemliga-profetia-ger-forklaringar-till-mordet-i-knutby-/. Accessed 28 Nov 2015.
———. 2005b. Barnmisshandel i Knutby församling. *Expressen*, October 18. http://www.expressen.se/debatt/barnmisshandel-i-knutby-forsamling/. Accessed 28 Nov 2015.
———. undated-a. Knutby del 7: Åsa Waldaus hemliga självprofetia. *Magasinet Paragraf*. https://www.magasinetparagraf.se/nyheter/knutby-artikel/42918-del-7-asa-waldaus-hemliga-sjalvprofetia/. Accessed 28 Nov 2015
———. undated-b. Barnen i Knutby. *Magasinet Paragraf*. https://www.magasinetparagraf.se/nyheter/kronikor/43420-barnen-i-knutby/. Accessed 28 Nov 2015.
Salomonsson, Dan. 2005. Tragedin som skakade Knutby. In *Pingströrelsens årsbok 2005*, 8–9. Stockholm: Pingströrelsens informationscentrum.
"Södermalmskyrkan mister vigselrätt." 1989. *Pingströrelsens årsbok 1989*, 6. Stockholm: Pingströrelsens informationscentrum.
Stark, Rodney, and William Sims Bainbridge. 1985. *The Future of Religion: Secularization, Revival, and Cult Formation*. Berkeley/Los Angeles/London: University of California Press.
Wahlström, Magnus. 2007. Fria församlingar och starka organisationer: Gemensamma verksamheter alternativ till samfund. In *Pingströrelsen: Verksamheter och särdrag under 1900-talet*, ed. Claes Waern and Jan-Åke Alvarsson, vol. 2, 301–316. Örebro: Libris förlag.
Waldau, Åsa M. 2007. *Kristi brud—vem kan man lita på?* Skara: Heja Sverige ABM.
Weber, Max. 1964. *The Theory of Social and Economic Organization*. Edited and with an introduction by Talcott Parsons. New York: The Free Press.

———. 1968. *Max Weber on Charisma and Institution Building: Selected Papers*. Edited and with an introduction by Shmuel. N. Eistenstadt. Chicago/London: University of Chicago Press

———. 1978. *Economy and Society: An Outline of Interpretive Sociology*. In , ed. Guenther Roth and Claus Wittich, vol. 2. Berkeley/Los Angeles: University of California Press.

INTERVIEWS AND INFORMAL CONVERSATIONS

Informal Conversations 1: Different members of the community 2011–2014. Notes were taken.

Informal Conversations 2: Pastor Peter Gembäck, 2011–2015. Notes were taken and the content has been checked with the Pastor.

Interview 1. Interview with Åsa Waldau, May 28, 2014.

Interview 2. Anonymized interview with a member, May 29, 2014.

Interview 4. Telephone interview with Pastor Peter Gembäck, July 22, 2015.

Interview 5. Telephone interview with Magnus Wahlström, the Pentecostal Movement, September 3, 2014.

Interviews 3. Several anonymized interviews with teenagers in Knutby Filadelfia, May 28–30, 2014, for the project Children in Minority Religions, sponsored by the Swedish Research Council.

Open Access This chapter is distributed under the terms of the Creative Commons Attribution 4.0 International License (http://creativecommons.org/licenses/by/4.0/), which permits use, duplication, adaptation, distribution and reproduction in any medium or format, as long as you give appropriate credit to the original author(s) and the source, provide a link to the Creative Commons license and indicate if changes were made.

The images or other third party material in this chapter are included in the chapter's Creative Commons license, unless indicated otherwise in a credit line to the material. If material is not included in the chapter's Creative Commons license and your intended use is not permitted by statutory regulation or exceeds the permitted use, you will need to obtain permission directly from the copyright holder.

PART 3

Novelties and Contemporary Innovation

CHAPTER 7

Faith Healing Revisited: A Charismatic Christian Intervention to the Therapy Culture in Finland

Tuija Hovi

Healing with the help of the Holy Spirit has traditionally been a pivotal theme in Pentecostal and Charismatic churches throughout the world. In recent decades, Pentecostalism in its various forms has rapidly expanded globally, raising interest and gaining more adherents, especially in Latin America, Asia, and Africa, though it still has a firm foothold in the Western world (see e.g., Anderson 2004). This expansion on every continent has been largely interpreted as a result of the cultural adaptability of Pentecostalism, especially of its doctrinal message, which focuses on healing. For instance, Candy Gunther Brown points out that the recognized limits of scientific biomedicine fuel therapeutic experimentation with divine healing, as they do with other alternative remedies, many of which invoke aid from personal or impersonal spiritual sources (Brown 2011, 8). Healing in diverse Pentecostal contexts is not understood only in medical terms but also in a more holistic way including, if not even requiring, an individual's personal spiritual transformation. Especially among the Third Wave Charismatics, the holistic understanding of healing also covers "this-worldly" material well-being. For this reason, the branch in question

T. Hovi (✉)
University of Turku, Turku, Finland

has been branded the Health and Wealth Gospel or Prosperity Theology by adherents of the established churches, as well as by Classic Pentecostals (cf. Brown 2011, 10).[1]

In the study of Christianity, the term "faith healing" is sometimes seen as ridiculing and pejorative. Brown, for her part, chooses "divine healing" instead, accepting the definition of the practitioners themselves, who wish to emphasize God's love instead of merely human faith or an impersonal spiritual force as a source of healing (Brown 2011, 4–5.) Nevertheless, without deliberately giving any value-laden connotations to the terms, I prefer to use "faith healing" as an umbrella term for the above-mentioned healings; that is, for those that are practiced with the help of prayer or other forms of ritual practices, including the notion of being in contact with a superhuman power. With "divine healing" I refer to healing in Christianity generally, whereas "charismatic healing" refers specifically to healing which is understood as a result of the gifts of the Holy Spirit (i.e. "charisms").

In this chapter, I focus on the relationships between well-being and religion in the context of the Christian intercessory prayer service called the Healing Rooms in present-day Finland.[2] The Healing Rooms (HR) concept was developed in its contemporary form in the 1990s in the United States, and has thereafter grown into a worldwide lay-based network. The underlying purpose of HR activity is evangelization and preparing people for the apocalyptic "end times," and to "save" as many as possible by awakening them to spiritual growth as Christian believers. However, this mission is not implemented by preaching, as is usually done in congregations and at revival meetings. Instead, it is carried out only implicitly by praying for people individually and privately, according to their personal requests. Intercessory prayer, as both a communal and private act, is an elementary part of Christian spirituality. The peculiarity of this prayer movement is the way in which the idea of intercession is put into practice: The HR operates at premises called "prayer clinics," giving the impression of spiritual health centers.

The central issue in this analysis concerns how traditional Christian notions and practices of divine healing, especially charismatic healing, fit modern Nordic society, with its highly developed and specialized healthcare system and psychologized therapy culture. I also explore how the international, originally American, HR has been accommodated in the traditionally Lutheran, but today rather secularized Finnish culture, and discuss how this interdenominational, lay-based organization defines and justifies its position in the country's religious landscape.

I begin with a short overview of the Christian scene in Finland to provide a backdrop to the context in which the HR operates. Thereafter, I move on to discuss the psychologization of culture and how it has been adopted by the national Christian scene, which comprises the context for my analysis. Next, I introduce the HR with a brief summary of its history and the basic idea of the practice, as well as the empirical material of the study. The description of the setting and procedure at the prayer clinics precedes the discussion on faith healing as an intervention to therapy culture. By the term "therapy culture," I mean the whole range of more or less psychologized, semi-professional practices that aim at creating better coping strategies for a more balanced, successful, and healthy life.

The Christian Scene in Contemporary Finland

In order to contextualize alternative and interdenominational or independent Christian practices, such as the HR, it is useful to employ a postsecular framework. This calls into perspective several factors that are helpful for understanding the HR's emergence: the resurgence of religion in the public sphere; the fragmentation of the religious landscape; and individualization, in terms of emphasis on personal needs. These processes have been recognized by Jürgen Habermas and many other scholars studying contemporary societies and the role of religion and spirituality in them (Habermas 2006; see also Bahram 2013; Moberg et al. 2012). What further characterizes religious life in contemporary Finland is increasing competition between traditional religious alternatives and other spiritual supply including westernized meditation and yoga pracices as well as New Age oriented energy healing and angel therapy, just to mention a few examples. This development intertwines with questions such as the complex relations between individualism and collectivism, and the various themes of believing, practicing, and belonging. Moreover, the boundaries of several sectors of knowledge, previously treated as juxtaposed—such as scientific, religious, esoteric, and knowledge of therapeutic discourses and practices—are blurring (cf. Utriainen et al. 2012).

The Christian scene in Finland is predominantly Protestant. The Catholic Church (ca. 12,000 members) and the Orthodox Church (ca. 60,000 members) have recently increased their membership numbers, mainly because of immigration, but their rates are still rather modest compared to the mainline church. Most Finns are members of the Evangelical Lutheran Church of Finland (ELC). At the end of 2016, the membership rate was 71.9 percent of a population of nearly 5.5 million inhabitants (ELC 2017). Actual participation in church activities, however, is considerably lower.

According to the latest quadrennial report of the ELC, based on data collected in 2012–2015, approximately 37 percent of church members participated in services at least once a year, Christmas Eve being the most popular liturgical occasion (ELC 2017; cf. Palmu et al. 2015, 93). Over the present decade, the membership rate of the ELC has gradually decreased. Nevertheless, the ELC still dominates the religious landscape. Even though it is not an institutional state church, it nevertheless plays a visible role in the country (cf. Nynäs et al. 2015, 15–16).[3] Contributing to society, it provides social welfare in the form of diaconal work, maintenance of cemeteries, and international humanitarian aid. The role of the ELC is also important in public debates, where its opinions are, on the one hand, often sought, but on the other, are also criticized. Today, the inclusive and multidimensional character of the ELC is visible also in that it is home to five Pietist-inspired revival-based movements: the Laestadians, the Awakened, the Evangelicals, the Beseechers, and Evangelical Neo-Pietism, or the Fifth Movement, as the last one is usually called in Finland. In addition, the more recent Charismatic Renewal and the Taizé-inspired Friends of Silence are nowadays active within the ELC.

Despite the ELC's dominant role and the solid tradition of old Pietist revival movements, one also finds various Charismatic Christian communities in the country. Pentecostalism was introduced in Finland during the first decade of the twentieth century, and is today the third largest religious group in the country. With approximately 46,000 members, the classic, lay-based, Pentecostal Movement is the largest revival movement outside the ELC, including 238 Finnish-speaking and 26 Swedish-speaking congregations. At present, 48 of the Finnish-speaking congregations are organized under the umbrella organization The Pentecostal Church of Finland (PCF), founded in 2002. The rest are independent and locally organized as registered associations. Despite such organizational division, the classic Pentecostal Movement is quite homogenous (ELC 2017; Ketola 2007, 34–35; PCF 2017; PingstFi 2017).

The Evangelical Free Church of Finland (EFCF), for its part, is a Finnish revival movement, which combines elements of Evangelical theology and Charismatic Christian practices. Historically, it was inspired by the American Holiness Movement of the nineteenth century, which was introduced to Finland through Sweden. The EFCF has been operating in Finland for over 120 years. This denomination consists of 100 local congregations around the country in Finland and one in Spain (EFCF 2017). Other denominations originated in the nineteenth century or earlier, but remain of minor significance to the Christian landscape; their growth leveled out quite some time ago. By contrast, the rapid growth of new independent congregations, from the 1980s onwards, has been notable. These communities mostly represent Third Wave Charismatic Christianity. The number of these congregations is currently estimated to be over 100. However, the instability and mobility in the Charismatic scene makes it very difficult to give exact figures (Hovi 2009; Ketola 2007).

In sum, it is hardly appropriate to call Charismatic Christianity a single "movement," classified in terms of the sociological church/sect typology, considering all its global diversity both inside and outside the older churches (cf. Anderson 2010, 13; Beyer 2003, 373). Likewise, in Finland, it is a Christian spiritual trend that exists both inside and outside the ELC. There is, on the one hand, a vibrant congregational field inhabited by numerous independent local communities and evangelizing organizations. On the other hand, the Charismatic Renewal and similar alternative activities are found within the mainline church, albeit to varying degrees of organization and autonomy (Hovi 2009; Hovi and Haapalainen 2015).

Psychologized Discourse and Therapy Culture

The psychologization of everyday life—including religious life—takes place when ordinary people reflect upon themselves and their environment in accordance with psychological models, without primarily seeing psychology as a scholarly discipline. Psychologization can thus be defined as "psychological vocabulary and psychological explanatory schemes entering fields which are supposed not to belong to the traditional and practical terrains of psychology" (De Vos 2012). The breakthrough of psychologization and therapeutization in Finland is said to have happened with the help of historian Juha Siltala's studies on the anxiety disorder growing out of the Finnish mentality and culture (Siltala 1992) and the masculine conceptions of honor, which focused on the culturally inherited need of the Finnish man to overcome shame through success and achievements (Siltala 1994). In addition to Siltala's psychohistorical interpretations of Finnish mentality, a trilogy of studies on different aspects of "psycho-culture" by sociologist Janne Kivivuori in the 1990s ignited critical discussion on the psychologization of everyday life. According to Kivivuori, by the end of the 1980s, popular psychology had become increasingly visible in many ways, above all in the media, societal debate, commercial life, and everyday conversation in Finland (Kivivuori 1991; Kivivuori 1996).

Psychological concepts and ideas of emotional and social coping have also been adopted in religious discourses in various parts of the world, particularly in North America. One example is therapeutically inclined Christian counseling. The realms of medical care, psychological therapies, and spiritual coaching overlap in many Christian communities, especially those focusing on healing. Anthropologist Pamela E. Klassen has shown how North American liberal Protestants renewed theologies and pastoral care by combining psychological and Charismatic Christian approaches to the self. According to Klassen, as "diagnosticians of the moral self," such groups combined ideas of faith healing, Charismatic Renewal, and psychology (Klassen 2011, xxii). While she describes the beginning of the Charismatic Renewal among Anglicans, Episcopalians, and Roman Catholics in the United States and Canada in the 1960s, she also points out analogies to what today may be called mindfulness. One example is the "habitual fourfold process," with its focus on holistic healing. This process was employed in preparing Christians for God's healing power. The recommended process included (1) daily relaxation, (2) reminding oneself of life outside oneself, (3) inviting that life to increase in one's own body, (4) visualizing one's body, or for the more advanced, forgetting one's body and, instead, concentrating on the spiritual energies of God (Klassen 2011, 146). Furthermore, instead of seeing the subconscious merely as the site of demonic activity, as suggested earlier by the influential Catholic theologian Paul Tillich, the subconscious came to be regarded as a human resource to be trained and utilized as "a control center under orders of God" (Klassen 2011, 145–146).

Similar tendencies have been noted in studies of pastoral counseling and Christian therapy groups in Finland. Kivivuori recognized the psychologizing trend emerging also in the mainline Lutheran church (Kivivuori 1999), tracing the origins of the psychologized pastoral counseling to the idea of the "surgery of the soul" based upon the Oxford Group Movement of the 1930s and the Moral Re-armament Movement's principles. According to those principles, the criteria for authenticity of an individual's faith are the authenticity and health of his or her personality which can be restored in a close social interaction during pastoral counseling. Moreover, social and often emotional problems can be solved by guiding individuals to convert to the Christian faith (Kivivuori 1999, 67).

In Finland, psychologization discourse has paved the way for contemporary therapy culture and has since become integrated in everyday speech and thinking (Ihanus 2005). Psychological concepts like "searching inside oneself," "identity-work," "personal development," "spiritual growth," "self-realization," "depression," "trauma," and "therapy," have become practically self-evident in contemporary public discourse and everyday life. In the Evangelical Lutheran Church in the twentieth century, psychologization became visible, especially in pastoral care and diaconia (i.e. the established charitable work of the ECL), as more elements from psychotherapy were adopted. Gradually, religious discourse in general has absorbed more psychologically framed conceptualizations. For instance, instead of provoking a sense of guilt, psychologically oriented churches prefer to speak of health and authenticity, or of illness or pain instead of sin. One way to update religious life is, indeed, to change one's way of talking about it (cf. Pietikäinen 2000).

In Charismatic Christianity, for its part, its idea of holistic healing—covering physical, emotional, social, and spiritual well-being—makes it obviously easier for its members to adapt to a psychologized culture. A language of, for example, health and authenticity goes hand in hand with the idea of a benevolent God as opposed to a punishing one. Healing Rooms prayer clinics illustrate one way in which such discourse can be operationalized and utilized for purposes of evangelization in contemporary psychologized and postsecular Finnish society.

The Global and Local Healing Rooms

Third Wave Charismatic Christianity is difficult to categorize into colloquial categories such as "conservative" or "radical," seeing as it combines components traditionally associated with both, even though these labels refer to categories usually perceived as opposites.[4] In the first place, the acceptance of fundamentalist principles, such as a firm belief in the authority and inerrancy of the Bible, is a component that may be labeled "conservative." The Neo-Charismatic worldview also includes God and Devil as good and evil personified, as well as believing in the existance of evil spirits. At the same time, however, all Charismatics are radical in their view of revelation as continuous, and their expectations of new manifestations of God's power through the Spirit (Chryssides 1999, 123). The latter quality gives space for modernization and new interpretations of sacred text. Furthermore, there is a strong emphasis on individualism, personal growth, and healing, which makes Charismatic Christian healing movements an integral part of the cultural "subjective turn" (cf. Heelas and Woodhead 2005).

This ambivalence is also evident in the Healing Rooms, where biblical fundamentalism is represented in the sense of retaining the "biblical truth," as in Pentecostal and Charismatic Christianity. Focusing on the idea of divine healing and the opportunity for lay intercessors to use their personal gifts of the Holy Spirit to help others by mediating divine healing power, the HR promotes salient aspects of Neo-Charismatic thinking. Besides, their international networking, adaptable organization structures, and active use of digital media for advocating their message, link the HR closely to the fluid trend of Neo-Charismatic or Neo-Pentecostal Christianity (cf. Anderson 2010, 19–20). However, it is difficult to categorize the HR merely as a Pentecostal organization, as it operates across denominational boundaries.

The International Association of the Healing Rooms was founded in 2001, but the origins of this particular prayer service date back to the first decades of the last century. The idea was launched by John Lake, a Pentecostal pastor in Spokane, Washington state. Lake's healing meetings were discontinued soon after his death in 1935 and remained so for several decades. However, his ideas were revived in the 1990s by another Pentecostal pastor, Cal Pierce, who started spreading Lake's ideas by founding local HR prayer clinics, which is the name he gave this type of intercession service. Since then, the HR has spread rapidly to every continent, taking advantage of already existing and functioning local Christian infrastructure, but the headquarters of the movement remain in Spokane. Typically, the prayer clinics operate in churches and congregations.

In Finland, the HR is a newcomer in the religious landscape. It was intentionally imported to Finland and systematically launched by a Neo-Pentecostal married couple who got to know the prayer clinic service whilst on holiday in California, when they visited a local Vineyard congregation in Santa Barbara. After having negotiated with several pastors and Christian community leaders, they finally founded the first Finnish prayer clinic a year later, following the model of Spokane. Since 2006, 34 prayer clinics have been established around the country (Healing Rooms Finland 2017). In Finland, the HR prayer clinics are, for the most part, connected to classic Pentecostal and EFCF congregations, or to the mainline ELC. Still, a prayer clinic may also be located in nonreligious surroundings like shopping malls, municipal facilities such as club apartments, or in other public premises. Occasionally, prayer clinics are also arranged outdoors, especially during cultural events. In any context, the idea is that a prayer clinic should be accessible to everyone. According to this principle, an HR prayer clinic is never located in an actual church building because of the institutional framing, which may be alienating to many Finns, seeing as church attendance is generally low despite high membership rates.

The mission of the Finnish HR leaders has been to build cooperative relationships, above all with the ELC, to be able to launch the idea of prayer clinics across the country. Surprisingly, prayer clinics are hardly ever connected to any Neo-Charismatic congregation but only to more established Christian organizations.

Recently, the mission of the Finnish leaders to systematically plant HR further has resulted in a few prayer clinics opening in the neighboring countries Estonia and Sweden. However, there seems to be a greater interest in the HR in Estonia—where seven prayer clinics operate on regular basis—than in Sweden, where only two prayer clinics provide services (Healing Rooms Estonia 2017; Healing Rooms Sweden 2017). In addition, the HR Finnish leaders introduced the HR practice in Norway in 2014. They have also organized several meetings for European HR leaders (Laitinen 2013, 4).

Material

The empirical material was compiled at the turn of 2010 and 2011 by using ethnographic methods, such as interviews and participant observation. I interviewed 30 prayer team members representing five prayer clinics in different districts, including the leading married couple in Espoo, in the headquarters of the Finnish branch. The interviews were semi-structured with open-ended questions. The questions revolved around processes of becoming a practitioner and working at prayer clinics. I also asked the interviewees to tell me about their background, their personal motivations, and intentions as intercessors. The discussion with each interviewee took on average 1.5 hours. The oldest of the interviewees was a man born in 1937, and the youngest a man born in 1977. Most were middle-aged or recently retired, born in the 1940s and 1950s. Women make up the majority of the intercessors at the prayer clinics, and of the interviewees; 19 of them were women and 11 men. One third of the interviewees were Pentecostals while the majority were Lutherans. One elderly couple came from the Seventh-day Adventist Church and two from Neo-Charismatic congregations, while one local team leader represented the Free Church (EFCF). The age and gender groups as well as religious affiliations of the interviewees correspond quite well with the distribution of prayer team members in general in the Finnish Healing Rooms.

Important contextual information was obtained through participant observation. I visited clinical receptions as a client, naturally informing the prayer team members about my research interests.[5] I was warmly welcomed without any explicitly expressed hesitations concerning my academic intentions. I also visited homes where I interviewed prayer team members, and I received an opportunity to attend a closed meeting of a local prayer team. During my fieldwork, the first Nordic Healing Room conference took place in Helsinki, where I attended the event.

A short questionnaire was also distributed to the visitors at every prayer clinic in the country in May 2011, the number of which was 23 at that time. The purpose of the survey was to provide information on the background and experiences of HR clients. Since the questionnaire was distributed via the prayer clinics, it excluded those clients who had visited a prayer clinic only once and, for one reason or another, did not return. However, the received responses (N = 124) gave an impression of the prayer clinics having both regular and occasional visitors. Most of them—74.19 percent—belonged to the mainline ELC, like the majority of Finns. The rest identified as Pentecostals, Free Church members, or Charismatics. It was no big surprise that 78 percent of the respondents participated more or less regularly in Charismatic events, mostly in the context of the ELC. Most of the respondents were women (71 percent). The largest age group was people aged between 36 and 45 years (31.45 percent). Interestingly, few were below 30 or above 60 years of age; both very young and very old were absent. Thus, the HR clientele in the study represent people of working age (see also Hovi 2012).

The Individualized Prayer Service: Setting

The prayer team members consider the intercession service they provide to be very different than intercessiory prayers in congregational contexts. First of all, HR intercession is completely lay-based. However, it is still highly structured, thoroughly controlled, and carried out only by trained intercessors, unlike the intercessions by priests as a part of Sunday services in congregations. The HR arranges a two-day training course on the principles of the prayer service, which is a prerequisite for becoming a member of a prayer team. The Finnish training package has been created upon the principles of the headquarters in Spokane. The training course consists of learning the "biblical basis" for the intercessory prayer as well as demonstrations and exercises. All prayer team members are required to be committed believers and are expected to be actively involved in their home churches, which has to be proven by a pastor's recommendation. They are also interviewed by local team leaders to make sure that they understand and accept the HR rules before they are allowed to start working at a prayer clinic.

Openness and intimacy at HR clinics were also underlined as significant differences when compared to congregational contexts. The prayer team members emphasized the importance of the low threshold; a client's religious background is not enquired into, the personal intercession is carried out in private, and there is no obligation for action on the part of the client. A male prayer team member in his late thirties described the HR principles and the unique setting at prayer clinics in this way:

> Well, there are many [aspects] in it. First of all: this method. It is like the idea that anyone, I mean any Christian believer can be a part of this work. This is not only for pastors or … or for those who are in charge of certain activities or somehow with a special status in a congregation […] Anyone can take the training course and come with, anyone who has a vocation for it. And yes, there is the good training for this work, clear ground rules. It guarantees such safety, that even though there are very different persons involved, there are always those rules to be followed, and there are leaders at the clinics [to make sure that they are followed]. It provides safety for this work. And of course, there is a difference also in the way people are provided a very personal prayer service. This does not take place at an altar or in public, but privately so that nobody else can hear what is prayed for. […] And I can also add that you can come just to be prayed for, there is no need to participate in anything else or listen to a sermon or anything like that. You can come like you go to the doctor's and receive this prayer service. […] And if I may continue, it is also [the fact] that there is always a team that prays, it also provides a kind of safety, and I believe that it also provides God's presence when there are several people praying. It is actually based on God's word, like "where two or three gather in my name, there am I with them." Jesus put it like this and it's also a good thing. (IF mgt 2011/016: 2)[6]

Before the actual clinical reception opens to clients, the prayer teams prepare by praising and praying by themselves for an hour. This meditative get-together helps them to concentrate on their task and to be present for the clients. The members whom I interviewed regard this preparation time as a necessary step to enable them to take on the role as mediator, to be a "channel" between God and client, as they call themselves. After having done their spiritual preparations, the team members form groups of three intercessors. Serving as a prayer team practitioner does not require any specific outfit. The appearance of intercessors is expected to be casual, clean, and neutral, and they are advised not to use any perfumes because of possible allergies. The only visible sign that someone is a team member is a name tag with his or her first name on it.

The local HR clinics are arranged once a week or fortnightly, always at the same time: 18.30–20.30. In the prayer clinic, there is a waiting room where the clients wait for their turn to be prayed for in separate "prayer rooms." While clients wait for their turn, the receptionist gives them a form to fill in. Having written down their prayer requests, they are individually invited into a prayer room, where a team of three members spends 10–20 minutes praying for them, according to their request. The ideal prayer group consists of both men and women. The purpose of this arrangement is to ensure a safe and comfortable atmosphere for everyone. It is said to be ideal that at least one of the prayer team members represents the sex of the person to be prayed for. In addition, it is not desirable that clients either pick and choose certain persons to serve them, or that prayer team members refuse clients on the basis of their sex.

In the course of one clinic session, there are usually on average 10 clients and two-to-four groups working for them, depending on the location. The local prayer clinics are not encouraged to prolong the regular reception time of two hours in cases where a large group of people awaits intercession. Instead, the length of each prayer is adapted to the number of clients; the higher the number, the shorter the personal prayer service. Correspondingly, when they are only a few, the intercessions may last longer than 10 minutes. This arrangement is meant to keep the practice controlled and save the energy of the volunteer team members. In case no client appears, team members spend the time praying for each other or some general cause.

The Individualized Prayer Service: Encountering a Client

At a prayer clinic, two groups of people encounter one another. On the one hand, there is the inner-circle community of carefully selected and trained prayer team members and, on the other, there are clients, people who visit the prayer clinic in order to be prayed for. Even though it is of utmost importance that the prayer team members are "born-again" Christian believers, clients are not required to disclose their religious affiliations or to confess anything unless they wish to. The underlying purpose, however, is to spiritually awaken clients, but only in a way that respects their privacy. During one interview with a female respondent, I asked how she would guide a person who checks the "I don't know" box regarding whether she or he is a believer or not. She responded:

> Yeah, we may perhaps ask if he or she would like to know more. Nothing like ... we never try to push or impose [...] It is easy to see very quickly if the person is not receptive and then just pass it. But normally, people experience the prayer situation as a good thing, even if they are not at all aware of the things concerning the faith because it is the Holy Spirit that works there. We are, of course, just instruments, we only mediate God's love and his presence and it works in a client in a positive way, praying for another person. (IF mgt 2011/014: 3)

Team members are often reminded by the leaders that the conversation between intercessor and client is meant to be minimal, discreet, and highly confidential. The clients' prayer requests often deal with problems either in their physical, social, or emotional life. Examples may be an illness, a bodily disorder, or depression, but clients also bring up many other kinds of everyday issues, such as domestic problems as well as difficulties in working life, which they wish to be resolved through prayer. All these individual needs and problems are regarded as equally important in relation to a person's spiritual development, and each of them are prayed for in the hope of divine healing (Hovi 2012, 137). It is also explicitly emphasized that the HR service is not intended to replace pastoral counseling, which is regarded as a task that requires professional competence. Praying for various problems is the only service provided at the HR clinics, and in case they have other needs, clients are advised to turn to their home congregations, physicians, or other professionals.

Taking the postsecular culture into consideration, a certain neoliberal and individualist flavor can be sensed in the way the practice is arranged with an emphasized "customer orientation." The prayer team members themselves like to use that expression to highlight their discreet and gentle approach. This approach means that they are allowed to pray only according to the client's request and nothing more. Nor are prayer team members allowed to make a client feel guilty—an approach that differs radically from that of the old Nordic Pietism, as well as from traditional Pentecostalism. However, since spreading the Word and gaining new followers for Jesus is the underlying purpose, conversion is often incorporated as an implicit wish in a prayer for the Holy Spirit to "touch" clients also spiritually while healing their bodily disorders. According to the prayer team members, holistic well-being must include a Christian way of life; any transformation promoting that is interpreted as healing (e.g. Hovi 2013, 201).

The leading couple of the Finnish HR accentuated the importance of cultural sensitivity in launching the practice successfully. According to them, the setting of the prayer clinic has intentionally been arranged to fit the Finnish reserved mentality as well as the Lutheran culture. A client must be treated in a calm and discreet manner, so for instance, praying in tongues is not allowed in the presence of a client, because it may make him or her feel uneasy. Needless to say, glossolalia is not included in the Lutheran tradition, and it often provokes resistance in the active attendees of the mainline church. The general cultural rules for proximity are also consciously taken into account and respected, even though the same rules are not as relevant in the Pentecostal tradition. For example, the laying on of hands is a typical and widely used ritual gesture especially for blessing and healing in Pentecostalism (e.g. Cox 1995, 109). However, at the HR prayer clinics, clients are not physically touched without being asked for permission. Even though a prayer clinic allows both men and women to work together and on equal terms, a prayer team member is not supposed to touch a client of the opposite sex at all. This privacy-respecting conduct is explained as taking into account that clients may have personal reasons for not wishing to be touched; these include the possibility that a client may have traumatic memories of sexual abuse, or of other forms of violence that are too painful to be broached.

On the whole, the atmosphere at a prayer clinic is meant to be safe and comfortable and not judgmental—clients may not come back if they are treated aggressively. Approaching holistic healing as a gradual and time-consuming process, the clinics make clients welcome to visit as many times as they like and feel the need to.

Faith Healing Revisited: Holistic Treatment

As the name of the HR practice suggests, it is focused on holistic well-being. The method used for this purpose is praying for the clients. As the prayer team members put it in order to explain the function of their work, they are "channeling" the power of the Holy Spirit by actively using their "gifts." Strangely enough, the gift of healing was hardly ever mentioned by the interviewees. Rather, they often described situations when they had instead used the gifts of prophecy and words of knowledge while praying for others. Without exception, all interviewees emphasized their role in the healing process as instrumental; they did not want to be identified as "healers." This attitude obviously reflects the internalized HR instructions emphasizing the intercessors' status as mere mediators.

The meaning and function of the HR, as compared to those of the numerous other Christian organizations which offer corresponding supportive spiritual services, was very clear to the prayer team members whom I met. Even though they were familiar with healing through prayer, they saw intercession at the HR clinics as unique, and as such, a supplement to what is offered to people in other churches and congregations, such as pastoral care. Healing as a holistic process, covering physical as well as psychological and spiritual aspects of the individual, was seen as a potential starting point for the clients' journey towards personal Christian faith. As I asked one of my interviewees how she would define the meaning of the HR prayer clinics in her own words, she responded:

> Well, it's like bringing healing and wholeness to people … anybody can come to be prayed for, you don't have to be a believer. Basically, it is that you could find Jesus Christ as your savior that is the most important thing. Anyway, but God wants to heal you, and it's often so that when you have a chance to experience healing, you also start to look for Jesus in your life, because that's where the help comes from. […] I take it as a holistic healing. A human being heals only after getting completely whole as the result of becoming a believer, but he or she can feel improvement already here. (IF mgt 2011/014: 2)

When I asked about the main concern of the HR, and whether it was the body or the soul, I often received the answer: both equally. Since people are perceived of as psychosocial beings, the interviewees did not want to separate these elements in their prayer, which is understood as a divine assignment. They often took illness and pain as somatization of unsolved emotional difficulties connected to a nonfunctional spiritual life, "being away from God." Bodily disorders as well as mental and spiritual troubles were seen as being so tightly interwoven that the prayer team members found it difficult to distinguish between them. The most analytical account was given by an active prayer team member who was a neurologist by profession:

> Well, we hope, of course, soul. And I wouldn't even like to care for the mind there. I think mental care belongs to the psychiatrists. But naturally, we can pray for it and for healing, but we do not care for the mind at the prayer clinic. And the body … we don't actually *cure* anything else either, we just pray, we give prayer service. But perhaps … we don't really treat the soul either, it doesn't belong to us. We give prayer service and we hope that above all the soul would feel better afterwards. (IF mgt 2011/073: 15)

He also emphasized the idea of holism and drew a strict line between his professional work at the hospital and what he does at a prayer clinic:

> I distinguish between my work and what happens in the Healing Rooms, completely. Here [at the hospital] I strictly represent medical science [...] and there [at the prayer clinic] I see it purely as a spiritual process. So, I don't see here any paradox with regards to my work, but there I practice my faith as I have the legal right to do. And, well, I think that the healing that happens there, it is purely a spiritual thing. (IF mgt 2011/073: 13)

An important theme in Charismatic Christian healing narratives are "wounds of the soul." The term refers to how a variety of unsolved, traumatic earlier experiences can be encapsulated in bodily pains, as well as in mental disorders. "Inner healing" and "becoming whole" are prominent issues in the HR prayer clinics, too, as they are in Charismatic healing in general (cf. Matulevicius 2015). The members recognized, in many cases, problems deriving from clients' early childhood:

Interviewee: There are quite a lot of such troubles that people go through, [like] troubles in their childhood and in their relationship to their mother. There are a lot of such cases. So, they understand now what they missed as a child, because it was as it was. Then we, in a way, help them in that situation [...].
Tuija: That's interesting, the relationship to mother and childhood home, that it comes up like that, as you said. If you think of the age distribution among the clients ... they are people whose parents experienced the war.
Interviewee: Yes, that's right. Then, the culture of parenting was really rough in Finland. I am a specialist in upbringing by profession and I know, considering the emotional development of a child, what the results are, when there is not attention and space for children's emotions, and how the self-esteem, self-confidence is built up. In a way, they have to pick up the pieces, for instance, still at the age of 60. (IF mgt 2011/051)

Unresolved traumatic experiences constitute an intentional focus in the prayer service. The theme in the interview excerpt above corresponds to what anthropologist Thomas Csordas has analyzed as "healing the memories" in his study on Charismatic Catholic healing groups (cf. Csordas 1997, 109). In these groups, the procedure was considerably different, being more verbally interactive, and included pastoral care conversations and visualization of the Virgin Mary as healer of the participants' inner wounds. By contrast, in the Protestant HR rhetoric, it is Jesus who is seen as the gentle supporter and healer (Hovi 2013, 199).

Controversial Border-crossings

George Chryssides has pointed out that New Age and Charismatic Christian "holistic health therapies" share certain similarities. Both camps propagate the idea of "making people whole" in ways that cannot be offered by biomedicine. Regarding the differences between the two, in New Age healing, the methods of therapy are much more diverse. The "suppliers" offer a wide range of choices to their clients, not necessarily presupposing any particular belief system. In Christian traditions, "healers" (like the prayer team members in the HR) insist that their work is grounded in the healing power of Jesus Christ, that they are continuing the healing ministry in his name, and that praise and thanks must be offered to him (Chryssides 2000, 66; Neitz 2012).

The HR has been criticized in Finland, above all in Christian circles. Some confrontations take place locally among different Christian communities. As the HR crosses organizational boundaries and disregards conventional modes of operation, the movement is at times perceived as a menace to established forms of Christianity. In many fundamentalist circles, especially in Neo-Charismatic communities, there is aggressive critique of everything with a New Age flavor, even though, or perhaps because, many New Age practitioners propagate the same ideals as those communities, like well-being, a good life, and prosperity—ideals that nevertheless are promoted and understood on different grounds, interpreted with different rhetoric, and framed within another belief system. According to the Charismatic Christian logic, New Age practices are simply viewed as being based on an incorrect and spiritually dubious framework: they are "unbiblical." As an indication of this concern, the HR has even been criticized for representing New Age ideas because it propagates "healing" in its English name, rather than the vernacular terms commonly used in connection with Christian healing practices in Finland.[7] For the same reason, it has been interpreted as being occult, heretical, and delusional, as well as "too American." Above all, this kind of critique can be found in Christian chat forums and blogs on the Internet.⁸ The leaders of the HR in Finland have responded to the criticism by saying that the concept of healing was stolen by New Age thinkers, and that the HR, by contrast, actually wants to rehabilitate the concept by bringing it back to its original biblical meaning:

> We think that real healing comes from Jesus, but the New Age movement has stolen it. We want to bring it back to its original context. And another sector where we probably are criticized is that we actually work within the New Age sector. We go to these New Age fairs and happenings and open up prayer clinics there, yeah, and there, more than anywhere, reach the people who are searching! (IF mgt 2011/106: 20)

Meredith McGuire has indicated that the idea of healing, which is so characteristic of New Age thinking, seems to have roots in the spiritual New Thought (or Mind Cure) movement that emerged from transcendentalism and the thinking of Emmanuel Swedenborg, and has also been adopted by several healing-centered Christian organizations like, for instance, Christian Science (McGuire 2008, 133). Such historical links mean very little if anything to Charismatics, but accusations by more established Christian communities against a new Christian movement for representing the New Age movement is typical in situations where new kinds of rhetoric or new forms of action are being introduced, even when the basic biblical message is the same. The present situation, in other words, seems to support Stephen Hunt's observation that there appears to be a widespread need to protect a "symbolic universe of meaning" which underpins the attitude toward other religious groups in terms of boundary maintenance. As suggested by Hunt, this is especially prevalent in Charismatic Christian healing practices (Hunt 2000, 43).

To propagate their interpretation of biblical healing, following Jesus' work as an example, the HR prayer teams introduce their work programmatically at annual New Age events in Finland, the Fair of the Spirit and the Knowledge, and the I Am Fair (Body-Mind-Spirit). These are events at which various New Age practitioners present their services for a couple of days each year. The Finnish leaders of the HR explained that these events are an important forum for the HR, too. They take it as an opportunity to win new followers for Christianity by using the appealing theme of healing, which is a playground for mutual interaction. This supports what Harvey Cox has pointed out; among Charismatics, there is a certain concern, at times even anxiety, about the emergence of non-Christian spiritualities. Their answer to the challenge is healing—in its Christian meaning, making a person "whole in Christ." The message of holistic healing is used as a gateway through which new recruits are expected to enter the movement (Cox 2011, xviii). For the HR, one way of branching out has been participation in annual New Age events, thereby offering a Christian alternative to potential "seekers."

Positioning itself as undertaking biblical missionary work fighting non-Christian spirituality as well as secular ways of life, the HR crosses and blurs the borders of traditional Pentecostal evangelization methods. As another example of modernized outreach, in April 2014, the monthly newsletter of the Finnish HR informed its members about the summer activities that would take place while the prayer clinics were taking a break. All regular prayer clinics in the country are closed for a couple of months in summer. During this time, there is, for instance, an HR cruise on the Baltic Sea, which had already become an annual tradition by 2014. During the cruise, there is an HR program for the group, buffet meals, and some free time for shopping or going to the spa, as is customary on Baltic Sea cruises. However, the free time is not only for leisure. It is also an opportunity for "healing the sick on board," which could mean praying silently for passengers, as well as interacting with them (Healing Rooms kuulumiset 2014). This outreach is another example of how the HR has quite radically brought Pentecostal faith healing out of its typical congregational context and revival meetings, and attempted to redefine it as a contemporary Christian well-being practice integrated into modern ways of life.

An Intervention in Post-secular Therapy Culture

In their theory of the spiritual revolution, Paul Heelas and Linda Woodhead (2005) argue that interest in so-called "subjective life spirituality" is growing faster than for traditional religions. Today, well-being practices that combine Westernized Eastern traditions such as yoga, meditation, life coaching, and mindfulness, are turning into alternatives or supplements to the already established therapy culture, which draws upon more or less scientific-psychological conceptualizations. Historian of religion Anne-Christine Hornborg has recognized such holistic healing as a trend in the present decade in Swedish society. According to Hornborg, finding and developing one's inner self with the help of life coaches and lay therapists has become a means of improving one's quality of life in holistic ways (Hornborg 2012, 18). In Finland, the same trend is visible. Spiritually inspired therapeutic and coaching practices are based on various traditions from ancient religions and philosophies (such as meditation and yoga based on Buddhist and Vedic traditions) as well as New Age therapies (reiki, angel therapy etc.) or on ideas of modern psychology, for instance neurolinguistic programming and cognitive psychology. The current trend of mindfulness, however, draws on both sources, spiritual and psychological ones.

Similarly, increasing interest in self-awareness and personal growth are not exclusive to alternative, non-Christian, spiritual practices. Sociologist Mary Jo Neitz has pointed out that the Charismatic Catholic Renewal and the psychologically inspired self-awareness movement have a great deal in common. In both movements, people are expected to grow and develop their potential. This is achieved by getting in touch with one's "real self," with God, with a higher consciousness, or with a different reality. In addition, personal growth is seen as a key to social progress (Neitz 2012, 20). It can also be interpreted as seeking spiritual authenticity, which is regarded as a prerequisite for holistic health.

The rise of fundamentalist and conservative forms of religiosity during the last couple of decades has been viewed as a set of reactions to the often confusing postsecular trends in religious life: First, conservative religious attitudes have been interpreted as a reaction to globalization, which dissolves the autonomy of national institutions, traditional organizations, and communication systems. Second, they have been viewed as a reaction to cultural flexibility, which blurs the boundaries of membership and involvement in religious life. Finally, they have been considered to be a reaction to the perceived crisis of the patriarchal family (Frisk and Nynäs 2012, 57). Despite the apparent paradox, the combination of conservative Charismatic Christianity and postsecular complexity in Finland seems to be functioning quite smoothly. Similar observations have been made in other parts of the world. Many Neo-Charismatic Christian movements and organizations move with ease between the twenty-first-century ideals of globalization, individualism, and even neoliberalism. For example, anthropologist Birgit Meyer has interpreted the global growth of the Prosperity Gospel as an expression of neoliberalism, and its missionary activities as an intentionally globalizing project (Meyer 2010, 114).

However, the HR does not represent the hardcore Prosperity Gospel, with the latter's strong emphasis on material wealth as a sign of God's blessing. Yet, in response to having been criticized as "Americanizing," the Finnish HR practice has been purposely rethought and polished so as to be more culturally acceptable. According to the leaders of the Healing Rooms Finland, the movement is "culturized," as they put it, into the secular Lutheran milieu. Ecstatic worship or aggressive proselytization may invite negative reactions and thus be counterproductive. Instead of open evangelization, a carefully considered management technique, strategic planning, customer orientation, and the interest in a new type of interdenominational cooperation have been adopted in order to more easily adapt the HR to neoliberal postsecular Nordic culture. Being a global network with a flexible organization structure that transcends social, organizational, and institutional boundaries between Christian denominations, the HR offers a new kind of involvement that accommodates individual as well as collective activity for lay people (cf. Martikainen et al. 2015, 80–83). For prayer team members, it offers an active role for spiritual self-actualization, and a coherent and democratic community of believers. For clients, a prayer clinic serves as a forum to be used without obligations or commitments. It offers easily accessible, time-efficient, discreet, and individual care. It is free of charge, and nothing is demanded in return. It is simply a place to visit when spiritual care or treatment is needed to solve a problem or to feel better.

Conclusions

I have presented the HR as a Christian intervention and reaction to postsecular and psychologized culture on the basis of the movement's mode of operation as a spiritual health center. It draws close to the forms and means of contemporary Western customer-oriented therapy culture, which combines the search for well-being and everyday problem-solving with personal spiritual transformations. Unlike counseling based on psychotherapy, the prayer clinic service does not attempt to provide conversational counseling, even though this is sometimes expected by clients. Instead, it is a Christian spiritual practice based on the idea of "channeling" divine power with the help of intercessors' Charismatic gifts in order to heal a person holistically. It is tailored to support people with their, often emotionally difficult, everyday problems involving health and well-being. Even though the ultimate function and purpose of this practice is strictly religious, its actual implementation is carried out in a way that uses modern, popular psychological approaches as well as Christian spirituality.

Notes

1. In this chapter, I use several overlapping labels referring to Pentecostal and Charismatic Christianity. By "Pentecostalism" I mean the whole Pentecostal culture in its all diversity, whereas "Classic" or "Traditional" Pentecostalism is used for the movement with roots in the Azusa Street revival at the beginning of the last century. In Finland, Classic Pentecostalism was planted remarkably early, and has attained status as an established church. "Charismatic Christianity" refers to the accentuated role and meaning of the "Gifts of the Holy Spirit" in everyday religious life, as well as a current in Christianity—among Protestants and Catholics—often represented by lay-led activities within established churches. With "Neo-Charismatic" and "Neo-Pentecostal," I refer to the trend of independent congregations and churches that emerged in the United States as a result of Third Wave Pentecostalism during the 1980s and '90s, often characterized by doctrinal emphasis on health and material prosperity (cf. Anderson 2010, 19–20). However, in Finland, Neo-Pentecostalism has a slightly different meaning, pointing specifically to the renewal within the Pentecostal Movement in the 1970s, and its impact on activities within the Evangelical Lutheran Church later on. "Neo-Charismatic Movement" refers to the field of independent congregations that has appeared since the 1990s. In spite of these national nuances, I use these labels as more or less synonymous in this chapter. Moreover, "fundamentalism" is used to denote a meaning system that relies exclusively upon a sacred text, in this case literalistic interpretation of the Bible, whereas a movement labeled as "conservative" emphasizes reluctance to accept reform and innovation.
2. The study of the Healing Rooms at hand was funded by the Academy of Finland (2011–2013) and was simultaneously one of the case studies of the Center of Excellence project *Post-secular Culture and Changing Religious Landscape in Finland 2010–2014* at Åbo Akademi University in Turku.
3. As Finland was a part of Sweden until 1809, there was a state church tradition there as well, and the Lutheran Church held that position until 1870. The close ties between church and state started to loosen up in the nineteenth century because of European ideological influences: the Pietist revival movements and liberalism (Ketola 2008, 61). This means that the separation between church and state had already taken place in Finland before it gained national independence, during its period of autonomy within the Russian regime (1809–1917). The corresponding separation of church and state in Sweden was carried out only 130 years later, in the year 2000 (ELC 2017).
4. A recent attempt to classify the Third Wave-inspired communities not historically but functionally is made by Jessica Moberg (2015).
5. The term "client" may sound misleading in this context because it is usually understood to be connected with economic exchanges. Even though HR services are based upon voluntary work and are free of charge, I refer to the

visitors as "clients" because most of the members of the prayer teams in Finland do so. The Finnish word *asiakas* literally means "a client" in English. The interviewed prayer team members did not have any problem with the term, even though it has commercial connotations in other contexts. They also used the word "customer-oriented" while describing the principles of their practice. Occasionally, HR clients are called by other names, such as "attenders"/ "visitors" (*kävijät*) or "those who are prayed for" (*rukoiltavat*).
6. The interview material compiled by author is archived at Åbo Akademi University. The reference after quotations signifies the archived unit.
7. Apparently, HR is referred to by the same name all over the world and is not translated into the vernacular.
8. Likewise, the American Neo-Pentecostal evangelist David Herzog, who held a set of healing meetings at the Olympic Stadium of Helsinki in July 2014, raised the same kind of critique, even in the leading national newspaper *Helsingin Sanomat* (Sippola 2014).

References

Åbo Akademi University. *Post-secular Culture and Changing Religious Landscape in Finland 2010–2014.* http://web.abo.fi/fak/hf/relvet/pccr/. Accessed 23 Apr 2015.

Anderson, Allan. 2004. *An Introduction to Pentecostalism: Global Charismatic Christianity.* Cambridge: Cambridge University Press.

———. 2010. Varieties, Taxonomies, and Definitions. In *Studying Global Pentecostalism: Theories and Methods*, ed. Allan Anderson, Michael Bergunder, André Droogers, and Cornelis van der Laan, 13–29. Berkeley: University of California Press.

Bahram, Masoumeh. 2013. Habermas, Religion, and Public Life. *Journal of Contemporary Religion* 28: 353–368.

Beyer, Peter. 2003. De-centring Religious Singularity: The Globalization of Christianity as a Case in Point. *Numen* 50 (4): 357–386.

Brown, Candy Gunther. 2011. Introduction: Pentecostalism and the Globalization of Illness and Healing. In *Global Pentecostal and Charismatic Healing*, ed. Candy Gunther Brown, 3–26. Oxford: Oxford University Press.

Chryssides, George. 1999. *Exploring New Religious Movements.* London: Continuum International Publishing.

———. 2000. Healing and Curing: Spiritual Healing, Old and New. In *Healing and Religion*, ed. Marion Bowman, 59–68. Enfield Lock: Hisarlik Press.

Cox, Harvey. 1995. *Fire from Heaven. The Rise of Pentecostal Spirituality and the Reshaping of Religion in the Twenty-First Century.* Reading: Addison-Wesley Publishing Company.

———. 2011. Foreword. In *Global Pentecostal and Charismatic Healing*, ed. Candy Gunther Brown, xvii–xxxi. Oxford: Oxford University Press.
Csordas, Thomas J. 1997. *The Sacred Self: A Cultural Phenomenology of Charismatic Healing*. Berkeley: University of California Press.
De Vos, Jan. 2012. *Psychologisation in Times of Globalisation*. Hove/New York: Routledge.
Evangelical Free Church of Finland (EFCF). 2017. http://www.svk.fi. Accessed 23 Nov 2017.
Evangelical Lutheran Church of Finland (ELC). 2017. http://evl.fi/. Accessed 23 Nov 2017.
Frisk, Liselotte, and Peter Nynäs. 2012. Characteristics of Contemporary Religious Change: Globalization, Neoliberalism, and Interpretative Tendencies. In *Postsecular Society*, ed. Peter Nynäs, Mika Lassander, and Terhi Utriainen, 47–70. New Brunswick: Transaction Publishers.
Habermas, Jürgen. 2006. Religion in the Public Sphere. *European Journal of Philosophy* 14: 1–25.
Healing Rooms. 2014. Healing Rooms kuulumiset, huhtikuu. HR monthly newsletter by e-mail, April, 2014.
Healing Rooms Estonia. 2017. http://www.healingrooms.ee/. Accessed 23 Nov 2017.
Healing Rooms Finland. 2017. http://www.healingrooms.fi/. Accessed 23 Nov 2017.
Healing Rooms Sweden. 2017. http://www.healingrooms.se/. Accessed 23 Nov 2017.
Heelas, Paul, and Linda Woodhead. 2005. *The Spiritual Revolution: Why Religion is Giving Way to Spirituality*. Malden: Blackwell.
Hornborg, Anne-Christine. 2012. *Coaching och lekmannaterapi: en modern väckelse?* Stockholm: Dialogos.
Hovi, Tuija. 2009. Suomalainen uuskarismaattisuus. *Teologinen Aikakauskirja – Teologisk tidskrift* 114: 66–73.
———. 2012. Clinical Services Instead of Sermons. In *Post-secular Religious Practices*, Scripta Instituti Donneriani Aboensis, ed. Tore Ahlbäck, vol. 24, 128–144. Åbo: Donnerska institutet.
———. 2013. Meanings of Healing: Experiences of Prayers at the Christian Healing Rooms Prayer Service in Finland. In *Constructs of Meaning and Religious Transformation*, ed. Herman Westerink, 185–205. Göttingen: V & R Unipress.
Hovi, Tuija, and Anna Haapalainen. 2015. Omaehtoinen yhteisöllisyys 2000-luvun kristillisyydessä. In *Kansanuskosta nykypäivän henkisyyteen*, ed. Pasi Enges and Kirsi Hänninen, and Tuomas Hovi. 158–187. Turku: Turun yliopisto.
Hunt, Stephen. 2000. The 'Problem' with Alternative Medicines: Some Dynamics of Boundary Maintenance Amongst Neo-Pentecostal Healing Groups. In

Healing and Religion, ed. Marion Bowman, 35–57. Enfield Lock: Hisarlik Press.
Ihanus, Juhani. 2005. *Järjen äänestä minäkertomuksiin. Psyyken ja psykoterapioiden muodonmuutoksia*. Helsinki: Yliopistopaino.
Ketola, Kimmo. 2007. Spiritual Revolution in Finland? Evidence from Surveys and the Rates of Emergence of New Religions and Spiritual Organizations. *Nordic Journal of Religion and Society* 19: 29–39.
———. 2008. *Uskonnot Suomessa: Käsikirja uskontoihin ja uskonnollistaustaisiin liikkeisiin*. Kirkon tutkimuskeskuksen julkaisuja 102. Tampere: Kirkon tutkimuskeskus.
Kivivuori, Janne. 1991. *Psykokulttuuri: Sosiologinen näkökulma arjen psykologisoitumisen prosessiin*. Helsinki: Hanki ja jää.
———. 1996. *Psykopolitiikka: Paljastava psykologia suomalaisen yhteiskunnallisen keskustelun perinteenä*. Helsinki: Hanki ja jää.
———. 1999. *Psykokirkko: Psykokulttuuri, uskonto ja moderni yhteiskunta*. Helsinki: Gaudeamus.
Klassen, Pamela E. 2011. *Spirits of Protestantism: Medicine, Healing, and Liberal Christianity*. Berkeley: University of California Press.
Laitinen, Susanne. 2013. Klinikkaterveisiä maailmalta. *Kristillisen rukousklinikan tiedotuslehti Healing Rooms*, 2/2013. (Greetings from international prayer clinics. – *Newsletter of the Christian Prayer Clinic Healing Rooms*).
Martikainen, Tuomas, Måns Broo, Tuija Hovi, Marcus Moberg, and Terhi Utriainen. 2015. The Changing Forms of Religious Organisations. In *On the Outskirts of "the Church": Diversities, Fluidities and New Spaces of Religion in Finland*, ed. Peter Nynäs, Ruth Illman, and Tuomas Martikainen, 73–87. Zürich: LIT.
Matulevicius, Saulius. 2015. From Pentecost to 'Inner Healing': Religious Change and Pentecostal Developments in the Post-socialist Lithuanian Catholic Milieu. *Approaching Religion* 5: 67–78.
McGuire, Meredith B. 2008. *Lived Religion. Faith and Practice in Everyday Life*. Oxford: Oxford Universtity Press.
Meyer, Birgit. 2010. Pentecostalism and Globalisation. In *Studying Global Pentecostalism: Theories and Methods*, ed. Allan Anderson, Michael Bergunder, André Droogers, and Cornelis van der Laan, 113–130. Berkeley: University of California Press.
Moberg, Jessica. 2015. Pentecostal Currents and Individual Mobility: Visiting Church Services in Stockholm County. *Approaching Religion* 5: 31–43.
Moberg, Marcus, Kennet Granholm, and Peter Nynäs. 2012. Trajectories of Post-secular Complexity: An Introduction. In *Post-secular Society*, ed. Peter Nynäs, Mika Lassander, and Terhi Utriainen, 1–25. New Brunswick: Transaction Publishers.
Neitz, Mary Jo. 2012. The Charismatic Renewal and the Culture of Narcissism. In *Fundamentalism and Charismatic Movements: Charismatic and Conversion*

Movements, Critical Concepts in Religious Studies, ed. Humeira Iqtidar and David Lehmann, vol. 3. London: Routledge.

Nynäs, Peter, Ruth Illman, and Tuomas Martikainen. 2015. Rethinking the Place of Religion in Finland. In *On the Outskirts of 'the Church': Diversities, Fluidities and New Spaces of Religion in Finland*, ed. Peter Nynäs, Ruth Illman, and Tuomas Martikainen, 11–28. Zürich: LIT.

Palmu, Harri, Hanna Salomäki, Kimo Ketola, and Kati Niemelä. 2015. *Haastettu Kirkko: Suomen evakelisluteralainen kirkko vuosina 2008–2011*. http://sakasti.evl.fi/sakasti.nsf/0/.../$FILE/Haastettu%20kirkko.pdf. Accessed 8 Jan 2016.

Pentecostal Church of Finland (PCF). 2017. http://www.suomenhelluntaikirkko.fi/. Accessed 23 Nov 2017.

Pietikäinen, Petteri. 2000. Psykokulttuurin kritiikki. *Tieteessä tapahtuu* 18(8). http://journal.fi/tt/issue/view/4121. Accessed 20 Apr 2017.

PingstFi. Info om de finlandssvenska pingsförsamlingarna 2017. https://pingstfi.blog/. Accessed 23 Nov 2017.

Siltala, Juha. 1992. *Suomalainen ahdistus: huoli sielun pelastumisesta*. Helsinki: Otava.

———. 1994. *Miehen kunnia: Modernin miehen taistelu häpeää vastaan*. Helsinki: Otava.

Sippola, Jussi 2014. Ihmeitä lupaileva saarnaaja ei ota vastuuta puheistaan. *Helsingin Sanomat*, July 27.

Utriainen, Terhi, Tuija Hovi, and Måns Broo. 2012. Combining Choice and Destiny: Identity and Agency Within Post-secular Well-Being Practices. In *Post-secular Society*, ed. Peter Nynäs, Mika Lassander, and Terhi Utriainen, 187–216. New Brunswick: Transaction Publishers.

Open Access This chapter is distributed under the terms of the Creative Commons Attribution 4.0 International License (http://creativecommons.org/licenses/by/4.0/), which permits use, duplication, adaptation, distribution and reproduction in any medium or format, as long as you give appropriate credit to the original author(s) and the source, provide a link to the Creative Commons license and indicate if changes were made.

The images or other third party material in this chapter are included in the chapter's Creative Commons license, unless indicated otherwise in a credit line to the material. If material is not included in the chapter's Creative Commons license and your intended use is not permitted by statutory regulation or exceeds the permitted use, you will need to obtain permission directly from the copyright holder.

CHAPTER 8

Sharing and Holy Hugs: The Birth and Development of Intimization in Charismatic Stockholm

Jessica Moberg

Fifteen people have gathered for a "cell group meeting" in the basement of the Neo-Charismatic New Life Church. After the introductory worship, it is time for each of the participants to present an individual prayer request, or "to share," as some call it. The regulars quickly seize the opportunity, but a female newcomer in her mid-twenties is evidently reluctant to air her troubles in the new group. As the topics are prayed for at the end, a man of about the same age comments upon her hesitation by asking the Holy Spirit to "loosen the bonds of her tongue" so that she may "open up." Returning the subsequent week, the woman recounts a work-related conflict, asking the others to pray for its solution. As a response, she receives hugs.[1]

Charismatic Christianity in Sweden is currently undergoing changes in theology, organization, and practice—the episode above is illustrative of the latter. Some of these changes are the result of inner dynamics in the organizations, while others take place due to cultural and structural shifts in the society where they are embedded. Studies conducted in the United States and other parts of the Anglophone world have analyzed the impact of late modern ideas concerning personal development, authenticity, and

J. Moberg (✉)
University of Gothenburg, Gothenburg, Sweden

intimacy on Neo-Charismatic and Neo-Evangelical organizations, as well as in Charismatic Catholic communities (Csordas 1997; Griffith 1997; Hunter 1987; Miller 1997). However, the issue has not received the same attention in the study of Charismatic Christianity in the Nordic region.[2] The present chapter, which presents a case study of Stockholm County, scrutinizes a development that began in the 1990s but has boomed during the last five to ten years: the increased emphasis on the creation of intimate relationships between practitioners (Moberg 2013b, 45–49). The study introduces the birth of intimization and locates the tendency in the local Charismatic landscape, providing examples of how it is organized, materialized, ritualized, and understood. It also discusses how Charismatic norms and ideals inform and set limits to intimization. The phenomenon is discussed and analyzed in light of theories on late modern intimization, with particular emphasis on how this has unfolded on the national level. Furthermore, attention is paid to both national/regional processes, such as urbanization in Stockholm County, and influences from the international Charismatic milieu on the region in question. The main argument is that intimization in Sweden has taken the form of a strong current in the Charismatic churches, one that is characterized by particular practices and aesthetics. Like the *early* Pentecostal revival and the Jesus Movement of the late 1960s, the movement is carried by young Charismatics and is transorganizational; thus far, it has not spawned any distinct church structures.

The study draws upon ethnographic work in 16 congregations between the years 2009 and 2013, both Pentecostal and Neo-Charismatic.[3] The material consists of field notes from observations and conversations with approximately 300 practitioners, interviews with pastors and churchgoers, and websites. The section on small group practice analyzes material collected at New Life Church, although visits to and conversations with members of other organizations indicate that the contents and orientation of the small groups is similar in most of the local congregations.

Modernity, Intimacy, and Mobility

Relationships between modernity, community, and interpersonal bonds have been addressed within various fields of research. In Pentecostal studies, scholars have attributed some of the success of Charismatic movements to their ability to re-embed mobile, modern urbanities into new communities (see Miller and Yamamori 2007, 22–23; Robbins 2010, 162–163;

cf. Martin 2002, 24). Others have taken interest in what can be described as an "intimate turn" in Neo-Charismatic churches like the Vineyard Movement, Calvary Chapel, Hope Chapel, and Hillsong Church. In this connection, Donald E. Miller and Tetsunao Yamamori have noted the rise of intimate displays such as hugs and the will to communicate one's pain, flaws, and problems to others (Miller 1997, 13–18, 20–24; Miller and Yamamori 2007, 28; cf. Tangen 2008, 194–195).[4] In a similar vein, Marie R. Griffith (1997, 137–138) and Kelly H. Chong (2011, 100) have observed how sharing emotions has become firmly integrated into healing practices in Charismatic-inclined organizations. Miller and Griffith, dealing with the United States context, also emphasize similar driving forces behind such developments. Miller (1997, 20–24; cf. Csordas 1997, 41–51) understands this as a response and adaptation to the therapeutic, individualistic, and antiestablishment values of the counterculture of the 1960s, whereas Griffith (1997, 33–39) underlines influence from the broader American therapeutic milieu and the "recovery movement." These are doubtlessly important points. However, in order to conceptualize and theorize intimization in Stockholm, the discussion needs to be brought out of the North American context, and anchored both in broader changes in modern relationships, and in the particular way intimization has played out in late modern Sweden. The reasoning of Anthony Giddens, Eva Illouz, and Frank Furedi is helpful in this respect.

According to Giddens (2003, 59–65; cf. Furedi 2004; Illouz 2008) increased mobility is tightly interwoven with processes of detraditionalization, which have fundamentally altered and rearranged modern relationships and ideals surrounding them. In contrast to premodern cultures, in which they were interwoven with economic and social transactions, modernity has brought about "the pure relationship" (prevalent in friendships and marriages), disconnected from such bonds. Alternatively, this form of relationship is based on trust and disclosure of emotions, and upheld for the emotional and/or sexual gratification that it affords the involved parties. Giddens accounts for the connections between mobility and intimacy by referring to the emotion-based character of modern relationships, thus providing one of the theoretical perspectives informing this study. However, in order to analyze episodes like the one recounted above, Illouz's and Furedi's theories on a therapeutic shift in late modern self-understanding and communicative practice offer ways of finding cultural impulses. Illouz and Furedi propose that the West is undergoing therapeutization, whereby psychological models of self-understanding spread to other spheres of society. This process commenced during the 1960s (notably at the same time as Neo-Charismatic groups based in the United States emerged, featuring such elements) but has risen to prominence in recent years. Consequently, contemporaries are prone to interpret both their personal problems and those of others as the result of traumas, which can be solved by airing personal emotions and issues. In fact, revealing one's inner ("authentic") emotions to others has become an imperative, while keeping secrets is perceived to be potentially harmful (Furedi 2004, 17–19; Illouz 2008, 5). Discussing the advancement of therapeutization, Furedi suggests that it has influenced and further spread via new media, such as reality TV, in which people are expected to disclose the most private aspects of their lives to the viewers (2004, 66–72).

Inspired by the work of these scholars, I understand "intimacy" firstly as a phenomenon, real in the sense of being anchored in modernity's "pure relationship," which includes the venting of emotions as well as sexual and non-sexual embodied practices. Secondly, intimacy is understood and approached as an ideal, or a project, which late modern people, mainly in the West, aspire to in their own lives. Following Furedi and Illouz, I believe that the longing for intimate relationships has been further fueled by the late modern spread of therapy culture, which offers both ideals and models for how intimacy should be accomplished.

Intimization in Sweden

It is hardly surprising that scholars have detected therapeutic tendencies in Neo-Charismatic groups in the United States, where the "therapeutic turn" surfaced as early as the 1960s and has since grown to be particularly predominant. The work of Illouz and Furedi also accounts for therapeutization by drawing heavily on examples from the United States. In this respect, it should be stressed that the cultural climate in the Nordic region differs from that of the United States; concerning intimate communications, Swedes (like their Nordic neighbors) have traditionally been seen as withdrawn and unwilling to express emotions (Frykman 1993, 224–232). There is, however, evidence that Sweden—and Finland, as illustrated by Hovi in her contribution to this volume—have undergone a major shift in intimate direction since the 1990s. Not only have informal and intimate gestures such as hugs replaced the formal handshake among younger generations; therapeutic discourses have spread as well. It is likely that popular culture has been a major factor in this regard, with American talk shows such as *Oprah* and *Doctor Phil* having attracted large audiences since then. Indigenous remakes of international reality programs like *Paradise Hotel* and *Big Brother*, where participants' private lives and emotions are put on display, have also likely catalyzed the transformation.

In the new millennium, therapeutization has continued to influence government/state institutions, as well as various religious and secular milieus and organizations (Frisk and Åkerbäck 2015; Hornborg 2012). In a study from 2015, Liselotte Frisk and Peter Åkerbäck note the emergence and vitality of a large, alternative, holistic healing landscape. A few years earlier, the Swedish government had allocated large sums to state employment centers in order for them to employ "work coaches" that would help long-term unemployed Swedes to re-enter the work market. Many of these coaches had New Age ties and offered their clients what can be seen as religious-therapeutic solutions to their problems: teaching them to air their emotions and personal problems, or finding and tapping into the power of their inner potential and thereby finding a job (Hornborg 2012). Yet another fresh example indicating Sweden's intimization is the establishment of "hugging courses" in Stockholm and Gothenburg just a few years ago. These courses, named "Intimacy and Integrity" (Intimitet och integritet), offer the participants settings in which they learn to hug and verbally set and discuss limits concerning what forms of intimacy they are able to accept (Intimitet och integritet 2015).

An Overview of Stockholm County

Stockholm County, which constitutes the economic hub of Sweden, is one of the fastest growing regions in Europe. The area is not only home to hug-friendly Charismatics. Together, the central capital, its suburbs, and neighboring cities count over 2 million inhabitants, making Stockholm County the most populous area in the Nordic countries. Among its main characteristics are high levels of technologization and vast mobility, as well as ethnic, religious, and cultural pluralism. Collectively in 2012, inhabitants born outside Sweden made up around 22 percent of the population (Statistiska centralbyrån 2013). Thus, a visitor is likely to encounter not only the Church of Sweden and various Free Church denominations (some Charismatic), but also different strands of Islam, Orthodox Christianity, as well as new religious movements and New Age spirituality. The influx of new people is not showing any signs of exhaustion. Aside from international migration, the county is undergoing rapid urbanization, with many young people moving in from smaller cities in search of employment or education. Yet, despite increased overcrowding, Stockholm city stands out nationally and internationally with its high number of single households. As of 2014, 43 percent of Stockholm's population lived in single households (Statistiska centralbyrån 2015).

LOCAL CHARISMATIC ORGANIZATIONS

Charismatic Christianity has a hundred-year-old presence in the region, and the current scene offers a microcosmic view of its history of various movements. Many of the denominations have roots in the Pentecostal revival (*pingstväckelsen*) of the early twentieth century. The largest is the Pentecostal Alliance of Independent Churches, PAIC (Pingst: Fria församlingar i samverkan), which grew out of the 1913 exclusion of pentecostalized congregations in the "Baptist Union of Sweden" (Svenska baptistsamfundet). Having been expelled, they formed the network known as the "Pentecostal Movement" (Pingströrelsen), which slowly transformed into today's denomination. PAIC encompasses the large and historically important "Filadelfia Congregation" (Filadelfiaförsamlingen), "City Church" (Citykyrkan), as well as organizations in neighboring cities (Pingströrelsens årsbok 2013).[5] Except for PAIC, there is the "pentecostalized" denomination Interact (Evangeliska frikyrkan), which is the result of the fusion of three nineteenth-century denominations that embraced the Pentecostal revival.[6] Among its congregations are the "Söderhöjd Church" (Söderhöjdskyrkan), the "Elim Church" (Elimkyrkan) and the "Cross Church" (Korskyrkan) (Moberg 2015, 32–33).

Later movements and initiatives have also made their mark on the scene. The 1980s saw the establishment of the independent "Center Church" (Centrumkyrkan; Centrumkyrkan 2013), although the decade was otherwise dominated by the emerging Faith Movement, led by the Uppsala-based "Word of Life" (Livets ord). The new movement resulted in a network made up of, on the one hand, new organizations like Arken[7] and, on the other, transformed Pentecostal churches like "Södermalm's Free Congregation" (Södermalms fria församling) that disaffiliated itself from the Pentecostal Movement (cf. Coleman 2000, 97–103).[8] As pointed out by anthropologist Simon Coleman (2000, 55–65), Neo-Charismatic culture is remarkably global in many ways, and local churches often constitute nodes in international church networks. In this regard, the Swedish Faith Movement constitutes an early example of a trend that has since continued. In 1992, Vineyard Stockholm, part of the international Vineyard Movement,[9] was created, and the year after, New Life Church saw the light of day—an organization with connections to the Neo-Evangelical/Charismatic milieu in the United States (Moberg 2015, 32–33). Global migration, as well as the initiatives of local entrepreneurs, continue to pluralize the new millennium's landscape. Neo-Charismatic churches in particular are mushrooming, although many of them have short lifespans. The influx of Charismatic migrants from Latin America and from West and East Africa has been important in this respect (Malmström 2013, 75–78). Also significant for the increase of Charismatic bodies was the rise and fall of Karisma Center, a prosperity-inclined organization with megachurch ambitions that existed at the turn of the millennium. As it was dissolved due to bankruptcy in 2005, several of its pastors created their own churches. Two examples are Hillsong Church Stockholm (originally Passion Church) and "Peter Church" (Petruskyrkan). The latter, however, soon fused with United Stockholm (*Dagen* 2011). Other additions are SOS [Save Our Souls] Church, Yahwe's Revival Center (previously "Power Source", Kraftkällan) and Calvary Chapel Stockholm.

Patterns of Growth and Decline

We lack statistics on Charismatics in Stockholm County, since the majority have been counted as part of the total membership of the largest Free Church denominations. In 2010, Free Church members made up 1.3 percent of the population—a relatively low figure in comparison with other parts of Sweden (Skog 2010, 69–70). It should be kept in mind, though, that this includes both Charismatic and non-Charismatic denominations, but excludes independent Charismatic organizations, Lutheran and Catholic Charismatics, and network-based churches. At first glance, Charismatic Christianity appears to be growing after some decades of decline; figures from both PAIC and Interact show such growth (Lilja 2015). At the end of 2012, PAIC counted 12,457 members in the region (Pingströrelsens årsbok 2013, 46). The creation of new organizations also seems to support the growth thesis. However, the latter tend to draw members from existing organizations rather than attract new converts, and many are relatively short-lived—as illustrated by the fate of the Karisma Center and Peter Church. Also, the county per se is growing; between 1950 and 2012 the number of inhabitants doubled, and between 2000 and 2012 alone almost 300,000 people relocated to the county (Statistiska centralbyrån 2014). In other words, the number of Charismatics does not appear to be growing in terms of percentage of the whole population.

Although it is difficult to speculate in total numbers, it is possible to detect trends of growth and decline. The only suprastructure that seems to be losing affiliates as a whole is the Faith Movement network, otherwise growth and decline patterns cut across denominational boundaries. More important today are Charismatic groups' location and orientation. Firstly, it is possible to speak of a shift from organizations in the surrounding cities to Stockholm. The Filadelfia Congregation, City Church, and Södermalm Church exemplify this trend, and have all increased their membership in the course of the last few years, with a substantial number of the newcomers being immigrants.[10] However, Neo-Charismatic organizations founded over the last 20 years seem to attract the most people. New Life Church presently counts around 400 members, and has also founded sister congregations in the area, and in other Swedish cities (New Life Church 2015). At the end of 2012, Hillsong Church Stockholm counted 1520 members, and in 2015, SOS Church estimated that it had around 600 (Pingströrelsens årsbok 2013; SOS Church 2015). Recent "church plants" United Stockholm and Calvary Chapel also appear to attract contemporaries. Even though they are still small, with around 30 members each, the numbers of casual attendees seems considerably higher.

The Membership

Practitioners make up a mixed group in terms of class, age, and socioeconomic status, although female practitioners are slightly overrepresented across the Charismatic spectrum. The majority have also been raised in Charismatic organizations or in the broader Free Church environment. Even though people convert, converts still make up a minority; from what I have observed, conversion is also more common among residents with immigrant backgrounds than among ethnic Swedes. Regarding age, members of old Pentecostal congregations are (unsurprisingly) older, while the youngest are found in Neo-Charismatic churches. One influential category of people on the contemporary scene is that of young Charismatics who have moved in from smaller cities and the countryside; this group constitutes the backbone of many new and popular Neo-Charismatic organizations. On resettling, they tend to disregard their denominational background and join youthful organizations they find appealing, such as Hillsong Church, New Life Church, SOS Church or Calvary Chapel and United Stockholm (Moberg 2013a, 211; 2015). In sociological terms, the developments in Stockholm follow larger urbanization patterns in Sweden as a whole, of which the "Charismatic urbanization" of Stockholm forms a part. In an international comparison, Charismatic Christianity and urbanization are hardly odd bedfellows. In Sweden, however, this form of Christianity has been far from an exclusively urban phenomenon. The Pentecostal Movement, for instance, has had a strong standing in smaller cities and rural regions as well as in the larger cities (see Alvarsson 2007, 341–344). On the national level, Charismatic urbanization obviously has the effect of draining small- and medium-sized cities of young Charismatics, which in turn concerns rural Charismatics (Dagen 2014).

It is also worth noting the attitudes to organization among today's practitioners, particularly urbanized young Charismatics and immigrants. These groups are highly mobile, tend to disregard denominational boundaries and labels, and have a consumer-oriented approach to religiosity and affiliation; they visit, join, or drop out of churches depending on the churches' ability to cater to their preferences and needs for the moment (Moberg 2013a, 187–188, 199–212).

Intimization: Origins and Distribution in the Field

The first signs of intimization appeared in the 1990s. While the early intimizers were affiliated with international churches or milieus where similar features have been observed, the majority of these features were not instigated by foreign missionaries, but created on the initiative of locals and were later integrated into and adopted the names of those churches. One example is Vineyard Stockholm (and later Hillsong Church Stockholm), which was essential to intimization, particularly in terms of introducing interaction-friendly furnishing (see below). Another congregation that picked up and furthered the trend was the New Life Church, whose orientation in several ways is similar to that of Vineyard. Also indicating intimization in this decade was the choice of Evangeliska frikyrkan (literally "The Evangelical Free Church") to take the official English designation Interact in 1997—which bears strong relational connotations. Yet, it would be anachronistic to speak of intimization as a current before the new millennium, when a new generation of Neo-Charismatic congregations—Hillsong Church, United Stockholm, SOS Church, and Calvary Chapel—adopted such elements, and older organizations began to move in that direction. It is worth noting that although intimization remains strong in new-millennium organizations, they neither materialize nor embody the trend to the same extent, nor in the same ways. As explored later in this chapter, it is more prevalent at Calvary Chapel and Vineyard Church than at Hillsong Church and United Stockholm; the former host small-scale and interactive Sunday services, whereas the latter combine intimate features with Sunday services influenced by the Faith Movement.

Gaining strength as a current, intimate practices and therapeutic language have impregnated most Charismatic churches, and are visible in sermons, theology, slogans, activities, and practices. A contemporary visitor to a sermon in old Pentecostal Filadelfia may be informed that being a Christian is not only about being close to God, but about developing deep emotional relations to others. As I happened to pass by Södermalm Church one evening in 2014, I also noted a new emblem and the slogan "an open embrace for you" (*en öppen famn för dig*), covering one of its large windows. Most congregations have also begun to offer relationship courses and lectures, such as preparatory courses for engaged couples, where spouses to-be are offered tools with which to improve their communication skills. Such courses can currently be found in both new and old organizations. In the same vein, the Filadelfia Congregation recently launched a three-evening course in parenting teenagers (Filadelfiakyrkan 2015). Other forms of intimate arena and activity are also thriving across the field. The popular small-group meetings are the most important of these (i.e., gatherings at which members congregate in smaller numbers), and are vital to the cultivation of close relations. Although the small-group concept has a prehistory in Protestant revivalist settings, its present content is highly interaction-oriented and its purpose framed in intimate language. On Filadelfia's website (2013), the small groups are described as venues where people share each other's lives, discuss "the big questions" while growing—both in faith and as human beings—within the setting of a close community.

Furnishings as Facilitation of Small-Scale Communication

Religious cultures are not only embedded in ideas and language but anchored in the body and material culture. Taking an interest in early Pentecostal church buildings, Nils G. Holm (1978, 82) and Ulrik Josefsson (2007, 54) suggested an interpretation of the central placement of the pulpit as an indicator of the sermon's central standing. In agreement with this interpretation, it is possible to see how intimization has brought about change to

Charismatic material culture, evident in new approaches to furnishing and decorating church venues. Such novelties not only signal the breakthrough of a new ideal of peer-to-peer communication, but also invite and bring about new patterns of interaction among visitors.

In the 1990s, Vineyard Stockholm introduced what can be referred to as "the coffee-table model." Although the congregation kept a low stage at the front, the customary rows of seats were abandoned, and the floor dotted with small coffee tables surrounded by four to six chairs. This café-inspired setup divides the practitioners into smaller groups and situates them face to face. Soon thereafter, New Life Church adopted the same model. Visiting these two congregations today, it becomes apparent that they not only furnish with socializing in mind, but also set time aside for it. The service is usually divided into two parts intermediated by a coffee break, during which churchgoers are encouraged to chat over sandwiches or cinnamon rolls. To promote friendly chats, one of the leaders signals the start of this break from the stage, inviting visitors to take the opportunity to interact and get to know new people. On the one hand, such requests serve to establish the norm of participant-to-participant interaction while, on the other hand, they establish the temporal frame in which it is to occur. Going by the rather loud murmur of voices, the occasion is appreciated both by regulars and newcomers. As for the latter, the coffee-table model also serves a pedagogical purpose, introducing them to the peer-to-peer chats that occur in other contexts, such as the small groups.

Lately, communication-friendly furnishing has increased in popularity, and been adopted by older organizations like the Söderhöjd Church. As I visited this congregation, a female member in her mid-twenties recounted the congregation's furnishing history: A few years back, the old pews had been declared outdated, and were at first replaced by more spacious lines of chairs. Shortly afterwards, the congregation rearranged the interior once again, bringing in the coffee tables. The woman, proudly pointing them out to me, explained that she found them more "contemporary and easy-going" than the "traditional rows."

Socializing in New and Cozy Locations

While small tables may add an informal, café-like atmosphere to any church, some twenty-first-century organizations have taken further steps in this direction. Calvary Chapel, United Stockholm, and Hillsong Church Stockholm rent semi-public venues such as nightclubs, theaters, or actual cafés, which are then redecorated and turned into cozy and conversation-friendly sites. On visiting Calvary Chapel, I observed that the group resided in a rented locale consisting of a combined café and concert venue. Consequently, the furnishing—small tables surrounded by stuffed chairs and sofas—was already optimal, allowing visitors to chat and have coffee prior to and following the service. In order to further "cozy up" (*mysa till det*) the place, as a young male visitor told me, the organizers illuminated the otherwise rather dimly lit café with soft spotlights and candles.

Since its establishment, Hillsong Church Stockholm has rented music venues, a choice that reflects its strong emphasis on worship music. In 2009, it resided in Göta källare, a centrally located two-floor nightclub, with the bar and dance floor situated in the basement. In contrast to Calvary Chapel, where the whole service was held in the same interaction-friendly place, Hillsong divided the service into three parts, taking place in different rooms in the basement. In preparation, the innermost dance floor was sealed off from the bar section and turned into a softly illuminated café with sofas, where people drank coffee and mingled prior to the service. In this section, they could purchase Hillsong CDs and DVDs. The "inner room," or the dance floor, was furnished like many Faith Movement churches: with lines of chairs placed before an elevated stage. After service, churchgoers reassembled in the outer, café-like space. A similar threefold spatial–temporal division was applied by United Stockholm, which rented the theatre Teaterstudio Lederman. Utilizing the existing interior—an outer, café-like foyer, consisting of several small rooms, and an inner room where the theatre stage was located—the foyer was used for mingling and interaction before and after the service. The latter activities took place in the inner room. Adding to the already cozy atmosphere—enhanced with red-painted walls and soft lighting—the foyer was decorated with candles and flowers, and the regulars offered and served visitors non-alcoholic drinks. Upon being asked about their choice of venue, the organizers drew upon a rhetoric of evangelization, explaining that they wanted potential converts to see that they were not "a bunch of stiff and boring Christians," by offering informal and intimate communication in a cozy "low-threshold" setting.

Hugging the Faithful

As pointed out by Daniel E. Albrecht (1999) and Martin Lindhardt (2011), ritualized action is part and parcel of Charismatic identity, visible in practices like prayer with the laying on of hands, glossolalia, or Neo-

Charismatic worship. Historically, one form of ritualized action has been especially significant as an identity marker within the Swedish Pentecostal Movement: "Peace greetings" are a form of greeting where a firm handshake is combined with the phrase "peace" or "peace brother/sister," and was at one time central to signaling Pentecostal affiliation.[11] Today, elderly Pentecostals still use this greeting, although middle-aged practitioners from various Charismatic orientations usually do not. As for intimization, the movement has ritualized a new practice involving physical interaction, one which would otherwise be considered informal and mundane: the hug. Over the last 15–20 years, this gesture has gained a prominent position in many congregations and churches during greetings, as well as in connection with sharing and prayer. Being most common in the organizations founded in the 1990s and the new millennium, the hugging trend has spread to Faith Movement and Pentecostal churches as well. To a large extent, it follows generational lines, with younger Charismatics being more frequent "huggers," not unlike their secular counterparts.

Looking more closely at the practice, the Charismatic hug is obviously similar to its mainstream sibling, but has, nevertheless, a few distinct traits. Observing a "secular" hug involving two friends, their faces usually light up with smiles, their eyes widen somewhat and they look into each other's eyes for a short moment. They proceed by embracing each other, using either both arms or the less intimate "shoulder-to-shoulder" variety of hug. In the Charismatic milieu, all of these features are enhanced, particularly facial expressions. Upon spotting each other, practitioners look extraordinarily happy; smiles are broader and eye contact more extensive. Regarding gender, there are also a few differences worth mentioning. Women tend to smile, hug, and touch each other more frequently and more extensively than men. Female embraces also tend to last longer and include both arms, while men hug for shorter periods of time and tend to settle for the "shoulder-to-shoulder" hug.[12] To some extent hugging, especially outside the greeting situation, follows gender lines, with men hugging men and women hugging women, a topic to which I will return.

Mini-communities Within Congregations

During the last 20 years, small group gatherings led by lay persons have become popular as complementary to Sunday services. The groups, which go under different names (house groups, small groups, cell groups, city groups, or connect-groups), can be found basically everywhere, and participation is more or less mandatory; members are expected to be part of one, and those who do not attend on a regular basis are reminded by their peers. Usually, they contain 8–15 participants, who gather for an evening during the working week to socialize and lean on each other for emotional support. In terms of content, sharing a meal, praying, presenting testimonies, and prayer requests are steady components, whereas Bible reading and lay sermons occur less frequently, contrary to what one might assume.

Even though similar groups have been studied in international Charismatic settings (Chong 2011; Griffith 1997; Hovi 2011; Tangen 2008) the phenomenon is not unique to this religious tradition; on the contrary, it has been observed in various religious and semi-religious settings in different parts of the Western world. Danièle Hervieu-Léger (1993) and Robert Wuthnow (1996), discussing declining membership rates in old churches and denominations, have called attention to this thriving new form of community. Wuthnow (1996, 52) notes its presence in New Age circles, and in Charismatic and Evangelical milieus. The impetus for joining them is "the desire for intimacy, support, sharing and other forms of community," which participants find to be lacking in their lives. The small groups in this study are doubtless part of this larger trend, and as suggested by Hervieu-Léger and Wuthnow, they are vital fora for the cultivation of close and intimate bonds.

Interacting in and Revealing the Private Sphere

Gatherings usually take place in members' homes, sometimes in accordance with a rotating schedule. Evidently, this setting, which is already associated with close and informal relations, provides the meeting with a casual and intimate frame. However, since people rarely design their homes with this type of gathering in mind, adjustments are made to optimize interaction. Before starting, the host and early arrivals often rearrange a living room containing sofas and armchairs by bringing in additional chairs and cushions from other parts of the home. These are placed so as to form a circle, enabling eye contact in the same manner as the coffee tables do. While this home-framing and redecoration invites the cultivation of intimacy, hosting meetings may also be said to constitute intimization by means of disclosure, although not in the "therapeutic" sense. The very act of welcoming others into one's home, offering them food and soft drinks, implies putting one's private life on display, revealing preferences in aesthetics, music, food, literature, and so forth. In case the host is married, the visitors also have the opportunity to meet, and probably interact with the spouse, and perhaps the children as well. Since all members are expected to host meetings at some point, all participants are committed to revealing themselves in this way.

Prayer Requests as Sharing

In a study of female Neo-Charismatics in the American organization Women's Aglow, Griffith (1997, 137–138) proposes that revealing oneself to others through sharing secrets is central to cultivating closeness. The small groups in Stockholm County serve a similar purpose, whereby the airing of emotions, thoughts, and secrets allows participants to get to know each other's struggles rather early. In comparison with how the sharing secrets usually takes place, requiring that the speaker knows the listeners and has established trust in them, sharing in the small groups bypasses the often lengthy process through which trust is established, and gets "right to the point."

In Stockholm, the practice of sharing has been introduced into, and fused with, the Charismatic speech genres of prayer requests and testimonies; it also so happens that members use "sharing" as a term that includes and refers to those practices. In the small groups, sharing often takes the form of prayer requests, presented at the beginning and prayed over at the end. The participants normally stand or sit in a circle facing each other, encouraged by the leader to present a topic they want others to pray for. The leaders' actions are crucial to creating a comfortable and sharing-friendly environment. He or she often takes the initiative by calling upon others to "put their problems and fears on the table," assuring them that they are among friends and that the topics brought up will stay in the room. Occasionally, the leader adds that keeping secrets from one another, and from God, is potentially harmful, underlining that sharing is part of the process of surrendering to and getting closer to God: a central revivalist motif. Such statements not only frame the practice theologically, but also put pressure on members to "speak out," implying that reluctance to do so presents an obstacle on the path of serving God.[13] Themes are sometimes presented spontaneously, but usually, the members take turns presenting a topic. Following the norm, they highlight a troublesome issue, and express their concerns, then a wish that the others pray for God's intervention. Afterwards, the leader normally thanks each person, while the others offer emotional support in the form of a tap on the shoulder, a warm hug, a sympathetic word, or an assurance that they will continue to pray over the topic.

Limits to Disclosure

My observations revealed that frequently broached topics concerned troublesome relationships, work-related problems, and health issues. Many of them also reflected the difficulties of young urban people, including problems in securing an apartment or a job, or passing a school examination. In accordance with the rhetoric surrounding the gatherings, participation allows the involved parties to air their most personal issues. During interviews, participants often expressed deep appreciation for the gatherings, where they could "tell each other everything." From the perspective of an outsider, there were nevertheless rules regulating what could and could not be shared, setting boundaries for intimization (cf. Griffith 1997, 125–126). As one might expect, rules were internalized by regulars, and questions of what could or could not be said were never explicitly raised. Some were no different from rules in any other social context. Others appeared to be rooted in particular Charismatic notions and ideals. For instance, dislike of other members in the congregation was never aired. Also, it seemed more of a general rule not to bring up problems between Charismatics. The unwillingness to touch these matters is likely the result of the inherent belief that those who had submitted their lives to Jesus were expected to have good relations, especially with fellow congregants. Breaking this social taboo would not only result in worsening conflicts, but to call that image into question. Moreover, the state of one's relationships was often described as an indicator of one's spiritual state. Love, affection, and patience were often portrayed as qualities given by the Holy Spirit, and to publicly highlight conflicts and anger risked reflecting badly on the person who raised such matters.

Some issues were also considered too sensitive to bring up in the small group context, limiting these groups' function as venues for communicating the most intimate concerns. Among them were experiences of abuse, including sexual abuse. Practitioners who had such problems normally addressed them in even more confidential exchanges, either in pastoral care (*själavård*) or with a close friend within the congregation—generally a member of the same small group. The latter in fact indicates that the "mini-communities" also serve as greenhouses for the cultivation of more intimate friendships that enable members to discuss topics that are too delicate for the small group setting.

Ritualized Intimacy and the Fear of Eroticization

Although cultivation of closeness is a central mission to many Charismatics today, other motivations are occasionally at odds with it. It hardly comes as a surprise that this form of Christianity involves various forms of self-discipline. The people with whom I interacted carefully sought to manage their sexual behavior and impulses, and to uphold norms concerning proper relationships between men and women. Such norms regulated who they could be closely involved with, drawing boundaries for and gendering intimization. Even though some forms of physical and emotional interaction were encouraged and understood as positive and "godly intimacy," there were nevertheless worries that this could lead to the opposite: the formation of improper sexual intimacy. Such worries were typically articulated by young and unmarried Charismatics, who shared the standpoint that sexual relationships prior to and outside of heterosexual marriage were sinful, and who strived to stay chaste until having married a Christian partner. Maintaining sexual purity involved different forms of self-control. Many were concerned about their (unwanted) sexual desires and spoke lengthily about the methods they employed to rid themselves of them. For example, they would seek the company of supportive, like-minded people, pray regularly, avoid visual sexual stimuli (ads featuring semi-nudity, certain TV programs, etc.) and, importantly, restrain themselves from becoming emotionally involved with people they might feel attracted to. Since the Charismatic scene is strongly heteronormative, meaning that people are expected to be heterosexual, it was mainly interaction between men and women that was considered problematic in this respect. I have already accounted for the gendered hugging patterns, whereby most hugs were exchanged between Charismatics of the same sex. In a similar vein, many restrained themselves from becoming close friends with people of the opposite sex; a few women explained that they avoided meeting male congregants alone outside of church, since "troublesome" situations may arise. In some cases, even the setting of the church did not suffice; I was informed, and warned about, "men who go to church to flirt." Yet, physical gender-crossing interaction that took place in church was evidently perceived to be less problematic than informal "hanging out" outside of church activities.

One reason why certain activities were regarded as harmless whereas others were seen as threatening can be detected in their ritualization. Several scholars studying ritual have noted how the prestipulated character of ritualized action permits people to interact in otherwise impossible ways. Catherine Bell (1997, 81), who argues for a wide definition of ritual, including all forms of "ritualized" action, suggests that such action is comprised of strategic ways of allowing the involved actors to achieve aims that would be unthinkable in a nonritualized context. From Bell's perspective, both hugs and intercession include ritualized action, being prestipulated and formalized; one knows what to anticipate and when. Moreover, they are social acts everyone is expected to participate in. One cannot turn down a hug or a friendly invitation to be prayed over. In the Charismatic milieu, ritualization evidently plays a vital role in rendering potentially threatening physical interaction harmless, turning it into the desired form of "godly intimacy." Another feature that should not be underestimated is that hugs and prayers in a church setting are collective events at which participants socially monitor each other.

If ritualization establishes the special nature of certain forms of physical intimacy, the narrative portraying such action as an aspect of meeting and serving God further underscores its uniqueness. Yet, it would be wrong to consider these approaches airtight, since congregants nonetheless expressed doubts about others' motives for engaging physically, even during "holy hugs" and prayer. The topic however, was highly sensitive, and I never heard it openly discussed in a collective forum; it only came up during interviews and informal conversations between members. One male New Life Church member, while viewing physical contact as good and natural, brought up the possibility that psychologically "damaged" people might take it as an opportunity to clandestinely obtain sexual gratification. Adding that he has had such suspicions while being hugged for "too long," he assured me that none of the members in his present small group seemed to have such "impure" intentions.

Meeting Jesus and Restoring Natural Community

Therapeutic discourses, underlining the need for emotional communication, have also become intertwined with older Charismatic narratives and self-understanding. One theme that resurfaced in sermons and informal conversations across the Charismatic field was that of fellowship (*gemenskap*), often articulated in the trope: "being a Christian is all about relationships, with God and with people." In this rhetoric, the tight bonds which were seen to exist between "brothers and sisters in Christ," especially members of the same small groups, contrasted with the brokenness and isolation believed to exist among secular people and those of other faiths—both on a societal and an individual level. In several sermons, non-Christians were described as alienated from an original and natural way of life that would allow them to be in touch with their emotions, and be integrated into a community where these could be communicated. In such accounts, reference was often made to the regional context. In the Filadelfia Congregation and New Life Church, Stockholm was depicted as a city that was "broken" not only because of sin, but also because people lived isolated lives and had no one to turn to for support, which was seen as a major cause of contemporary depression. Loneliness was often connected to secularization, in the course of which Stockholmers (and Swedes in general) had become deeply lonely and removed "hyper-individualists" without a sense of caring for and interacting with others. Several pastors pointed out the central island Kungsholmen, labelling it "the loneliest island in the world"—a reference to its exceptionally high percentage of single households, a phenomenon seen here as a sign of loneliness. By the same token, many Charismatics proposed that non-Christians attempted to substitute meaningful human contact with drinking, overeating, "empty" sexual affairs, and the like. Becoming a Charismatic Christian and a members of a congregation was accordingly presented as a way of healing an unnatural separation from God by accepting Jesus, as well as breaking social isolation by returning to the close, emotional communities God had intended.

Disclosure, Healing, and Conversion

Late modern ideals such as the unfolding of the authentic inner self and psychological models of interpretation have also merged with Charismatic conversion, miracle, and healing narratives. Hence, submission to God, combined with emotional communication, was presented as the method for overcoming emotional problems and living authentic lives. Accepting the idea that people are broken because of previous relationship traumas, leaders and practitioners presented conversion and embedment in a close-knit Christian community as the solution. Central to this rhetoric was that secular Swedes deny their true feelings and pretend everything is fine since they lack a place in which to air their problems, which only adds to their distress. It was often pointed out that it was impossible to overcome trauma via secular therapies, since they were incapable of addressing a primary cause of human discontent: alienation from God. Drawing upon the theme of conversion, pastors and members explained that the one way to surmount such problems was submitting one's life to God, who would initiate a process that would heal emotional wounds and make people whole. Hence, secular people, regardless of personal success, would never know true happiness but always experience a sense of inner emptiness.

Apart from God's ability to work miracles, sharing among Christians was ascribed a central role in restoring and healing the individual. Becoming, and living as, a Charismatic meant no longer pretending that everything was fine, and openly admitting one's brokenness—to God, oneself, and fellow Charismatics. This was sometimes communicated in connection with sharing in the small groups. In New Life Church, one leader initiated meetings by telling the participants that it was time to "take off their masks," signaling both that people wore such masks in everyday life, and that they had come to a place that offered them the opportunity to take them off and reveal their "authentic" selves. Additionally, bonds cultivated through sharing were often seen as the work of the Holy Spirit, and stories about intimacy and disclosure were given a Charismatic twist; because the parties involved had accepted Jesus and therefore were "inhabited by the same Spirit," they were able to develop a deeper and closer form of intimacy than non-Christians.

A Movement born of a Mobile Doctor Phil Generation

Charismatic intimization in Stockholm is part of a broader Western cultural turn. Influences from global Neo-Charismatic networks, where intimate and informal features have been observed, have also been vital for fueling the current in Sweden, as illustrated by early intimizer Vineyard Stockholm. Yet, Charismatic intimization also mirrors the particular way in which Sweden has been intimized. In contrast to the United States, where churches like Vineyard and Calvary Chapel were created as early as the 1960s and 1970s, they did not appear in Stockholm until thirty years later. One important reason for this comparatively late introduction is that intimization in Sweden did not take root until the 1990s, meaning that there was no fertile soil for Charismatic enterprises of this kind prior to that time.

It is significant that both Vineyard Stockholm and New Life Church were founded in the very same decade in which Sweden saw the breakthrough of international therapy TV like *Doctor Phil*, and docusoaps, making these early features of Swedish intimization. The strengthening of the intimization current in the new millennium also mirrors Sweden's growing intimization, visible in the trend's spread to new societal spheres and institutions (see Hornborg 2012, 11–14). Looking at the membership of organizations that have furthered it in the twenty-first century, they are dominated by socialized Charismatics between 18 and 35; that is, they belong to the first Swedish generations brought up in a society saturated with therapeutic TV shows, ideals, and practices. This has evidently informed their religious preferences and choices. It is also possible to see how intimization has been fueled by mobility on the national level, with a substantial number of the members having relocated from smaller cities to Stockholm County as adults. Employing Giddens' terminology (2003) their "uprooting" in combination with the wider cultural turn seems to have further fueled their longings for intimacy and their seeking of communities of like-minded others, with whom they might develop new emotional ties. As illustrated, practices like sharing allow participants to form such bonds quickly. Uprooting also seems to have contributed to the creation of new Charismatic theology and norms. The dichotomization of the warm "Christian communities" on the one hand, and "lonely Stockholm" on the other, does appear to reflect the experiences of newcomers with few contacts with the native population. In conclusion, contemporary intimization is rooted in a wider therapeutic shift in Sweden, as well as in Charismatic urbanization. It has its institutional base in young Charismatic churches that offer solutions to the uprooting and contemporary longings of a mobile "Doctor Phil generation."

While intimization of older Charismatic organizations is part of the same trend, I believe it is fruitful to view it in light of the current mobility within the local Charismatic landscape. It is well known among pastors and churchgoers that younger Charismatics in particular visit, leave, and affiliate with organizations depending on their current needs and preferences. For older churches, particularly those with aging memberships, this has become a challenge; in order for them to thrive, or even survive, they depend on the interest and commitment of new generations. Speaking with middle-aged and elderly practitioners in some of the older churches, many expressed fear that "the young" would find "their" organizations boring and leave in pursuit of more youthful organizations. Against this backdrop, the introduction of Neo-Charismatic novelties like worship music and contemporary instruments in Pentecostal churches (often at the expense of the older psalms), and the creation of specific youth services, as well as therapeutic language and relation-building practices, are all means for securing continued engagement. It is telling that none of the relation-building courses are designed for the stable elderly membership (who are probably not interested in them either), but for those who belong to and have the opportunity to raise future generations; that is, congregants who are about to marry, and the parents of teenagers. These novelties are not always welcomed by elderly members. Visiting the Filadelfia Congregation a few years back, I observed a neatly dressed lady between 70 and 80 demonstratively covering her ears during the loud electric guitar solo that was part of the weekly worship. Interestingly, as social anthropologist Jan-Åke Alvarsson continues to discuss in the next chapter, old Pentecostals' disappointment with current developments in the churches may in turn give rise to further innovation.

Conclusions

I have proposed that Charismatic Stockholm has seen the birth of intimization, visible in the creation of communication-friendly environments, and the use of therapeutic language and new forms of ritualization and practice. Intimization took off in the 1990s with the establishment of Vineyard Stockholm and New Life Church, but did not gain significant strength as a current until the new millennium, when it was furthered by Hillsong Church, United Stockholm, and Calvary Chapel, and started spreading to older Charismatic organizations. Charismatic intimization in Sweden is part of a Western late modern cultural shift, and has developed parallel to overall intimization, which began at the same time, and is possible to detect in the wider Swedish context. For the most part, Charismatic intimization is carried forward by younger socialized individuals who have grown up in an intimized nation, many of whom have moved to the Stockholm region from smaller cities as adults, and lack social networks in the new setting. However, the current is also shaped by the tradition where it has taken root, and the forms of intimacy enacted by the Charismatics differ in some respects from intimate practices in other religious and secular settings, or those broadcast on TV. In particular, sexual norms and chastity training undertaken by practitioners engender intimization, informing them of who they may develop close relationships with. Moreover, the possibility of attaining aims such as becoming free of emotional trauma and finding one's authentic self have fused with Charismatic theology and been given a particular twist: this means that they are obtainable only in Charismatic settings, since they depend upon submission to God and intimate communication between practitioners "inhabited by the same Spirit."

Notes

1. I have borrowed the term "holy hug" from anthropologist Thomas Csordas (1997, 69) who used it to describe ritual practice among charismatic Catholics in the United States.
2. Exceptions are Tuija Hovi's (2010) studies of Neo-Charismatics in Finland and the work of Karl Inge Tangen (2008).
3. This chapter draws upon the classifications and terminology laid out in the introductory chapter. The congregations in question are: Arken, Calvary Chapel Stockholm, Centrumkyrkan, Citykyrkan, Korskyrkan, Hillsong Church Stockholm, Maranataförsamlingen i Stockholm (tent meeting), New Life Church, Filadelfiakyrkan, SOS Church, Kraftkällan, Söderhöjdskyrkan, Södermalmskyrkan, Tomaskyrkan, United Stockholm, and Vineyard Stockholm.
4. Donald E. Miller does not use the term Neo-Charismatic, but refers to Calvary Chapel, Vineyard Church, and Hope Chapel as "New Paradigm Churches."
5. Pingst: Fria församlingar i samverkan was instituted as a "national organization" (*riksförening*) in 2001, and decided to keep the name when it became a registered denomination in 2004 (Pingströrelsens årsbok 2013, 40).
6. The new denomination initially took the name "The New Building" (Nybygget), but soon changed it to Evangeliska frikyrkan.
7. The Swedish name Arken has an ambiguous meaning, and is possible to translate either into "The Ark" or "The Arch," both of which have biblical connotations. For this reason, the church is referred to by its Swedish name.
8. A few years ago it returned to PAIC.
9. "Nordic Vineyard" (Vineyard Norden) is not only part of the international Vineyard Movement, but also a registered denomination in Sweden.
10. This estimation is based on knowledge about known congregations–a study of underground churches might point in another direction.
11. Conducting fieldwork, I encountered several Neo-Charismatics with Pentecostal family backgrounds who reported that their Pentecostal grandparents had warned them that unless they used the "proper" peace greeting rather than a "good day" or an informal "hi," common in the majority culture, they would go to Hell.
12. The latter, chaster hug has sometimes been referred to by Charismatics and Evangelicals as "the Christian side hug."
13. On a few rare occasions, new members did object to such an interpretation, or questioned the need for them to "open up" to strangers so quickly. Such critique, however, was never uttered in the sharing context, but broached afterwards.

References

Albrecht, Daniel E. 1999. *Rites in the Spirit: A Ritual Approach to Pentecostal/Charismatic Spirituality*. Sheffield: Sheffield Academic.
Allt fler blir döpta i sekulariserade län. 2014. *Dagen*, March 28. http://www.dagen.se/allt-fler-blir-d%C3%B6pta-i-sekulariserade-l%C3%A4n-1.93271. Accessed 6 Mar 2016.
Alvarsson, Jan-Åke. 2007. Pigor och arbetare har blivit solid medelklass: Pingströrelsens klassresa i det svenska samhället. In *Pingströrelsen: Verksamheter och särdrag under 1900-talet*, ed. Jan-Åke Alvarsson and Claes Waern, vol. 2, 338–359. Örebro: Libris.
Bell, Catherine M. 1997. *Ritual: Perspectives and Dimensions*. New York: Oxford University Press.
Centrumkyrkan. 2013. http://www.centrumkyrkan.se. Accessed 3 July 2013.
Chong, Kelly H. 2011. Healing and Redomestication: Reconstruction of the Feminine Self in South Korean Cell Group Ritual Practice. In *Practicing the Faith: The Ritual Life of Pentecostal-Charismatic Christians*, ed. Martin Lindhardt, 98–128. New York: Berghahn Books.
Coleman, Simon. 2000. *The Globalisation of Charismatic Christianity: Spreading the Gospel of Prosperity*. Cambridge: Cambridge University Press.
Csordas, Thomas J. 1997. *Language, Charisma and Creativity: The Ritual Life of a Religious Movement*. Berkeley: University of California Press.
Filadelfiakyrkan. 2015. http://www.filadelfia.nu. Accessed 5 Aug 2013; 14 May 2015.
Frisk, Liselotte, and Peter Åkerbäck. 2015. *New Religiosity in Contemporary Sweden: The Dalarna Study in National and International Context*. Sheffield: Equinox.
Frykman, Jonas. 1993. Nationella ord och handlingar. In *Försvenskningen av Sverige: Det nationellas förvandlingar*, ed. Billy Ehn, Jonas Frykman, and Orvar Löfgren, 119–201. Stockholm: Natur och kultur.
Furedi, Frank. 2004. *Therapy Culture: Cultivating Vulnerability in an Uncertain Age*. London: Routledge.
Giddens, Anthony. 2003. *Runaway World: How Globalization Is Reshaping Our Lives*. New York: Routledge.
Griffith, R. Marie. 1997. *God's Daughters: Evangelical Women and the Power of Submission*. Berkeley: University of California Press.
Hervieu-Léger, Danièle. 1993. Present-Day Emotional Renewals: The End of Secularization or the End of Religion? In *A Future for Religion? New Paradigms for Social Analysis*, ed. William H. Swatos, 129–148. London: Sage Publications.
Holm, Nils G. 1978. *Pingströrelsen: En religionsvetenskaplig studie av Pingströrelsen i Svenskfinland*. Åbo: Stiftelsen för Åbo akademiska forskningsinstitut.
Hornborg, Anne-Christine. 2012. *Coaching och lekmannaterapi: En ny väckelse?* Stockholm: Dialogos Förlag.

Hovi, Tuija. 2010. Gender, Agency and Change in Neo-Charismatic Christianity. *Aura: Tidskrift för akademiska studier av nyreligiositet* 2: 38–62.

———. 2011. Praising as Bodily Practice: The Neocharismatic Culture of Celebration. In *Religion and the Body*, ed. Tore Ahlbäck, 129–140. Åbo: The Donner Institute for Research in Religious and Cultural History.

Hunter, James Davison. 1987. *Evangelicalism: The Coming Generation*. Chicago: University of Chicago Press.

Illouz, Eva. 2008. *Saving the Modern Soul: Therapy, Emotions, and the Culture of Self-Help*. Berkeley: University of California Press.

Intimitet och integritet. 2015. http://www.i-and-i.se. Accessed 4 Nov 2015.

Josefsson, Ulrik. 2007. 'Det är saligt att samlas i tron': Möten, gudstjänster och samlingar. In *Pingströrelsen: Verksamheter och särdrag under 1900-talet*, ed. Jan-Åke Alvarsson and Claes Waern, vol. 2, 50–63. Örebro: Libris.

Lilja, Josefin. 2015. Evangeliska frikyrkan växer i sekulariserade delar av Sverige. *Dagen*, March 24. http://www.dagen.se/evangeliska-frikyrkan-v%C3%A4xer-i-sekulariserade-delar-av-sverige-1.346634. Accessed 6 Mar 2016.

Lindhardt, Martin. 2011. Introduction. In *Practicing the Faith: The Ritual Life of Pentecostal-Charismatic Christians*, ed. Martin Lindhardt, 1–48. New York: Berghahn Books.

Malmström, Nils. 2013. Pentekostala invandrarkyrkor. In *Pentekostalismen i Sverige på 2000-talet: Rapport från ett forskningsprojekt på IPS 2012–2013*, ed. Jan-Åke Alvarsson, 75–92. Uppsala: Forskningsrapporter från Institutet för pentekostala studier.

Martin, David. 2002. *Pentecostalism: The World Their Parish*. Oxford: Blackwell.

Miller, Donald E. 1997. *Reinventing American Protestantism: Christianity in the New Millennium*. Berkeley: University of California Press.

Miller, Donald E., and Tetsunao Yamamori. 2007. *Global Pentecostalism: The New Face of Christian Social Engagement*. Berkeley: University of California Press.

Moberg, Jessica. 2013a. *Piety, Intimacy and Mobility: A Case Study of Charismatic Christianity in Present-Day Stockholm*. PhD dissertattion, Södertörn University.

———. 2013b. Pentekostal spiritualitet i Stockholms län: En ansats till typologisering. In *Pentekostalismen i Sverige på 2000-talet: Rapport från ett forskningsprojekt på IPS 2012–2013*, ed. Jan-Åke Alvarsson, 41–73. Uppsala: Forskningsrapporter från Institutet för pentekostala studier.

———. 2015. Pentecostal Currents and Individual Mobility: Visiting Church Services in Stockholm County. *Approaching Religion* 5: 31–43.

New Life Church Stockholm. 2015. http://www.newlife.nu. Accessed 5 Oct 2015.

Petruskyrkan uppgår i United. 2011. *Dagen*, March 15. http://www.dagen.se/petruskyrkan-uppg%C3%A5r-i-united-stockholm-1.130053. Accessed 6 Mar 2016.

Pingströrelsens årsbok 2013. 2013. Stockholm: Pingströrelsens informationscentrum.

Robbins, Joel. 2010. Anthropology of Religion. In *Studying Global Pentecostalism: Theories and Methods*, ed. Allan Anderson, Michael Bergunder, André Droogers, and Cornelis van der Laan, 156–178. Berkeley: University of California Press.
Skog, Margareta. 2010. *Frikyrklighet och ekumenik kring millennieskiftet: I Berndt Gustafssons fotspår: Tre studier*. Lund: Lunds universitet.
SOS Church. 2015. http://missionsos.org. Accessed 15 Oct 2015.
Statistiska centralbyrån. 2013. *Utrikes födda 2012*. Last modified August 21, 2013. http://www.scb.se/sv_/hitta-statistik/artiklar/fortsatt-okning-av-utrikes-fodda-i-sverige/. Accessed 2 Nov 2015.
———. 2014. http://www.scb.se/. Accessed 18 May 2014.
———. 2015. *Åtta av tio delar hushåll med någon*. Last modified September 10, 2015. http://www.scb.se/sv_/Hitta-statistik/Artiklar/Atta-av-tio-delar-hushall-med-nagon/. Accessed 6 Apr 2017.
Tangen, Karl Inge. 2008. *Ecclesial Identification Beyond Transactional Individualism? A Case Study of Life Strategies in Growing Late Modern Churches*. PhD dissertation, University of Oslo.
Wuthnow, Robert. 1996. *Sharing the Journey: Support Groups and America's New Quest for Community*. New York: Free Press.

Open Access This chapter is distributed under the terms of the Creative Commons Attribution 4.0 International License (http://creativecommons.org/licenses/by/4.0/), which permits use, duplication, adaptation, distribution and reproduction in any medium or format, as long as you give appropriate credit to the original author(s) and the source, provide a link to the Creative Commons license and indicate if changes were made.

The images or other third party material in this chapter are included in the chapter's Creative Commons license, unless indicated otherwise in a credit line to the material. If material is not included in the chapter's Creative Commons license and your intended use is not permitted by statutory regulation or exceeds the permitted use, you will need to obtain permission directly from the copyright holder.

CHAPTER 9

Televangelism in Sweden—Now? Is Channel 10 in Älmhult in Fact a Telechurch?

Jan-Åke Alvarsson

Ever since televangelism[1] started in the United States, Sweden has been considered an impossible arena for that type of enterprise. At the time, almost all Swedes were formal members of the Swedish Lutheran Church, were heavily secularized, and were considered to be anti-Charismatic, and fairly anti-American in some regards. Unlike secularized American popular culture, which has generally been well received, Swedes have tended to be averse to the United States' international politics, or its expressions of "public" religiosity, like televangelism. Furthermore, up until that time, the state monopoly of Swedish radio and television had closely regulated the transmission of church services, and thus had impeded any such evangelization initiatives via TV.

Nevertheless, in 2005, when televangelism's heyday seemed to be over in the United States, a new Charismatic TV channel was founded in Älmhult in Småland, a place in the south that, prior to the channel's establishment, was known for only one thing; it was the birthplace and home to the head office of IKEA, the worldwide furniture company. The new channel was called "Channel 10" (*Kanal 10*). "Kanal" was a neutral designation witout any religious connotations and the number "10" was not

J.-Å. Alvarsson (✉)
Department of Cultural Anthropology, Uppsala University, Sweden

© The Author(s) 2018
J. Moberg, J. Skjoldli (eds.), *Charismatic Christianity in Finland, Norway, and Sweden*, Palgrave Studies in New Religions and Alternative Spiritualities, https://doi.org/10.1007/978-3-319-69614-0_9

used by any television channel in Sweden at the time. Since then, another, bigger channel, called TV10, has led to some confusion as to the identity of these two different channels.

In 10 years, Channel 10 has grown into a successful business whose principal product is Pentecostal or Charismatic preaching.[2] The business idea is based on experiences from televangelism's heyday in the United States, in the 1980s. The present article initially asks the question: How can it be that televangelism attracts Swedes today, when it was considered impossible for it to do so only 30 years ago?

In the text, the actors behind the channel, its contents, and the reception of the programs are presented in light of contemporary changes taking place in the Pentecostal landscape, especially where these concern intergenerational conflicts of interest and ongoing mediatization. The material presented is discussed from a theoretical perspective on identity, inspired by Paul Ricoeur (2005), Erik Erikson (1964), and nostalgia as advocated by Clay Routledge et al. (2006, 2014).

The source material for this study is based on participant observation in Pentecostal churches, Pentecostal TV programs, interviews, websites, and academic works on Pentecostalism. The discussion also benefits from material gathered by the journalist Joakim Lundgren, who in 2013 carried out thorough research on Channel 10, commissioned by the Christian newspaper "The Day" (*Dagen*).[3]

Pentecostalism in Sweden

Pentecostalism reached Sweden as early as November 1906, through Swedish-American Andrew G. Johnson, who brought it over directly from 312 Azusa Street, the birthplace of international Pentecostalism in Los Angeles. In the beginning, it was an ecumenical movement, especially preponderant among Methodists and Baptists. After the initial outpouring of the Spirit in Skövde, Örebro was the center of activities for some time. In 1907, the focus gradually transferred to Gothenburg. Not until the 1910s did Stockholm start to play a part, always with Gothenburg as a questioning sceptic.[4]

In the late 1910s, the situation had changed considerably and a particular denomination, the Swedish "Pentecostal Movement" (Pingströrelsen; SPM),[5] was founded in 1919. Through the firm leadership of Lewi Pethrus, the denomination united different pentecostalized groups and managed to become a leading movement on the Swedish, as well as on the European scene. In the 1980s, SPM's membership numbers surpassed 100,000 and it became the largest Free Church in Sweden. In 1937, the Baptist movement was divided into two denominations, the Örebro and the Stockholm Baptists, two branches that were well visible long before the split. The so-called "Örebro Mission" (Örebromissionen) became the second Pentecostal movement in Sweden, while the Stockholm Baptists turned more Evangelical and conservative. However, the Örebro Mission never managed to equal the Swedish Pentecostal Movement in its size or activities.

In 1962, a notable split occurred in the SPM when Maranata was founded by Norwegian Arne Imsen. The movement had initial success and lured back many old revivalists with its use of popular songs, "back to basics" preaching, renewed radicalism, and nostalgia for the "good old revival times." This heyday was short, however, and after a couple of years most of the enthusiasts had left the movement. In 1983, another notable Charismatic movement was born, Word of Life (Livets Ord) in Uppsala, led by Ulf Ekman, a former Lutheran priest who was heavily influenced by Neo-Pentecostals like Kenneth Hagin and Kenneth Copeland in the United States. The movement had great influence in Eastern Europe after the fall of the Iron Curtain, but its success in Sweden peaked at the turn of the century with some 3000 followers in the mother congregation in Uppsala and slightly more in a few scattered congregations in the rest of Sweden. In 1983 the Swedish Lutheran Church had its first Charismatic Movement in the Oasis Movement (Oasrörelsen). In due course, several other minor waves of Pentecostalism or Pentecostalized movements, like the Australian Hillsong Church, reached Sweden. Simultaneously, dividing lines between churches became blurred again, and people moved more freely between denominations (Moberg 2013, 187–188).

The arrival of these new waves of Pentecostalism also affected Classic Pentecostal churches. They changed their music style, introduced "worship music," often in English, and drew inspiration from concert culture, visible in their utilization of colorful lighting and, at times, smoke machines. Many churches were rebuilt to resemble concert halls and, while the centrality of the podium had previously reflected the importance of preaching in the service, the focus on the stage now emphasized the music as the main event, causing a generational divide and leaving a good number of the Classic Pentecostals alienated (cf. Moberg 2013, 106–107).

THE SITUATION OF SWEDISH RADIO AND TELEVISION

The Swedish radio broadcasting service was founded as a monopoly on March 21, 1924 under the name of "Radio Service Ltd" (AB Radiotjänst), hereafter referred to as 'Swedish Radio' (which from 1956 also broadcast television) and (after 1979 when television was separated and placed in a special foundation) 'Swedish Television', the more commonly used designations.[6] The first program was broadcast on January 1, 1925; incidentally this consisted of a church service from the Sankt Jacob Lutheran church in Stockholm. In 1956, the company started transmitting television programs six days a week, at first only for a few hours per night. The limited time given was seen as an opportunity to reach the public, used by the authorities to inform, educate, and enlighten the Swedes. The telecasting from this single channel was therefore censored and without commercials. It was considered to be "public service." In 1969, a second television channel was created: TV2. This addition was intended to give the illusion of variety, while the channel tried to meet the growing challenges from international media. Not until 1979, when the whole company was divided into four subsidiaries and reorganized, did Sweden see the first legal alternatives to this monopoly, in the form of community radio. As we shall see, Pentecostals felt immediately inspired to utilize that possibility. A major threat to Swedish national television appeared in December 1987, when the commercial channel TV3 started telecasting via satellite from London. Swedish authorities tried to stop the enterprise with legislation, but failed; in 1991 they capitulated and allowed a new Swedish commercial TV channel: TV4. Since then, commercial radio and TV channels have proliferated, but lip service is paid to the idea of "public service" broadcasting in that the fact that possession of a TV set is still subject to a quarterly fee.

The Pentecostal Use of Media: The Swedish Background

Classic Pentecostalism in Sweden reflects many of the traits found in international Pentecostalism: It started in 1906, it promotes a Charismatic spirituality, and it utilizes the latest media trends.[7] In its earliest days in 1906, and for quite some time afterwards, newspapers and journals were used to inform and inspire its adherents. At Azusa Street in Los Angeles, the revival's journal was called *The Apostolic Faith*. In Sweden, Pentecostalism was welcomed and promoted by editor Richard Edelberg in his Örebro-based, Evangelical journals "The Närke Paper" (*Närkesbladet*)[8] and "The Swedish Tribune" (*Svenska Tribunen*). But for the impatient Pentecostals, these were not enough. Therefore, the first genuinely Pentecostal periodical, "Embers from the Altar" (*Glöd från altaret*), was published in Gothenburg in 1909. When this journal was discontinued, another one took its place almost immediately in Stockholm in 1911: "The Voice of the Bridegroom"

(*Brudgummens röst*). The editor-in-chief was Carl Hedeen and his co-editor was Olov Leonard Björk—both well-known figures in the early Pentecostal Movement. A young, up-and-coming preacher, the new pastor of the small Filadelfia Congregation in Stockholm, was invited to become an assistant editor. His name was Levi Petrus, soon to be changed to Lewi Pethrus. Among other contributions, he provided the journal with self-composed hymns. However, in the mid-1910s, when Pethrus saw the growing number of independent and incipient Pentecostal congregations in Sweden, he considered that "The Voice of the Bridegroom" was still insufficient to inform and inspire the rising movement. Maybe there was also already a slight crack in the collaboration between Pethrus and the other leaders— such a split would become obvious at the end of the decade. Nevertheless, in 1916, Pethrus launched a journal of his own: "The Gospel Herald" (*Evangelii Härold*)—the main organ of the Pentecostal Movement until 1993. In 1921, the journal hired a new and brilliant editor, recently converted poet and writer Sven Lidman. In 1922, the success of "The Gospel Herald" drove "The Voice of the Bridegroom" out of the competition, and the latter had to be closed down. In 1945, under the leadership of Lidman, "The Gospel Herald" reached its peak with a circulation of 72,500 copies that, at the time, made it the largest journal of its kind in Sweden.

"The Gospel Herald" was aimed at a readership of Pentecostals throughout Sweden. In the 1940s, however, Pethrus and others saw the need for a means of reaching out to the greater Swedish society and influencing political debate. Consequently, he started the newspaper "The Day" in 1945, supported financially by Pentecostal industrialist Karl G. Ottosson—and opposed internally by Sven Lidman. The latter thought that a pure Pentecostal movement should not be soiled by mundane business. In spite of this, Pethrus and Ottosson were able to carry through their endeavor at a time when many newspapers were going out of business, and establish a Pentecostal mouthpiece in Swedish society.

In 1912, when Pethrus was still fairly unknown and the Filadelfia church was still a member of the Baptist Union of Sweden,[9] he was encouraged by many of his members to publish a series of sermons as a book on Pentecostal eschatology called "Jesus Is Coming" (*Jesus kommer*). Interestingly, the Swedish title could be interpreted both as meaning "Jesus is returning" [now] and "Jesus is coming back soon." However, when he approached the Baptist publishing company, B-M.:s bokförlag, the editor asked, "Who would want to read a book of sermons, and by an unknown preacher?" Pethrus' manuscript was turned down—something that turned out to be a historical mistake on the part of that publisher; the book is still in print and has gone through 15 editions. Furthermore, Pethrus' efforts to publish the book led to the foundation of "The Filadelfia Publishing House" (*Förlaget Filadelfia*), for many years the major publisher of Christian books in Sweden, producing hundreds of titles, many of them in several editions. Publishing was discontinued in 1997 due to waning sales returns (Stävare 2007, 322).

In the 1940s and 1950s, healing was again on the public agenda. This aspect had been controversial even at the start of Pentecostalism in Sweden, but now the secular press focused upon it again. Newspapers like "The Daily News" (*Dagens Nyheter*) and "The Evening Paper" (*Aftonbladet*)[10] wrote story after story about the threat of Pentecostalism to conventional medicine and to scientific progress. In 1946, agitation against the Pentecostals led the state-owned "Sweden's Radio" (*Sveriges Radio*) to cancel a planned broadcast from the Stockholm Filadelfia Church because it had been claimed in a previous service that a person had been healed after intercession (Stävare 2007, 329). The experience of being banned outraged Pentecostals; Pethrus, the informal denominational leader, decided to challenge the Swedish radio monopoly and start an independent "pirate radio station." In 1949, Swedish Pentecostals were able to tune in to Radio Luxembourg to triumphantly listen to programs produced by their own denomination. But the quality of reception was poor and broadcasting was discontinued after a short time. In 1953, a second attempt was made from a "pirate ship" placed on international waters in the Baltic Sea. This attempt, however, was also short-lived.[11] None of these efforts were explicitly illegal, because they could not be subjected to Swedish law, but they exasperated the Swedish authorities and threatened the idea of a state monopoly in broadcasting.[12]

In 1955, the endeavors to create a Swedish Pentecostal radio station came to fruition. With the foundation of the IBRA (the International Broadcasting Radio Association) earlier that year, the Pentecostal movement was able to secure a firm location[13] for its broadcasts in Tangier, in today's Morocco, which at the time qualified as "international territory", and was therefore exempt from the strict broadcasting restrictions of Swedish law at the time. On July 29, 1955, Lewi Pethrus and Karl G. Ottosson flew into Tangier to inaugurate the new Swedish Pentecostal Radio Station. Thousands of expectant Pentecostals tuned in to the station. The station's aim of evangelizing Sweden via radio was quickly expanded to include missionary work in other countries. Thus, for a period of four and a half years, hundreds of programs, not only in Swedish, but in 23 different languages, were broadcast and provided Swedish Pentecostalism with a new medium for evangelization and supplementary missionary work (Stävare 2007, 329). When broadcasting from Tangier ceased in 1959, IBRA Radio continued to broadcast from a series of local radio stations in Asia, Africa, and Latin America.[14]

As stated above, the Swedish Radio monopoly was partially dismantled in April 1979, when the authorities allowed the creation of local radio stations, called "community radio" (*närradio*), which were in general run by non-profit organizations. The first one to make use of this opportunity in Sweden was the Pentecostal church of Jönköping, followed by their sister church in Linköping (Stävare 2007, 331). Soon, other Pentecostal congregations and many other different actors followed. This led IBRA to discontinue its production of programs for the Swedish listeners.[15] By now, almost all Pentecostals had their own local radio station anyway. The year after, in 1980, the Swedish authorities also allowed the establishment of community television stations. The municipality of Huddinge, located just south of Stockholm, was the first to attempt this. Their key to success was cooperation with media students from the neighboring Pentecostal community college, Kaggeholm. Thus, Pentecostals once again played a part in a new media initiative in Sweden (Stävare 2007, 331).

In the 1980s, the Pentecostal Movement formed a partnership with the Canadian TV program *100 Huntley Street*. This led to new ideas about television as a means for evangelizing in new regions, especially an increasingly secular Europe. During the annual Pentecostal conference outside Jönköping, Nyhemsveckan, in June 1983, this vision was presented at one of the sessions. The response was overwhelming; the following collection amounted to more than 1 million Swedish *kronor*s (SEK, "Swedish crowns"), the largest offering to date in Swedish Pentecostal history. The Pentecostals had once again demonstrated their confidence in the use of modern mass media. A two-year television training course was launched at Kaggeholm in 1984,[16] and TV production was initiated the same year by one of the Pentecostal companies called TV Inter. The sister churches in Denmark, Finland, and Norway joined in the enterprise. Only three years later, in 1986, the productions had reached such a professional level that the Swedish state television company (Sveriges Television) agreed to broadcast eight programs.[17] The same year, TV Inter bought an old cinema hall in Stockholm and transformed it into a TV studio. In 1989, a series of 20 TV shows for children were produced. In 1992, the Stockholm studio was considered too small and production was moved to more spacious facilities in Linköping. During the 1990s, TV Inter continued its struggles to establish itself as a significant player on the Swedish media scene. During its first five years, TV Inter was able to broadcast at least one program each weekend, in this period on the new commercial TV channels *TV4* and *Kanal 5*. The programs transmitted included "Morning Air" (*Morgonluft*), "A Friend for Life" (*En vän för livet*), and the children's show *Lenas Peplon* (Wahlström 2007, 337).

In the 1970s, a series of programs featuring traditional revivalist songs, "The Whole Church Sings" (*Hela kyrkan sjunger*), led by Margit Borgström from the Pentecostal church of Umeå, were shown on Swedish television. The programs were widely discussed and Borgström became something of a celebrity in Sweden. Twenty years later, in 1997, mindful of the original program's success, TV Inter attempted to create a sequel: "Do You Remember the Song?" (*Minns du sången*). This time inspiration was also taken from American singing duo Bill and Gloria Gaither's *Homecoming* programs in the United States. Under the direction of Anders Jaktlund and Urban Ringbäck, around 100 Christian artists, mostly Pentecostal, were brought to the studio in Linköping to participate in the program series. The sequel became even more popular than the original, and as a result Swedish television broadcast 25 episodes and a number of reruns between 1998 and 2000 (Wahlström 2014a, 307; 2014b, 467).

After 1995, Pentecostal TV production faced increasing costs and around the year 2000, TV Inter concluded that the production of conventional TV programs for the Swedish market was no longer feasible. In 1999 the TV studio in Linköping was disposed of and its activities brought back to Stockholm. A series of people were dismissed and costs considerably reduced (Stävare 2007, 332). Today, attempts at televangelism seem to have vanished altogether. TV Inter now produces occasional Sunday morning services for Swedish state television. Otherwise, they concentrate on producing for—sometimes streaming on—the Internet. Programs on the Internet constitute a new mass media area, and are far less costly than conventional TV production. Apart from local initiatives by Pentecostal congregations, some successful websites have been launched, e.g. "Good News" (*Goda Nyheter*) with the subtitle: "The art of growing through the difficult issues of life."[18] The website provides instruction and counseling in areas like: "forgiveness," "unemployment," "recently divorced," "private economy," "guilt," "loneliness," and the like.

What has been accounted for so far pertains to the initiatives of the Swedish Pentecostal Movement. This denomination has been the leading actor, not only because of its size, but also because of its continuous interest in evangelization. Other Pentecostal movements, like the Örebro Mission and Maranata, have published books and journals but to a smaller extent. With the foundation of Word of Life in Uppsala, however, another significant actor appeared on the Christian media scene.[19] From the start, books by Ulf Ekman and cassette tapes with recorded sermons were distributed on a large scale. In 1989, Word of Life also started a journal, "The Magazine" (*Magazinet*), which was continued until 2001 when it was replaced by "The World Today" (*Världen i dag*). Starting in 1991, for a short time, television programs were produced for a European audience. In 1993, Word of Life acquired a license to broadcast radio programs in Uppsala, but the practice was soon discontinued because of the high expense (Coleman 2000, 168; Gerdmar 2014). In 1996, Word of Life acquired its first website and as of today all services are streamed and transmitted via the Internet.

In a brief recapitulation of Pentecostal media history, we may thus conclude that, within the Swedish Pentecostal movement, there has been an ever-present desire and openness to make use of the most recent mass media available. A desire to evangelize through these media has also been present ever since Pentecostalism started. The results of these campaigns have varied, but the desire to reach out has been palpable.[20] In this more limited sense, Swedish Pentecostalism has attempted to make use of the television medium as "televangelism." However, if we define televangelism in the way many American researchers do, as connected to the creation of a "telechurch," televangelistic attempts by Swedish Pentecostals do *not* amount to true televangelism. In this context, I define a *telechurch* as an electronic church where the pastor acts from a studio with a few people who stand in as "members" while the real constituency, who make up the electronic church, are situated in front of their TV screens at home, communicating with their pastor only through donations and prayer requests (Hedges 2002, 1118). This type of endeavor is a very different genre, and it has never been attempted on the Swedish scene because of the emphasis on congregationalism and collective leadership in Swedish congregations. A telechurch, as such, is based on the fame, skill, and charisma of a single preacher who creates a virtual church of his own. This kind of focus on one, central, charismatic figure thends to be frowned upon in traditional Swedish society in general, and in the congregationalist Pentecostal Movement in particular.[21]

Televangelism: A General Background

In the United States, televangelism began as early as the 1950s, in the infancy of television. And Pentecostals were there from the beginning. Oral Roberts' televised camp meetings from 1954 are considered to be the starting point.[22] From 1960 onwards there was an "Oral Roberts special" every Sunday morning. This, in fact, became the basis for a new telechurch pastored by Roberts. As of 1969, Oral Roberts' ambitions were higher and the program was moved to "prime time." With the help of invited Hollywood stars, the number of viewers increased notably. Reverend Roberts made use of this opportunity to ask for money. He had recently founded Oral Roberts University in Tulsa, Oklahoma and needed more funds for its existence. When Roberts solicited money via this medium, the response was overwhelming. Roberts received more money that he could have dreamed of (Hedges 2002).

A colleague of Roberts, Southern Baptist Minister Pat Robertson, had started a similar enterprise in 1959, but he did it in a different way. He bought a TV station threatened by bankruptcy, and started broadcasting daily programs, transforming it into a Charismatic Christian TV channel. Robertson attracted more and more adherents, and at the height of his career, he seems to have had around 30 million "subscribers" that paid a "membership fee" and furthermore donated large sums of money.[23] The result was a vast variety of programs including news, entertainment and, for a short time, also a soap opera. The surplus receipts covered the construction of the flamboyant Crystal Cathedral in California and, among other things, the unsuccessful Pat Robertson presidential campaign in 1988. Robertson reached many Americans, but not enough to reach the White House.[24]

The success of Oral Roberts and Pat Robertson attracted other preachers to televangelism, but the lure of money and massive followings also entailed temptations. From a present-day standpoint, it appears that televangelism in the United States declined notably during the 1990s. The flamboyant lifestyles and outright scandals connected to two of the big televangelists, Jim Bakker and Jimmy Swaggart, brought the whole business into disgrace. Both Pat Robertson's CBN (Christian Broadcasting Network) and Jim Bakker's PTL (Praise the Lord) network have now closed down. Today, there is only one major Charismatic TV station left in the United States, Trinity Broadcasting Network, or TBN. Daniel J. Hedges, Assistant Professor at Oral Roberts University in Tulsa, summarizes televangelism in the United States in the following way, emphasizing that Pentecostals and Charismatics have been the main protagonists of the business from the beginning, along with Oral Roberts:

> No other segment of Christianity has employed television for evangelism and religious influence as successfully as charismatics and pentecostals [...] The overall result has been that television has taken both the best and the worst of charismatic and pentecostal Christianity into the home of virtually every family in America (Burgess and van der Mass 2002, 1118).

Harvey Cox elaborates on mediatization in the following way, from a perspective especially important to the comprehension of televangelism:

> [T]he power of the television medium transforms and magnifies the ordinary [...] Television is a modern technology that has a curious similarity to the magic of shamanism. The shrinking of distance, the larger-than-life presence, the compression of time, the sense of belonging suggested by the congregation's response, the appeal to emotion rather than logic—all integral to the topography of television. (Cox 1996, 278)

There are also other countries where televangelism has played a prominent role. Brazil might be the best example. One of the major Neo-Pentecostal denominations in the country, "The Universal Church of the Kingdom of God" (Igreja Universal do Reino de Deus) televised programs as one of its distinguishing characteristics from the beginning (Ruuth 1995, 195). In 1990, the leader of this denomination, Bishop Edir Macedo,[25] bought two of the major TV channels in Brazil: TV Record in São Paulo and *TV Rio* in Rio de Janeiro. The cost was estimated at $ 45 million (Burgess and van der Mass 2002; Ruuth 1995, 201).

In summarizing what he believes to have been the purpose of this bold venture, ecclesiologist Anders Ruuth states that the intention was:

> [t]o reach as many people as possible with the message of the church. Radio and television are seen as the best instruments for reaching out. As we have seen, the message can be summarized as: *Pare de sofrer. Existe uma solucao!* ("Stop suffering! There is a solution!"). (Ruuth 1995, 207, author's translation)

It is interesting to note, however, that Bishop Macedo, who is all in favor of televangelism, seems to be against a particular form of telechurch. He states that:

> I am against an electronic church of the type that we find in the United States, where the pastor is on the television screen and people are at home and attend the doorbell, if someone comes by, or the cat, if it is meowing. In my church we prefer direct contact with the people. (Ruuth 1995, 207, author's translation)

In this quotation, Macedo opposes the idea of a telechurch, referring to his vision of "direct contact" with the audience. One hypothesis to explain the success of American telechurches is the predominance of individualism in the United States. Maybe Macedo reckons that this is not as true of Brazil, even though the medium of TV is just as strong there. In Sweden, individualism has increased notably during the last decades.[26] Has this opened up opportunities for a telechurch?

THE PURPOSE OF CHANNEL 10

As was stated in the introduction, there is one particular case that seems to thwart the view of Sweden as a country that is infertile ground for telechurches: Channel 10 in Älmhult in southern Sweden. According to its founder, Börje Claesson, Channel 10 wants to practice televangelism, and has been doing so for a number of years. The first question that will be discussed here is whether, on the one hand, this endeavor reinforces the local churches leading to "a direct contact with the people" in accordance with Macedo's idea or if it, on the other hand, should be considered a new "telechurch" based on my definition of such a phenomenon stated above.

The birth of Channel 10 is intricately entwined with the aforementioned Claesson, a Pentecostal businessman from a traditional Pentecostal family. Claesson has several close relatives who are leading Pentecostal pastors within the SPM, a fact which has contributed to his securing a central position in the movement. He retired early from his business activities and initiated a local church in Älmhult. When he sold his company, a corporation that provided an electronic phonebook on the Internet, he made a gross profit and decided to invest the money in a Charismatic TV channel, something possible in Sweden in 2005 because of the restructuring of the media landscape described above.

In an interview in 2013 in "The Day,"[27] Claesson was referred to as a "Smålandish Media Magnate" (*smålandsk mediamogul*; Lundgren 2013, 11, author's translation). His statement in the same interview does nothing to diminish that estimation: "I was a total failure, and nobody thought that I would start a TV channel. That goes against everything [that people think of me]. Nevertheless, I know that I will soon start a TV channel in Syria. I just know it" (Lundgren 2013, 11, author's translation). On Channel 10's website (2015) the ambition of the TV station is stated in the following way:

> Channel 10 is Sweden's Christian TV channel. Here you will find a wide variety of programs, all with a clear Christian focus. Our telecasts include feature films, news, children's shows, education, debates, worship and intercession programs. One week each month we also broadcast our esteemed Café and Campaign Evenings. We offer a mix of music performances, interviews,

and conversations directly from our studio in Älmhult. Channel 10 is a Christian channel, which is clearly evident in the programs we broadcast. We profess the Apostles' Creed, with Jesus clearly in focus. Channel 10 is not tied to any denomination but seeks as much breadth as possible. We telecast programs from the Oasis Movement within the Swedish church, to various free churches in Sweden. A few of our programs are broadcast in English, but most of them are either in Swedish or subtitled. Our goal is to broadcast as many of our programs as possible in Swedish. We broadcast Christian television around the clock, divided into three eight-hour blocks—one eight-hour block between 4 p.m. and midnight, and then a rerun of the programs until 4 o'clock p.m. the next day.[28]

The manifesto of Channel 10 demonstrates that it is an ecumenical, or at least a transdenominational collaborative, initiative that includes most of the Charismatic sector of Swedish Christianity, from the Oasis Movement within the Swedish Lutheran Church to, as we shall see below, Neo-Pentecostal enterprises like The Arch (Arken) and Word of Life. Studying the program schedule, we can also include the Swedish Pentecostal Movement, and Pentecostal preachers with their own ministry. Channel 10's own summary of its history reads:

> Channel 10 began broadcasting in 2005. It has developed and has been growing steadily ever since. Since the inception, we have made major changes to the content of the programs, and we continually increase our viewer numbers. Today, apart from using the satellite disc (the Sirius Satellite), you can also order Channel 10 as an optional channel from the Freeserve and Telia selections. You can also follow Channel 10 via our Web TV.[29]

In the interview in "The Day," Claesson professes that he has been inspired by the business strategy of the neighboring company IKEA:

> The channel should be considered as a spiritual IKEA, which has a popular appeal. It started on a small scale, on the soil of Småland, but with time it became one of the most well-known trademarks in the world. From IKEA, I bring with me the idea of working as a team and that anyone can contribute with his or her gift. The company is a success today, but it was not like that in the beginning. (Lundgren 2013, 12, author's translation)

In this quotation it is hard to separate what Claesson alludes to as being IKEA's strategy from his own vision. But it becomes increasingly clear that his ambitions are not limited to a small church or a weekly television program. Claesson wants to reach out worldwide, just like IKEA. And just like IKEA's wide assortment, he claims, Channel 10 offers a great variety of programs. According to the Channel 10 website, these include: "TV shows from different parts of the world, from different communities and for different audiences: from the current talk shows and church services, news, children's shows and music programs." (Author's translation. Information found online at 'kanal10.se' April 12 2014.)

The program schedule of Channel 10 may be divided into six different kinds of programs: (a) news programs, (b) conventional church services, (c) teaching and counseling, (d) missionary activities, (e) testimonies, and (f) programs for children and youth. Each section is represented by at least two different programs: ambitions are high. Some of the programs, for example one of the news broadcasts, are produced in cooperation with a sister channel in Norway, "Channel 10 Norway" (Kanal 10 Norge).

The schedule referred to reflects the intention of Channel 10 to represent the breadth of Charismatic Christianity in Scandinavia. The news anchor is Tomas Ander, a Charismatic preacher of SPM origin. The leader of the program "Life with Jesus" is Linda Bergling, pastor of the Arch, a free Charismatic ministry in Stockholm, with historical ties to the Faith Movement. One of the missionary programs is led by Morgan Carlsson, who is the administrative secretary of Media Mission International (MMI), an organization that claims to be "the largest missionary organization in Europe, using mass media as a tool." One of the programs based on personal testimonies is called "From Darkness to Light," led by Hans and Eva Marklund, the pastor couple of the Faith Movement congregation in Alingsås. One of the children's programs, "Youngsters," is hosted by Lennart Henricsson from the Oasis Movement. Channel 10 has a standing element that is not accounted for in the program schedule: Börje Claesson asking for money. In between programs, and in the style of a commercial, Börje Claesson explains the vision of Channel 10 and asks the viewer to support his cause.

The enterprise is not limited to television, however. Channel 10 also provides encounters between viewers/sponsors and Charismatic celebrities, probably to encourage giving. In September 2014, for example, Christian business owners were invited to meet Sverre Larsson, the former director of "The Day Group" (Dagen-gruppen) of the Swedish Pentecostal Movement (see above). Another strategy for attracting attention is to let Charismatic profiles and celebrities write blogs on the Channel 10 website. In late 2014, former Word of Life leader Ruben Agnarsson asked the rhetorical question: "Do the missiles from the Palestinians really exist?" in one of the fairly frequent pro-Israel blogs featured on the site.

Seen as a whole, the selection of programs and other activities seem to provide an extended version of what was once the contents of a traditional Pentecostal revival meeting. This contained Bible teaching, hymns, testimonies, and intercession—and youth activities as well as a Sunday school for children. During one of the hymns after the sermon, participants were regularly asked for an offering. Missionary reports were also often a part of the service. Seemingly, Channel 10 provides all the details that used to constitute this type of Pentecostal service: hymns, Bible teaching, testimonies, missionary reports, and pleas for support.

Financing Channel 10

In 2012, Channel 10 had 30 employees, around 100 volunteers (including Börje Claesson's staff), and, according to its own estimates, reached between 50,000 and 100,000 Swedish viewers per week. Potentially, however, 2 million Swedes could also watch its programs via their cable networks. These are impressive figures. But how does Claesson finance these extensive activities? According to Claesson himself, Channel 10 is partially financed by commercials, "but above all from the 9000 private donors and the 172 congregations that provide funds regularly" (Lundgren 2013, 12, author's translation). In 2012, Channel 10 actually collected some 20 million *kronor*s and accounted for a profit of half a million *kronor*s. When it comes to the identity of the supporters, Claesson is secretive. According to Lundgren:

> Who they are, [Pastor Claesson] does not want to disclose, but for those who have watched Channel 10's programs, it soon becomes obvious that money is not an insignificant issue in this context. Blessings are promised to those who contribute—an attitude that the channel has been much criticized for. (Lundgren 2013, 12, author's translation)

The Channel 10 website (Kanal 10.se, 2014) provides us with a hint as to how the donations are acquired and administered. It echoes the petition by Börje Claesson in his frequent "commercials":

> Channel 10 carries out great work to spread the gospel of Jesus. For the most part, the work is financed by voluntary donations. You can donate to Channel 10 in several different ways. Not only can you call or text a one-time gift using the numbers above. You can also make a donation through your account or credit card below. The most valuable [choice] for Channel 10 is of course if

you want to become a monthly partner. You can also become one by clicking the button below "Become a partner." 1. Choose; 2. My gift; 3. My Details; 4. Check and complete. I want to: give a gift, become a partner.

Today, these partners obviously amount to more than 9000; on average, they provide more than 2000 *kronor*s each per year (Lundgren 2013, author's translation). This is a considerable sum when it comes to donations from the general public.[30]

AUDIENCES OF CHANNEL 10

Personally, I first came into contact with Channel 10 through my father, an old Pentecostal pastor, who was connected to the Comhem cable network and could watch the programs through that. He appreciated what he called "a tone of revival" (*en väckelseton*) that he recognized from his early years in the Pentecostal Movement. When I watched the programs together with my father, they often brought back memories from my childhood of revival campaigns and tent meetings. Some of the participants were even the same, for example Målle Lindberg, who calls himself "a gypsy preacher" and who made the front page of several evening papers with his spectacular performances in the 1960s. At that time, he was related to the short-lived, "wild" Pentecostal movement of Maranata (Dahlgren 1982, 139–42).

It is obvious that not only my father, but many elderly Pentecostals appreciate the Channel 10 programs. According to an article in "The Day," 75 percent of all incoming telephone calls come from elderly people. Journalist Lundgren states that: "There is no doubt about the fact that the channel means a lot to many in this age group. A collection of incoming letters leaves no doubt and [they] express pure gratitude" (2013, 13, author's translation). In one of my interviews, a female member of the Pentecostal Movement stated the following about Channel 10:

> I watched a Bible study on marriage that was one of the best I ever heard. I saw a fine report about poverty in South America that illuminated the problems but also the efforts that have been made, in a very informative way. I have seen touching interviews that expressed needs for intercession, but also peoples' testimonies about how they have been helped through Channel 10.[31]

This testimony, as well as many others, accounts for the appreciation for Channel 10 that is shown by viewers of a Pentecostal/Charismatic background.

The Effects of Televangelism

The bold vision of Börje Claesson, however, is televangelism. He claims that through his TV channel, "God's fire will spread all over Scandinavia, with hundreds of thousands saved as a goal." Furthermore, he states that: "This is revival. It is our calling to transmit the message to the Swedes, to be a tool for revival in Sweden and confer hope to the congregations" (Lundgren 2013, author's translation). This quotation clearly demonstrates Claesson's own vision: Channel 10's televangelism will reach out to secularized Scandinavians, bring them to salvation, and thus transform the whole region. Scandinavia will be ignited by and burn with Pentecostal fire. In the process, the local Pentecostal or Charismatic congregations will be filled with hope.

The results from earlier studies of televangelism in the United States do not point in that direction, however. Daniel J. Hedges concludes that "the impact on society at large appears to be relatively small; fundraising rhetoric notwithstanding, religious television appears to reach mostly the converted and have little evangelistic impact" (2002, 1120). Experience from other televised attempts in Sweden would suggest the same. Above, we have described initiatives like "Do You Remember the Song?" produced by the Pentecostal missionary organization TV Inter, but broadcast on Swedish state television. These programs were viewed by a great many people and were much talked about. But the effect can probably be labeled "nostalgia," rather than "conversion." Innumerable church services all over Sweden were later called "Do You Remember the Song?" but there were extremely few new converts to Pentecostalism as a result, if any.[32] The intention may have been televangelism, but the effect was most probably nostalgia and the nostalgia produced did not result in conversion.

As stated above, SPM's TV Inter has concluded that producing this type of program is too expensive considering the meager results. Thus, they have almost abandoned televangelism in Sweden. Börje Claesson and Channel 10, however, think otherwise. The format and the vision of this channel differ considerably from any other endeavor so far in Swedish history. With the "tone of revival" from bygone days, music accompanied by accordions and guitars, and emotional sermons, Claesson and his revivalist friends intend to "save" not only Sweden, but all of Scandinavia. And in one respect, they have succeeded where others, like SPM and Word of Life have failed. They have been able to finance a Pentecostal Charismatic TV channel for years.

As noted above, Claesson claims that: "This is revival!" There are a number of issues that pull that claim into question, however. The people that travel to Claesson's "City Church" in Älmhult are already believers seeking healing, consolation, or maybe just nostalgia. As we have seen, the majority of those making phone calls and donating money are elderly people, most of whom are obviously believers. When it comes to the programs broadcast by Channel 10, we may also call into question the character of these programs. The style is often old-fashioned compared to today's Pentecostal and Neo-Pentecostal church services. The songs are old and popular Pietist hymns. But what is most surprising is the type of speech employed on these programs. The language used is full of Bible references and Pietist expressions, fully comprehensible to an old believer, but probably incomprehensible to the nonbeliever that Claesson wants to reach. Lundgren states that: "The question is—Does the channel reach the people it opts for? Is the classical revivalist language understood by secularized Swedes that, in a fragmented existence, never find enough time as it is?" (2013, 13, author's translation).[33]

Is Nostalgia the Key to Channel 10's Success?

According to the arguments presented above, Channel 10 is not likely to become the ideal of televangelism that Claesson wants it to be. It does not reach out to "Scandinavia," not even to secularized Sweden. But why has it become a success, at least if we consider it from the perspective of "survival" in a tough media business? Channel 10 has obviously stayed alive for a long time—longer than could have been expected, considering the size of Claesson's initial investment of funds. To explain this, we must instead look at the situation of Pentecostal believers in Sweden today to find the answer. As hinted at above, classical Pentecostal churches have undergone a dramatic transformation in just one or two decades. The spirituality of the 1940s and 1950s, the time when today's elderly people were young, is all gone. There are no more prophetic messages, speaking in tongues, prayer nights, revivalist hymns, no more string instrument orchestras or church organs, not even any hymn books. All these classical expressions of revivalism are more or less gone (cf. Moberg 2013, 106–107). Many old-time believers have a hard time recognizing their old churches, even more so in taking a liking to them. They are faithful and do not leave the church officially, but they do not feel at home and they are more and more often becoming absent friends.

The rapid alteration of religious expressions such as classical Pentecostal church services can be attributed to several factors. First, individualism has spread rapidly in Sweden during the last few decades. People do not bother as much about what others think. The predominantly rural and collectivist culture of Sweden has been replaced by an urban and individualist one. Furthermore, people increasingly vote with their feet. Whereas old-time Pentecostals were most faithful to their congregations, Jessica Moberg (2013) has shown that today's members are mobile and choose a congregation according to what they consider the best for that moment. This has led to a nervous adaptation to new circumstances in many churches. This whole rapid transformation of churches and church culture opens up a new field to actors like Claesson, and media enterprises like Channel 10. Alienated Pentecostals are looking for a new home—but wish to do so without having to do what was once considered almost a sin, that is, to abandon their congregation. This is where Claesson's TV channel comes in. In the programs from Channel 10, they recognize "a tone of revival" and more. They feel at home again.

At the same time, another process is going on in Swedish society: mediatization, i.e., the influence of mass media on Swedish culture in a broad sense: "In all fields of culture, the presence of the media changes the rules of aesthetic creation, dissemination and the use of sound, images, and texts. To a high degree, mediatization affects reading and listening, education and the book industry, theater and the music, film and visual culture in both fine arts and popular culture" (Fornäs 2011, 5). It goes without saying that the author also should have included church services. In line with the transformation of Swedish TV media from sober information services to "commercial populism" in the 1980s (Furhammar 2006), or the more recent trend of "digital storytelling," Channel 10 has produced a popular form of revival, maybe not of the heart, but definitely of the culture of bygone days in Pentecostalism. And, just like in the old days, people are happy to open their wallets and donate money to something that is to their liking—and especially to a TV channel that claims that it is going to bring old time revival to Scandinavia!

Through his work on identity, Paul Ricoeur (1992) has taught us that we are dependent on narratives to create and maintain a personal identity. By telling and retelling stories of our lives, we integrate a reconstructed past and an imagined future, and we mediate discrepancies to produce a more coherent version of continuity. In the same way, we opt to provide life with some type of purpose. Stuart Hall speaks of the "production of identity" and claims that this process is "not an identity grounded in [Foucaultian] archaeology, but in the re-telling of the past" (1990, 224). Dan McAdams and Kate McLean further suggest that "a narrative identity builds slowly over time as people tell stories about their experiences to and with others. Over developmental time, selves create stories, which in turn create selves" (2013, 233). Erik Erikson emphasized the importance of continuity in the notion of personal identity: "The key problem of identity, then, is (as the term connotes) the capacity of the ego to sustain sameness and continuity in the face of changing fate [...] Identity connotes the resiliency of maintaining essential patterns in the process of change" (Erikson 1964, 95–96). In a situation where a positive interpretation of the present is difficult to attain or create, an individual often turns to the past, something we call "nostalgia." Up until recently, nostalgia was considered a deficient character trait. Recent research, however, has shown that nostalgia is a common and transcultural phenomenon that "bolsters social bonds, increases positive self-regard, and generates positive affect" (Routledge et al. 2006, 975).

In the case of elderly people in the classical Pentecostal Movement, the construction of an identity and purpose in life becomes increasingly difficult in the radically transformed environment of the local Pentecostal church. The perception of continuity is suddenly disrupted. Thus they revert to nostalgia, returning to the past. This explains the success of programs like "Do You Remember the Song?" that feature old-time revival songs as well as mediatized versions of old-school Pentecostal services. In these programs, viewers are helped to return to the past. The programs from Channel 10 are not just passive nostalgia, however. Through the repeated pleas for donations from Börje Claesson, followed by nostalgic satisfaction in return, as well as the chance to submit prayer requests, etc., the interchange results in a mutual interdependence. The talk around coffee tables around Sweden—or visits to the City Church in Älmhult—also provide individuals with chances to retell the stories of their lives, thus renewing their perceptions of their personal identities and creating new meanings and new purposes in life for them.

Indulging in nostalgia is a convenient way to feel better and open up to others. It opens the heart and boosts generosity, which accounts for the fact that it has been possible for Claesson to generate the large sums that he needs. This has made it possible for him and his collaborators to create what I consider to be Sweden's first telechurch. Around Sweden, what is broadcast from Ängelholm is now the talk of the coffee tables of elderly Pentecostals and other Charismatic believers. And day after day, former churchgoers now sit in front of the screen, awaiting new inspiration, reinforced by nostalgia. While still remaining members of a local church, elderly and disappointed members of Pentecostal and Charismatic origin can increasingly identify with a media version of a church—a telechurch. What Bishop Macedo did not want, is exactly what Pastor Claesson has achieved—in a time that no one thought was "right" for religious television. According to this interpretation, Channel 10 is most certainly the answer—but, in the eyes of Börje Claesson, and many of his sponsors, probably to the wrong question. The channel may not have met the supposed needs of nonbelievers, but it has definitely brought new meaning to the lives of the older believers who feel alienated in their own churches.

NOTES

1. The term *televangelism* is usually considered to be an (American) abbreviation of "evangelization via television." However, the term also indicates a translocative capacity of broadcasting activities that take place elsewhere, thus making them available for "take-away"—for remote consumption or participation.
2. I use "Pentecostal" as an encompassing term for the type of spirituality that originated among African Americans in the United States in the early twentieth century, regardless of its current location. To single out this type of Pentecostalism, I sometimes use the term "Classic Pentecostalism." This stands in contrast to the type of Pentecostalism that surged towards the end of the twentieth century, which is more related to "health and wealth" theology. I use the term "Neo-Pentecostal" for the latter. To define Pentecostalized movements within other types of churches, like the Swedish Lutheran Church, I use the term "Charismatic." The latter may also be used as an encompassing term to define spirituality common to Classic Pentecostalism, Neo-Pentecostalism, and the Charismatic Movement (for a more detailed discussion, see Alvarsson 2007b).
3. The material, consisting of several interviews, a visit to the location of TV production in Älmhult, and an analysis of viewer statistics, was presented as a spread in "The Day" (*Dagen*) Sept. 6, 2013.
4. For an overview of the different Pentecostal movements in Scandinavia, see Alvarsson (2011) and for the Swedish Pentecostal Movement in particular, see Alvarsson (2007a).
5. In this article I use "The Swedish Pentecostal Movement" and the abbreviation SPM for the main Pentecostal movement in Sweden. From 2001 this movement was more officially organized and called Riksföreningen Pingst Fria församlingar i samverkan; in English "The Pentecostal Alliance of Independent Churches" or "PAIC." As most of the historical events in

this article took place before 2001, however, I will keep the abbreviation "SPM" throughout the text.

6. Initially, the company was organized as a foundation, founded by the Swedish government as a Public Service company, but corporately owned by interested parties, like the press, the news agency "TT," and radio companies. It was supposed to be independent of the government or any economic interests, but it was still closely identified with the Swedish state. After 1979, when Sveriges Television (Swedish Television) was founded as a separate foundation, the board has been constituted by representatives of all the political parties in the Swedish Parliament, with a president who is politically independent.

7. For more detailed information, see Alvarsson (2014a).

8. Närke is the name of the province of the city of Örebro.

9. Most Pentecostal congregations were founded as independent entities resulting from the revival. However, some of them, like the Filadelfia Church in Stockholm, were originally Baptist congregations, even though there was also an influx from Methodists and later the Swedish Covenant Church. The Filadelfia Church in Stockholm was explicitly expelled from the Baptist Union in 1913, only one year after the publication of "Jesus is Coming," while other congregations left the Union in protest or because of differences in spirituality.

10. See e.g. *Dagens Nyheter*, Feb. 1, 1950, *Aftonbladet*, Feb. 2, 1950, and *Expressen*, Feb. 17, 1950. cf. the conditions in the 1920s in Stävare (2010, 70–74).

11. This attempt was followed by the founding of Denmark's most successful pirate radio station, the commercial and secular Radio Mercur in 1958, and its Swedish imitators, Radio Syd outside southern Sweden the same year, and Radio Nord, outside Stockholm in 1961. All of these attempts naturally increased the pressure on Swedish authorities to open up the country to more commercial media.

12. Lewi Pethrus also tried to realize his vision through legal methods by negotiating with the Minister of Communication on several occasions, but without result (Stävare 2007, 329).

13. With the foundation of IBRA, the Pentecostal Movement was able to escape the limiting currency regulations in force in Sweden at the time, because no Swedish citizen could be prevented from being a member of a foreign association or send his or her membership fee to that association (Djurfeldt 2007, 203).

14. In 1971, Radio Trans Europa in Lisbon became a new center for IBRA activities. In 1985, IBRA broadcast in 53 languages and reached 150 peoples in more than 100 countries. Seventeen million Swedish *kronors* per year were invested in IBRA at the time (Stävare 2007, 330).

15. IBRA Radio discontinued broadcasting in Swedish in March 1980 (Björk 2007, 291).
16. The Kaggeholm community college already had a mass media education program which was responsible for the community television project in Huddinge. On the basis of that experience, and inspired by the Canadian *100 Huntley Street* (and with two presenters from that TV station), formal television education began in 1984 (Björk 2007, 292). This channel has produced many of the present technicians, anchormen, sound technicians, and cameramen working for Swedish Television (Kanal 1 and TV2) as well as TV4.
17. At this stage, to cut costs, Swedish Television started buying programs from freelance companies who were also based in Sweden. However, the quality requirements were high, and it was a surprise to some skeptics that the SPM passed the audition. Four of the programs mentioned in the text were broadcast during 1986 and the rest during 1987 (Björk 2007, 292).
18. In Swedish: "Konsten att växa genom livets svåra frågor." (Author's translation). The address is http://www.godanyheter.nu/.
19. In his study of Word of Life, Simon Coleman has highlighted the interesting fact that mass media were also "incorporated into members' spiritual lives and practices," i.e. they were used as complements to regular church services (Coleman 2000, 168).
20. One evangelization campaign, launched by German-born international evangelist Reinhard Bonnke in the 1980s, attempted to reach all Swedish households with Bonnke's pamphlet "From Minus to Plus" (*Från minus till plus*) which was generally a magnificent failure. No new converts were seen. In the aftermath, many Pentecostals ironically reversed the title of the campaign.
21. For the Swedish mentality, see Daun (1989). For Pentecostal views on congregations, see Josefsson (2005, 97–108).
22. Pentecostal evangelist Kathryn Kuhlman also contributed to a number of TV programs with features from her healing campaigns in the 1950s and the 1960s, broadcast on CBS (Columbia Broadcasting System), at the time one of the major TV companies in the United States.
23. In the United States, religious groups' collections are exempt from taxation.
24. Scandals and conflicts have since struck the Robertson family. The TV channel decreased in importance and no one was ready to take over from the aging Robertson. The Crystal Cathedral had to be disposed of. Today, it is owned by the Catholic Church.
25. In many Pentecostal denominations, especially in African American ones, the first pastor takes the title "Bishop" in accordance with 1 Tim. 3:1: "the office of a bishop" (i.e. *not* as part of an idea of succession). This is also the case in IURD and some other Latin American churches.

26. See the World Values Survey (2015), according to which Sweden is now considered the most individualistic country in the world.
27. As stated above, *Dagen* was founded in 1945 by Lewi Pethrus and was for a long time associated with the SPM. Today, however, a consortium of Christian actors, ranging from SPM to a Norwegian Lutheran organization, jointly finance and supervise the production of *Dagen*.
28. Author's translation of the statement found online at 'kanal10.se' April 12, 2014.
29. Author's translation of the information found online at 'kanal10.se' April 12, 2014.
30. According to *Dagens Nyheter* of Aug. 12, 2014, official Swedish statistics state that the average Swede donates 600 *kronor*s per year to nonprofit organizations in general. Donors to Channel 10 probably also give money to other causes, e.g., their own local churches, which indicates that this number is indeed exceptional.
31. Interview with Pentecostal woman, 65–70 years of age, April 14, 2015.
32. The response to the show, in particular the proliferation of church services called "Minns du sången", actually caused Swedish Television to discontinue the broadcast of the series (*Dagen*, Nov. 6, 2001).
33. Lundgren's observations coincide exactly with my own, gathered from watching many programs produced by Channel 10.

References

Alvarsson, Jan-Åke. 2007a. Pingstväckelsens etablering i Sverige: Från Azusa Street till Skövde på sju månader. In *Pingströrelsen: Händelser och utveckling under 1900-talet*, ed. Jan-Åke Alvarsson and Claes Waern, vol. 1, 10–45. Örebro: Libris.

———. 2007b. Pentekostal, evangelikal och karismatisk: Definitioner av några viktiga begrepp. In *Pingströrelsen: Verksamheter och särdrag under 1900-talet*, ed. Jan-Åke Alvarsson and Claes Waern, vol. 2, 40–49. Örebro: Libris.

———. 2011. The Development of Pentecostalism in Scandinavian Countries. In *European Pentecostalism*, ed. William K. Kay and Anne E. Dyer, 19–39. Leiden/Boston/Tokyo: Brill.

———. 2014a. *Om Pingströrelsen... Essäer, översikter och analyser*. Skellefteå: Bokförlaget Artos.

Björk, Annica. 2007. Pingströrelsen blev största frikyrkan: Fler än 25.000 döptes under en tioårsperiod. In *Pingströrelsen: Händelser och utveckling under 1900-talet*, ed. Jan-Åke Alvarsson and Claes Waern, vol. 1, 289–315. Örebro: Libris.

Burgess, Stanley M., and Eduard van der Mass, eds. 2002. *International Dictionary of Pentecostal and Charismatic Movements*. Grand Rapids: Zondervan.

Coleman, Simon. 2000. *The Globalisation of Charismatic Christianity: Spreading the Gospel of Prosperity*. Cambridge: Cambridge University Press.

Cox, Harvey. 1996 [1994]. Fire from Heaven: *The Rise of Pentecostal Spirituality and the Reshaping of Religion in the Twenty-First Century*. Reading: Addison-Wesley Publishing Company.
Dahlgren, Curt. 1982. Maranata: En sociologisk studie av en sektrörelses uppkomst och utveckling. PhD dissertation, University of Lund.
Daun, Åke. 1989. *Swedish Mentality*. University Park: The Pennsylvania State University Press.
Djurfeldt, Olof. 2007. Missionsintresset växte i förnyelseväckelsen: Allvarliga profetior i krigets skugga. In *Pingströrelsen: Händelser och utveckling under 1900-talet*, ed. Jan-Åke Alvarsson and Claes Waern, vol. 1, 177–219. Örebro: Libris.
Erikson, Erik. 1964. *Insight and Responsibility*. New York: Harper & Row.
Fornäs, Johan. 2011. Medialisering: Introduktion. In *Medialisering av kultur, politik, vardag och forskning: Slutrapport från Riksbankens Jubileumsfonds forskarsymposium i Stockholm 18–19 augusti 2011*, ed. Johan Fornäs and Anne Kaun, 5–13. Huddinge, Mediestudier vid Södertörns högskola.
Furhammar, Leif. 2006. *Sex, såpor och svenska krusbär: Television i konkurrens*. Stockholm: Ekerlid.
Gerdmar, Anders. 2014. Livets Ord. In *Svenskt Frikyrkolexikon*, ed. Jan-Åke Alvarsson, 274–277. Stockholm: Bokförlaget Atlantis.
Hall, Stuart. 1990. Cultural Identity and Diaspora. In *Identity: Community, Culture, Difference*, ed. Jonathan Rutherford, 222–237. London: Lawrence & Wishart.
Hedges, Daniel J. 2002. Television. In *International Dictionary of Pentecostal and Charismatic Movements*, ed. Stanley M. Burgess and Eduard van der Mass, 1118–1120. Grand Rapids: Zondervan.
Josefsson, Ulrik. 2005. Liv och över nog: Den tidiga pingströrelsens spiritualitet. PhD dissertation, University of Lund.
Kanal 10. http://www.kanal10.se. Accessed 6 Mar 2016
Lundgren, Joakim. 2013. Kanal 10 – första tv-kyrkan i Sverige. *Dagen*, September 6.
McAdams, Dan P., and Kate C. McLean. 2013. Narrative Identity. *Current Directions in Psychological Science* 22: 233–238.
Moberg, Jessica. 2013. Piety, Intimacy and Mobility: A Case Study of Charismatic Christianity in Present-Day Stockholm. PhD dissertation, Södertörn University.
Ricoeur, Paul. 1992 (1990). *Oneself as Another (Soi-même comme un autre)*. Chicago: University of Chicago Press.
———. 2005. *The Course of Recognition*. Harvard: Harvard University Press.
Routledge, Clay. 2015. *Nostalgia: A Psychological Resource*, Essays in Social Psychology. Abingdon/New York: Routledge.
Routledge, Clay, Tim Wildschut, Constantine Sedikides, and Jamie Arndt. 2006. Nostalgia: Content, Triggers, Functions. *Journal of Personality and Social Psychology* 91: 975–993.
Routledge, Clay, J. Juhl, A. Abeyta, and C. Roylance. 2014. Using the Past to Promote a Peaceful Future: Nostalgia Proneness Mitigates Existential Threat Induced Nationalistic Self-Sacrifice. *Social Psychology* 45: 339–346.

Ruuth, Anders. 1995. *Igreja Universal do Reino de Deus: Gudsrikets universella kyrka: en brasiliansk kyrkobildning*. Uppsala/Stockholm: Almqvist & Wiksell International.
Stävare, Nils-Eije. 2007. En mediemedveten väckelserörelse: Dagen flaggskepp i bred massmediesatsning. In *Pingströrelsen: Verksamheter och särdrag under 1900-talet*, ed. Jan-Åke Alvarsson and Claes Waern, vol. 2, 319–359. Örebro: Libris.
———. 2010. Pingstvännerna – värstingkristna för hundra år sedan. In *Värstingkristna i drevet*, ed. Kerstin Elworth et al., 51–84. Artos: Skellefteå.
Wahlström, Magnus. 2007. Omprövning av tidigare principer: Kvinnlig ledarskap exempel på rörelsens nyorientering. In *Pingströrelsen: Händelser och utveckling under 1900-talet*, ed. Jan-Åke Alvarsson and Claes Waern, vol. 1, 317–353. Örebro: Libris.
———. 2014a. Minns du sången. In *Svenskt Frikyrkolexikon*, ed. Jan-Åke Alvarsson, 307. Stockholm: Bokförlaget Atlantis.
———. 2014b. TV-Inter. In *Svenskt Frikyrkolexikon*, ed. Jan-Åke Alvarsson, 467. Stockholm: Bokförlaget Atlantis.
World Values Survey. 2015. http://www.worldvaluessurvey.org/WVSContents.jsp?CMSID=Findings. Accessed 23 Dec 2015.

ETHNOGRAPHIC MATERIAL

Interview with Pentecostal woman, 65–70 years of age, April 14, 2015.

Open Access This chapter is distributed under the terms of the Creative Commons Attribution 4.0 International License (http://creativecommons.org/licenses/by/4.0/), which permits use, duplication, adaptation, distribution and reproduction in any medium or format, as long as you give appropriate credit to the original author(s) and the source, provide a link to the Creative Commons license and indicate if changes were made.

The images or other third party material in this chapter are included in the chapter's Creative Commons license, unless indicated otherwise in a credit line to the material. If material is not included in the chapter's Creative Commons license and your intended use is not permitted by statutory regulation or exceeds the permitted use, you will need to obtain permission directly from the copyright holder.

CHAPTER 10

Postscript: Embers from a Global Fire

Jessica Moberg and Jane Skjoldli

Historically, the symbolic vocabulary of Charismatic Christianity is littered with fire metaphors and analogies, especially connected to the agency of the Holy Spirit. Fire can be unpredictable, like wildfire; it can be controlled, as when lighting a torch; or, it can simply go out. Drawing on such a rich symbolic tradition allows us to paint a dynamic and lively picture of Nordic Charismatic history and the contemporary scene, in which a global blaze finds its expression in more humbly burning embers. In line with these analogies, this anthology opened with the emergence of Pentecostal religiosity in the Nordic countries, tracing paths among ashes from fires that have burned brightly in the scattered sites and cities of Nordic landscapes.

Among these fires, the scholars contributing to this volume have shown how individuals and groups have tapped into, and contributed to, local, national, and global developments; torches have been passed from American revivalist movements, through religious exchanges organized by, with the help of, or as collaborations between local sites, feeding into the global blaze. As torchbearers migrated and returned, they let the

J. Moberg (✉)
University of Gothenburg, Gothenburg, Sweden

J. Skjoldli
University of Bergen, Bergen, Norway

© The Author(s) 2018
J. Moberg, J. Skjoldli (eds.), *Charismatic Christianity in Finland, Norway, and Sweden*, Palgrave Studies in New Religions and Alternative Spiritualities, https://doi.org/10.1007/978-3-319-69614-0_10

flames they brought with them coalesce in Nordic countries, laying the foundation for the diverse Charismatic expressions we see manifest today. There is no one contemporary Nordic Charismatic Christianity, but many linger around the bonfires at the time of writing. Some groups have gone in a therapeutic direction, with popular music and sermon styles, and enjoy growth; their bonfires attract present lingerers. Others gather around the embers of old-fashioned Pentecostal psalms and sermons. These variations result from transformations native to the Nordic countries and internal dynamics in Charismatic bodies, as well as influences from the international, mainly Americanized Charismatic cultures.

Nordic Particularities

The chapters written by Mikaelsson and Stensvold have illustrated the strong significance of contact through transatlantic networks in the early establishment phase, in terms of national and international infrastructures of communication. Such webs of contact, including migrant networks, enabled traveling preachers to spread their message within, without, and between the Nordic countries. As shown by Mikaelsson, the role of women missionaries, previously poorly attended to in research literature, was essential to Pentecostal establishment processes.

Even though member numbers remain relatively small, this religious minority has taken up, and continues to take up space in the public spheres, including the media realm. Moreover, Charismatics have wielded media channels themselves, producing daily papers, newsletters, periodicals, TV shows, and YouTube sermons. However, despite adopting and adapting to contemporaneous mainstream trends, it seems as though the spell of peculiarity associated with this brand of Christianity has not been lifted—at least not yet.

Existing research has tended to emphasize tensions between Charismatic Christianity and national churches. Yet, as the contributions to this volume elucidate, the predominant picture of Nordic state churches as hegemonic structures is in need of nuance and problematization. While it is important to recognize their occasionally oppressive side, national churches have also benefitted Charismatic Christianity. As demonstrated by Stensvold, revivalist movements within Lutheran churches served to bridge mainstream and Charismatic Christianity. More recently, Charismatic movements within Lutheran churches have contributed to creating a new organizational base for the former.

This book has also shed light on contemporaneous and contemporary trends in all Nordic countries, many of which have found expression in Norway, Finland, and Sweden. One of these trends regards how member recruitment has primarily taken place through socialization rather than by conversion. Another trend concerns the growth of new collaborative forms across Charismatic and non-Charismatic boundaries, pointing towards a general, but not ubiquitous pull towards ecumenism, where Charismatic discourse used to be more exclusivist. This is connected to the overall disintegration of denomination-based identities and increased mobility within the Charismatic field, in which socio-religious anchors are moved from conventional labels to the self on the one hand, and the broader revivalist scene on the other. Whereas old boundaries are deconstructed, new ones are formed around age and generation, class, and ethnic groups. As examined by Mantsinen and Alvarsson, preferential differences between generations present challenges, particularly to Pentecostal communities.

Yet another growing trend is pointed out by Hovi, Moberg, and Skjoldli, who demonstrate that Faith Movement-influenced rhetoric, strategies, practices, and theologies have given way to therapeutization, intimization, and self-censorship regarding Charismatic practices. One conspicuous aspect of this is the declining use of the previously prominent fire-laden metaphors. One might describe this new Charismatic profile as more low-key than the earlier public profile of the Faith Movement.

Nordic Issues in a Global Light

The category of Charismatic Christianity has proven valuable for capturing historical and contemporary developments in different parts of the world. However, as the anthology clarifies, what used to be easily identifiable as "Charismatic" or "Pentecostal" in Nordic contexts has become increasingly vague and blurred by the developments sketched herein. This bears implications on how Pentecostal studies researchers construct, define, and approach their objects of study from a wider, global perspective.

Elements that were previously central to the definition of these objects seem to be losing some of their relevance, demanding the construction of categories that better capture contemporary identities, practices, alliances, and priorities. If speaking in tongues, prophecy, and healing have become marginal in several groups, how can we justify defining Charismatic Christianity based on these particular components? Still, the fact that Charismatic practices are toned down in wider collaborative situations displays consciousness of the social boundaries that might result from them. We believe this reflects ongoing negotiations of boundaries regarding Christian fellowship, identity, and consciousness over Charismatic primacy and uniqueness. Such developments have also been noted in the wider global Charismatic field, in which ecumenical imperatives, which used to garner suspicion, show signs of integration among Charismatics.

Future Research Prospects

Much work remains to be done in the study of Nordic Charismatic Christianity. We find three themes particularly worthy of inquiry. The first pertains to geographic coverage. Our greatest regret as editors is the lack of case studies from Denmark and Iceland. The fact that Charismatic Christianity has been relatively unsuccessful in these countries begs the question of what beneficial conditions were in place in Norway, Sweden, and Finland, that were absent in Denmark and Iceland. Second, we call for better and more nuanced statistics regarding the number of Charismatics in the Nordic region, where transdenominational aspects are considered. In this regard, we find it crucial to look at developments outside conventional denominations, in new networks and cooperative fora. Finally, Pentecostal studies would benefit from research on Charismatic movements within Nordic national churches. This "organizational embrace" of the former outsider and opponent may not only contribute to discussions about Charismatization as transformation of other denominations, but also illuminate the refashioning and possible taming of the global Charismatic fire.

Open Access This chapter is distributed under the terms of the Creative Commons Attribution 4.0 International License (http://creativecommons.org/licenses/by/4.0/), which permits use, duplication, adaptation, distribution and reproduction in any medium or format, as long as you give appropriate credit to the original author(s) and the source, provide a link to the Creative Commons license and indicate if changes were made.

The images or other third party material in this chapter are included in the chapter's Creative Commons license, unless indicated otherwise in a credit line to the material. If material is not included in the chapter's Creative Commons license and your intended use is not permitted by statutory regulation or exceeds the permitted use, you will need to obtain permission directly from the copyright holder.

Index[1]

A

Adventism, 38, 114
Americanization
 critique of, 3, 4, 28, 177, 183n8
 as process, 12, 26, 42, 45, 166, 201
Anderson, Allan H., 2–5, 7, 8, 12–15, 44, 54, 59, 72n10, 73n17, 83, 84, 86, 113, 161, 168, 182n1
"Arch, the" (Arken), 209n7, 225, 226
Assemblies of God, 56, 72n4, 118
Augsburg Principle, 28
Authority
 political, 68, 149
 spiritual, 140
Azusa Street revival, 3, 7, 41, 182n1

B

"Banda Mission, the" (*Bandamisjonen*), 56, 59, 61
Baptism, 3, 8, 31, 37–39, 41, 42, 51, 53, 54, 57, 67, 72n10, 114, 115
 adult, 37, 38, 42
 in the Holy Spirit, 3, 8, 39, 41, 51, 53, 54, 57, 72n10 (*see also* Glossolalia)
 infant, 31, 37, 114
"Baptist Union of Sweden, the" (*Svenska Baptistsamfundet*), 192, 217
Barratt, Thomas Ball, 8, 25, 26, 41, 42, 49, 51–54, 56–62, 66, 69, 71, 71n3, 73n18, 73n21, 115
Bauman, Zygmunt, 113, 114
Bible, Books of, 74n33, 90, 155n6, 155n7
 1 Timothy 3:1, 235n25
 1 Corinthians 14: 24–25; 12; 14: 24–25, 84, 86
 2 Corinthians 11: 2, 155n7
 Ephesians 4: 11–12, 90
 Genesis 22, 153
 Isaiah 54: 5, 74n33
 John 4: 24, 155n6
 Matthew 28: 18–20; 24: 14, 53, 54
 Revelation 21: 9–27; 7: 3-8, 39, 155n7

[1] Note: Page number followed by 'n' refers to notes.

© The Author(s) 2018
J. Moberg, J. Skjoldli (eds.), *Charismatic Christianity in Finland, Norway, and Sweden*, Palgrave Studies in New Religions and Alternative Spiritualities, https://doi.org/10.1007/978-3-319-69614-0

Bible College, 85, 87, 89, 90
Bible school, 12, 66, 118–120, 122, 138, 140
Bloch-Hoell, Nils, 3, 8, 9, 15, 25, 41, 51, 52, 54, 57, 71n2
Bourdieu, Pierre, 16, 112, 113, 128, 131
Bride of Christ, 137, 144, 145, 148, 149, 152, 153
Brofeldt, Pietari, 114
Bundy, David, 7, 14, 17n2, 49, 51–53, 55, 57, 59, 61, 62, 65, 66, 69, 71n3, 72n9, 72n14, 73n18, 74n28

C
Calvary Chapel, 12, 189, 193–198, 206, 208, 209n3, 209n4
Castrén, Hanna, 114
Catholic Church, the, 14, 30, 163, 235n24
"Channel 10" (*Kanal 10*)
  Norway, 226
  Sweden, 224–227
Charisma
  as emic concept, 6, 83
  Weberian, 4, 16, 82, 83, 85, 89, 93, 94, 100, 103, 104, 115, 120, 124, 149
Charismatic gifts, 128, 181
Charismatic Movement, the, 10
  in the Catholic Church, 163
  in Protestant churches, 10
  (*see also* Oasis Movement, the)
China Inland Mission (CIM), 52, 55
Church of Jesus Christ of Latter-day Saints, 34
  See also Mormons
CIM, *see* China Inland Mission
"City Mail, the" (Byposten), 41, 71n3
Claesson, Börje, 224–227, 229–233

Coleman, Simon, 12, 83, 144, 148, 192, 221, 235n19
Congregationalism, 9, 61, 63, 69, 124, 152, 165, 170, 171, 221
Conventicle Act, 29
Converts, 1, 8, 30, 37, 42, 43, 45, 54, 65, 66, 104, 111, 118–120, 130, 166, 193, 194, 198, 229, 235n20
Cox, Harvey, 3, 174, 178, 179, 223
"Credo Church, the" (*Credokirken*), 16, 81, 82, 84, 88–92, 96, 97, 99, 101–104
Csordas, Thomas, 10, 177, 188, 189, 209n1

D
"Day, the" (*Dagen*)
  Norway, 88
  Sweden, 9, 214, 233n3
Democracy, 28, 143
Demons, 117
  See also Evil spirits
Devil, the, 167
Dissension Act, 31, 33

E
Edvardsen, Aril, 68, 74n30
Ekman, Ulf, 12, 84, 144, 148, 215, 221
"Embers from the Altar" (*Glöd från altaret*), 216
Engström, Dagmar, 54, 56–59, 61, 68, 69, 72n11, 72n13, 73n15
Eschatology, 43, 217
Evangelicalism, 35
Evangelical-Lutheran Church of
  Finland, 6, 7, 109, 115
  Norway, 2, 6, 11, 27, 39, 44, 52, 57
  Sweden, 2, 6, 11, 215

Evangelization, 17n1, 58, 67, 73n16, 120, 122, 162, 167, 179, 181, 198, 213, 218, 220, 233n1, 235n20
"Evidence of Faith World Evangelization" (*Troens Bevis Verdens Evangelisering*), 67–68
Evil spirits, 167
See also Demons

F
Faith healing, 161–181
Faith Movement, the, 1, 2, 6, 11, 12, 16, 72n4, 87, 94, 144, 154, 192, 194, 196, 198, 199, 226, 241
Filadelfia Congregation in
  Knutby, 137–155
  Oslo, 8, 37, 41, 62, 63
  Stockholm, 194, 205, 217, 218, 234n9
"Flaming Fire" (*Flammende Ild*), 87
Flåten, Enevald, 85–89
Fossmo, Helge, 137, 138, 140, 141, 144, 146–149, 151–154, 155n5, 156n14
Free Friends (*Frie venner*), 52, 56, 61, 62
"Free Pentecostal Movement of Finland, the" (*Suomen vapaa Helluntaiherätys*), 10, 116
"Friends"
  of Hauge, 29–32
  of Pentecost, 8, 51, 115

G
Gembäck, Peter, 141, 143, 145, 155n9
Gender roles, 119, 145
Generation conflicts, 124, 130, 214

Gifts of the Spirit, 3
Glossolalia, 39, 54, 84, 87, 101, 102, 198
  prohibition, 102, 174
  See also Speaking in tongues
"Good News, the" (*Det gode budskap*), 55
"Gospel Herald, the" (*Evangelii härold*), 217
Grace, 34, 38, 84, 93–95, 98–101
Gulbrandsen, Chrissie, 56, 65
Gulbrandsen, Parley, 51, 56, 61, 65

H
Habitus, 110–114, 119, 120, 123, 125–133
Hagin, Kenneth E., 12, 215
Hauge
  Hans Nielsen, 28, 52, 53
  movement, the, 30, 52
Healing Rooms, 16, 162, 167–169, 176, 179, 182n2
  See also Prayer Clinic
Helsinki Saalem, 121
Hillsong Church, 2, 12, 189, 193–198, 208, 209n3, 215
Holiness Movement, the, 34, 52, 55, 164
Holistic healing, 166, 167, 174, 175, 179, 191
Hollenweger, Walter J., 3, 5, 113
Hugs, 16, 187, 209n12

I
Imsen, Arne, 10, 215
"Inner Mission, the" (*Indremisjonen*), 30–32, 34, 35, 37–39, 42, 44, 45, 57
Intercessory prayer, 1, 162, 170

International Broadcasting Radio
 Association (IBRA), 218, 219,
 234n13, 234n14, 235n15
Intimization, 187, 241
 See also Therapeutization
Islam, 11, 87, 191

J
Jesus Movement, the, 9, 144, 188
Johnson, Andrew G., 8, 214

K
Karisma Center, 193

L
Lake, John, 168
"Lammers Movement, the"
 (*Lammersbevegelsen*), 31

M
Macedo, Edir, 223, 224, 233
Mahmood, Saba, 112
Maranata Movement, the, 10,
 144, 228
Martin, David, 3, 7, 189
McGuire, Meredith, 10, 178
Members
 class, 33, 39, 43, 111, 112,
  114, 115, 119, 129, 131,
  132, 194
 education, 9, 43, 53, 54, 57,
  119, 120, 192, 224, 231,
  235n16
 gender, 169
 socialized, 9, 111, 118–120,
  128–133, 207, 208
Methodism, 26, 34, 36, 39, 114
Methodist Church, 36, 42, 52,
 61, 73n17

Migration
 to Nordic countries, 6–9, 11, 12,
  14, 15
 to North America, 32, 189
Monopolies
 in media, 6, 88, 89, 118, 119, 137,
  138, 141, 142, 149, 150, 152,
  165, 168, 190, 216–221, 230,
  231, 233, 234n11, 240
 in religion, 2, 11, 13, 15, 16, 27,
  28, 71, 111, 115, 130, 138,
  149–152, 162, 163
Moravians, 52, 72n5
Mormons, 34, 36, 39
Mukti Mission, the, 58, 59, 73n17

N
Neitz, Mary Jo, 4, 177, 180
Neo-liberalism, 173, 180, 181
New Age, 177–180, 191, 200
New Life Church, 187, 188, 193–195,
 197, 204–206, 208, 209n3
New Religious Movements, 11, 16,
 137, 156n13, 191
New Thought, 178
Nordquelle, Erik Andersen, 52, 55, 61
"Norway's Free Evangelicl Heathen
 Mission" (*Norges Frie Evangeliske
 Hedningemisjon*), 56, 60
"Norwegian Pentecostal
 Congregations' Outer Mission,
 the" (*De norske pinsemenigheters
 ytremisjon*), 63
Nostalgia, 17, 93, 214, 215,
 229–233

O
Oasis Movement, the, 10
 Denmark, 10
 Finland, 10
 Norway, 10

Sweden, 10, 215, 225, 226
    See also Charismatic Movement, the
Örebro Mission (*Örebromissionen*), 215, 220
Östberg, Emma, 8

P
Pentecostal Alliance of Independent Churches, the (PAIC), 147, 156n12, 192, 193, 209n8, 233n5
Pentecostal Church of Finland (*Suomen helluntaikirkko*, SHK), 110, 121–129, 131–133, 164
Pentecostal People (*Helluntaikansa*, HK), 110, 122–125, 127–129, 131–133
"People of the Cross" (*Ristin Kansa*), 122
Petersen, Ole Peter, 33, 36
Pethrus, Lewi, 8, 62, 66, 147, 214, 217, 218, 234n12, 236n27
Pierce, Cal, 168
Pietism, 28–30, 35, 114, 173
Postmodernity, 113
Prayer, 1
    houses, 32
    requests, 162, 172, 173, 187, 200, 201, 221, 232
Prayer clinic, 162, 163, 167–172, 174–176, 178, 179, 181
Prophecy, 54, 84–90, 93, 94, 99, 100, 102–104, 141, 153, 174, 241
Prophetic speech, 85, 86
Prosperity Gospel, 180
Psychologization, 163, 165–167
    See also Therapeutization

R
Ramabai, Pandita, 58, 59, 73n17
Reformation, the, 4, 7, 27, 28
Ritualization, 203, 204, 208

Roberts, Oral, 10, 221, 222
Robertson, Pat, 222, 235n24
Rønhovde, Olav, 88–92
Rymker, Fredrick Ludvig, 37

S
"Sanctification Union, the" (*Helgelseförbundet*), 139, 155n3
Satan, 57
Second Coming of Christ, 43
Secularization, 9, 11, 44, 45, 124, 126, 205
Seventh-day Adventist Church, 169
Sexuality, 146
Sharing, 187–208, 209n13
    See also Testimony
Sinfulness, 30, 32
Small group meeting, 82, 196
Speaking in tongues, 1, 3, 25, 39, 41, 101, 102, 114, 128, 130, 230, 241
    See also Glossolalia
Spirit manifestations, 39, 40, 57, 82, 83, 95, 98, 101, 103, 167
Spiritual Revolution, the, 179
Spiritual warfare, 146
"Star of Hope, the" (*Toivon tähti*), 114
Subjectification, 37, 53, 54, 70, 83, 84, 89, 96, 101, 104, 111, 112, 127, 128, 144, 149, 152, 216, 218

T
"Tabernacle, the" (Tabernaklet), 41, 60
Telechurch, 213
Televangelism, 213–233, 233n1
Testimony, 85, 88, 200, 201, 226–228
    See also Sharing
Thelle, Agnes, 56–59, 61, 69, 72n14

Therapeutization, 11, 16, 189–191, 241
  See also Psychologization
Third Wave Charismatics, 161, 165, 167
Tollefsen, Gunnerius, 61, 63, 66, 73n23
"Traditional Pentecostal Churches" (*Perinteinen helluntaiseurakunta*, PHS), 122, 124–126, 145
TV Inter, 219, 220, 229

U
Urbanization, 7, 32, 42, 188, 192, 195, 207

V
"Victory of the Cross"
  Finland (*Ristin Voitto*), 116, 118, 122
  Norway (*Korsets Seier*), 54, 71n3, 72n9
Vineyard Movement, 6, 12, 189, 192, 209n9

"Voice of the Bridegroom" (*Brudgummens röst*), 216, 217

W
Waldau, Åsa, 137–146, 148–154, 155n1
Weber, Max, 26, 82, 83, 89, 93, 94, 103, 110, 120, 149
Welfare state, 9–11, 116
Word of Life (*Livets ord*), 12, 84, 88, 104n3, 138, 144, 148, 192, 215, 220, 221, 225, 226, 229, 235n19
Words of Knowledge, 84, 98, 104, 174
Worship music, 12, 17, 118, 132, 198, 207, 215
Wounds of the soul, 176

X
Xenolalia, 54

Y
Yli-Vainio, Niilo, 116–118

The manufacturer's authorised representative in the EU is Springer Nature Customer Service Centre GmbH, Europaplatz 3, 69115 Heidelberg, Germany. If you have any concerns regarding our products, please contact ProductSafety@springernature.com

Printed and bound by CPI Group (UK) Ltd, Croydon, CR0 4YY

23/03/2026

02076663-0005